Brother Swaggart, Here Is My Question About Bible Prophecy

Brother Swaggart, Here Is My Question About Bible Prophecy

By Jimmy Swaggart

Jimmy Swaggart Ministries
P.O. Box 262550 • Baton Rouge, Louisiana 70826-2550
Website: www.jsm.org • Email: info@jsm.org
(225) 768-7000

ISBN 978-1-934655-55-9

09-106 | COPYRIGHT © 2010 Jimmy Swaggart Ministries®

14 15 16 17 18 19 20 21 22 / CW / 10 9 8 7 6 5 4 3 2

TABLE OF CONTENTS

INTRODUCTION – *"Brother Swaggart, Here Is My Question About Bible Prophecy"*   1

CHAPTER 1 – What Is The Rapture Of The Church? . . . 15

CHAPTER 2 – When Will The Antichrist Be Revealed? . . 41

CHAPTER 3 – What Is The Great Tribulation? 91

CHAPTER 4 – What Is The Battle Of Armageddon? 135

CHAPTER 5 – What Is The Second Coming? 183

CHAPTER 6 – What Is The Kingdom Age? 217

CHAPTER 7 – What Is The Perfect Age To Come? 277

INTRODUCTION

The word *"eschatology"* simply means the study of Endtime events according to the Word of God. So, this book is about Endtime events.

DISPENSATIONS

I personally believe that *"Dispensations"* is a Biblical explanation of the manner and way in which God has dealt with the human race. I also feel that without an understanding of Dispensations, one cannot properly understand the Word of God as one should. The following are Dispensations as the Bible gives them to us:

THE DISPENSATION OF INNOCENCE

• The Dispensation of Innocence: this pertains to the time frame of Adam and Eve from the time they were created unto the time of their Fall (Gen., Chpts. 1-3). As to how long the Dispensation of Innocence lasted, we aren't told. Inasmuch as the number *"40"* is the number of probation in the Bible, it is my thinking that they lived for 40 days and nights in a state of innocence before their Fall.

THE DISPENSATION OF CONSCIENCE

• The Dispensation of Conscience: the time frame of this Dispensation was approximately 1,600 years. It was from the time of the Fall of Adam and Eve to the time of Noah (Gen., Chpts. 4-8). This means that God dealt with the human race of that time through the conscience. Inasmuch as man is now a fallen creature, it did not turn out too well. In fact, the Scripture says concerning this time:

THE WICKEDNESS OF MAN

"And God saw that the wickedness of man was great

in the Earth *(these 'men of renown,' the giants of Verse 4, were developing more and more ways of wickedness)*, **and that every imagination of the thoughts of his heart was only evil continually** *(Due to this infestation, the evil began with the very thought processes and incorporated every human being; this was a continuous action of evil which never let up, and constantly grew more degrading)*.

THE GRIEF OF THE LORD

"**And it repented the LORD that He had made man on the Earth** *(God does not change as it regards His Nature; however, the fact that the Lord repents presents the truth that God, in consistency with His Immutability, assumes a changed position in respect to changed man)*, **and it grieved Him at His Heart.** *(This is not merely an anthropomorphic statement, as some claim, but a true statement regarding the Nature of God; sin grieves the Lord!)*" **(Gen. 6:5-6).**

THE DISPENSATION OF GOVERNMENT

• **The Dispensation of Government:** this Dispensation lasted about 400 years from the time of Noah to Abraham (Gen., Chpts. 9-12). During this Dispensation of Government, the Lord instigated various Laws. They were:

THE COVENANT

"**And God blessed Noah and his sons, and said unto them, Be fruitful, and multiply, and replenish the Earth** *(the Blessing that God gave to Noah was, in effect, a Covenant; the Covenant concerned the subject matter of the Verse)*.

"**And the fear of you and the dread of you shall be upon every beast of the Earth, and upon every fowl of** the air, upon all that moves upon the Earth, and upon all the fish of the sea; into your hand are they delivered *(to be delivered into the hand of man refers to the fact that man would be able to tame and reduce certain animals to be of help to him)*.

BLOOD WAS NOT TO BE EATEN

"Every moving thing that lives shall be meat for you; even as the green herb have I given you all things. *(All the animals, if so desired, could serve as food, as well as could vegetables; Gen. 1:29 implies that man was exclusively vegetarian before the Flood.)*

"But flesh with the life thereof, which is the blood thereof, shall you not eat *(man is prohibited from eating blood; there were several reasons; however, the main reason was because the shedding of blood in Sacrifices typified the Great Atonement, which would be carried out by Christ in the shedding of His Life's Blood)*.

CAPITAL PUNISHMENT FOR CAPITAL CRIMES

"And surely your blood of your lives will I require; at the hand of every beast will I require it, and at the hand of man; at the hand of every man's brother will I require the life of man *(this Verse condemns suicide, as well as homicide; this is a solemn proclamation of the sanctity of human life)*.

"Whoso sheds man's blood, by man shall his blood be shed *(in this Covenant, we actually have the institution of Government; the Passage speaks of cold-blooded murder; that being the case, the State has the right to take the life of such a murderer)*: for in the Image of God made He man *(capital punishment is not meant by God to serve as a deterrent, but rather, to portray the inherent worth of man)*.

THE PRODUCTIVITY OF THE EARTH

"And you, be you fruitful, and multiply; bring forth abundantly in the Earth, and multiply therein *(were it not for demonic religion and man's rebellion against God, the Earth could easily care for 100 billion people).*

"And God spoke unto Noah, and to his sons with him, saying *(the problem with the world is that it ignores what God has said),*

"And I, behold, I establish My Covenant with you, and with your seed after you *(the Covenant that God established with Noah was to be extended to all thereafter; in fact, it still stands)*;

"And with every living creature that is with you, of the fowl, of the cattle, and of every beast of the Earth with you; from all that go out of the Ark, to every beast of the Earth. *(This Covenant includes all of God's creation on Earth.)*

THE PROMISE OF GOD

"And I will establish My Covenant with you, neither shall all flesh be cut off anymore by the waters of a flood; neither shall there anymore be a flood to destroy the Earth. *(This Covenant guarantees that the world will never again be destroyed by water.)*

THE RAINBOW

"And God said, This is the token of the Covenant which I make between Me and you and every living creature that is with you, for perpetual generations *(means that generations of people will continue forever)*:

"I do set My bow in the cloud, and it shall be for a token of a Covenant between Me and the Earth *(the whole creation rests, as to its exemption from a second deluge, on the eternal stability of God's Covenant, of which the bow is the token).*

"And it shall come to pass, when I bring a cloud over the Earth, that the bow shall be seen in the cloud *(the rainbow)*:

THE COVENANT OF GOD

"And I will remember My Covenant, which is between Me and you and every living creature of all flesh; and the waters shall no more become a flood to destroy all flesh *(it doesn't mean that there will not be local floods, but rather, a flood to destroy the entirety of the Earth).*

"And the bow shall be in the cloud; and I will look upon it, that I may remember the Everlasting Covenant between God and every living creature of all flesh that is upon the Earth *(in this Passage, we are told that this Covenant is everlasting; in the Hebrew, it means 'the Covenant of Eternity').*

"And God said unto Noah, This is the token of the Covenant, which I have established between Me and all flesh that is upon the Earth *(the Covenant being universal, the sign of the rainbow is also universal).*

THE ENTIRETY OF THE POPULATION OF THE EARTH

"And the sons of Noah, who went forth of the Ark, were Shem, and Ham, and Japheth: and Ham is the father of Canaan. *(The entirety of the population of the Earth, and for all time since the Flood, are descendants of Shem, Ham, and Japheth; 'Canaan' is mentioned because his lineage will prove to be bitter enemies of Israel about 800 years into the future.)*

"These are the three sons of Noah: and of them was the whole Earth overspread. *(This means that every single person on the Earth died in the Flood, with the exception of this family)*" **(Gen. 9:1-19).**

THE DISPENSATION OF PROMISE

• **The Dispensation of Promise: this Dispensation lasted from the time of Abraham to the time of the giving of the Law to Moses, a time frame of approximately 400 years. This time of Promise is bound up in the Abrahamic Covenant. It is the greatest Dispensation yet, simply because, in this Covenant given to Abraham, we have the Promise in clarity of the coming Redeemer. It says:**

THE ABRAHAMIC COVENANT

"**Now the LORD had said unto Abram** *(referring to the Revelation which had been given to the Patriarch a short time before; this Chapter is very important [Gen. 12], for it records the first steps of this great Believer in the path of Faith)*, **Get thee out of your country** *(separation)*, **and from your kindred** *(separation)*, **and from your father's house** *(separation)*, **unto a land that I will show you** *(refers to the fact that Abraham had no choice in the matter; he was to receive his orders from the Lord and go where those orders led him)*:

I WILL MAKE YOU A BLESSING

"**And I will make of you a great Nation** *(the Nation which God made of Abraham has changed the world, and exists even unto this hour; in fact, this Nation 'Israel' still has a great part to play, which will take place in the coming Kingdom Age)*, **and I will bless you, and make your name great** *(according to Scripture, 'to bless' means 'to increase,' the builders of the Tower of Babel sought to 'make us a name,' whereas God took this man, who forsook all,* *and 'made his name great')*; **and you shall be a blessing:** *(concerns itself with the greatest blessing of all. It is the glory of Abraham's Faith. God would give this man the meaning of Salvation, which is 'Justification by Faith,' which would come about through the Lord Jesus Christ, and what Christ would do on the Cross. Concerning this, Jesus said of Abraham, 'Your father Abraham rejoiced to see My day: and he saw it, and was glad' [Jn. 8:56]).*

IN YOU SHALL ALL FAMILIES OF THE EARTH BE BLESSED

"And I will bless them who bless you *(to bless Israel, or any Believer, for that matter, guarantees the Blessings of God)***, and curse him who curses you** *(to curse Israel, or any Believer, guarantees that one will be cursed by God)***: and in you shall all families of the Earth be blessed.** *(It speaks of Israel, which sprang from the loins of Abraham and the womb of Sarah, giving the world the Word of God and, more particularly, bringing the Messiah into the world. Through Christ, every family in the world who desires blessing from God can have that Blessing, i.e., 'Justification by Faith')*" **(Gen. 12:1-3).**

The account of this Dispensation in the Bible is from Genesis, Chapter 12, to Exodus, Chapter 19.

THE DISPENSATION OF LAW

• **The Dispensation of Law: this Dispensation lasted from the time of Moses to Christ, a time frame of approximately 1,600 years. The Biblical account covers everything between Exodus, Chapter 19, through the last Chapter of Saint John. It must be remembered that the four Gospels, Matthew, Mark, Luke and John, although in the New Testament, still pertained to Old Testament times. In other words, even though Grace and**

Truth came by Jesus Christ, still, it was not fulfilled until the Sacrifice of Christ on the Cross, His Resurrection, Ascension, and then the sending back of the Holy Spirit.

The Law of Moses, which was actually the Law of God, came in three parts, one might say. They are:

1. The Ceremonial: this included all the Feast Days and the very core of this Law, which was the Sacrificial System.

2. The Civil: this pertained to all the various Laws between men, all given by God. These Laws covered every aspect of life and living as it regarded Israel.

3. The Moral: this was basically the Ten Commandments, which pertained to man's relationship with God and his relationship with his fellow man.

This great Law commenced with the Twentieth Chapter of Exodus and continued through the Book of Leviticus. All the balance of the Old Testament, along with the four Gospels, had to do with the way that Israel tried to keep this Law and, more than all, failed in the attempt.

THE DISPENSATION OF GRACE

• The Dispensation of Grace: this Dispensation began with the coming of the Holy Spirit in a new dimension on the Day of Pentecost and continues unto this hour. In the Word of God it covers everything from the First Chapter of Acts to the Twentieth Chapter of Revelation. This time is referred to, as well, as the *"New Covenant."* Of all the many Chapters which refer to this Covenant, the meaning of which was given to the Apostle Paul, perhaps one could say that Romans, Chapters 4 and 5, deal with this matter of Grace as no other Chapters. Perhaps the following two Verses proclaim to us its intent:

JUSTIFICATION BY FAITH

"Therefore being Justified by Faith *(this is the only way one can be justified; refers to Faith in Christ and what*

He did at the Cross), **we have peace with God** *(justifying peace)* **through our Lord Jesus Christ** *(what He did at the Cross)*:

"By Whom also we have access by Faith into this Grace *(we have access to the Goodness of God by Faith in Christ)* **wherein we stand** *(wherein alone we can stand)*, **and rejoice in hope** *(a hope that is guaranteed)* **of the Glory of God** *(our Faith in Christ always brings Glory to God; anything else brings glory to self, which God can never accept)*" **(Rom. 5:1-2).**

SANCTIFICATION BY FAITH

In Romans, Chapters 4 and 5, we are told how to be Saved, i.e., *"to be justified by Faith,"* **and now in Romans 6, we are told how to be Sanctified by Faith, that is, how one is to live for God. The great Apostle said:**

"Know you not, that so many of us as were baptized into Jesus Christ *(plainly says that this Baptism is into Christ and not water [I Cor. 1:17; 12:13; Gal. 3:27; Eph. 4:5; Col. 2:11-13])* **were baptized into His Death?** *(When Christ died on the Cross, in the Mind of God, we died with Him; in other words, He became our Substitute, and our identification with Him in His Death gives us all the benefits for which He died; the idea is that He did it all for us!)*

BURIED WITH HIM BY
BAPTISM INTO DEATH

"Therefore we are buried with Him by baptism into death *(not only did we die with Him, but we were buried with Him as well, which means that all the sin and trans-gression of the past were buried; when they put Him in the Tomb, they put all of our sins into that Tomb as well)*:

TO WALK IN NEWNESS OF LIFE

"**That like as Christ was raised up from the dead by the Glory of the Father, even so we also should walk in newness of life** *(we died with Him, we were buried with Him, and His Resurrection was our Resurrection to a 'Newness of Life')*.

THE LIKENESS OF HIS DEATH

"**For if we have been planted together** *(with Christ)* **in the likeness of His Death** *(Paul proclaims the Cross as the instrument through which all Blessings come; consequently, the Cross must ever be the Object of our Faith, which gives the Holy Spirit latitude to work within our lives)*, **we shall be also *in the likeness* of *His* Resurrection.** *(We can have the 'likeness of His Resurrection,' i.e., 'live this Resurrection Life,' only as long as we understand the 'likeness of His Death,' which refers to the Cross as the means by which all of this is done)*" **(Rom. 6:3-5).**

THE MEANING OF THE CROSS IS THE MEANING OF THE NEW COVENANT

The Cross of Christ, i.e., *"Christ and Him Crucified,"* is that to which all the Patriarchs and the Prophets of old pointed. This, the Cross, is the story of the Redemption of mankind, which was typified by the millions of lambs which were offered in sacrifice in the some 4,000 years between Adam and Eve and the time of Christ. One might say and be theologically correct that the Cross of Christ is the only thing standing between man and the Wrath of God. God cannot abide sin in any form. He deals with man, consequently, only on the basis of Justice satisfied, which it was at Calvary's Cross, which requires Faith on our part in that Finished Work. As we stated in the heading, the meaning of the Cross is the meaning of the New Covenant, as the meaning of the New Covenant is the meaning of the Cross.

Every single blessing that man receives, whether Salvation for the sinner or Sanctification for the Saint, all the work of the Holy Spirit within our lives, every blessing and of every description, is made possible by the Cross of Jesus Christ, i.e., *"what He there did."* Paul referred to it as *"The Everlasting Covenant,"* meaning that it will never have to be replaced, amended, or changed in any capacity (Heb. 13:20).

What Jesus did at the Cross makes it possible for the fallen sons of Adam's lost race to be Saved, and what He did at the Cross, makes it possible for Believers to live a victorious life, victorious over the world, the flesh, and the Devil. It only requires that our Faith be exclusively in Christ and what Christ has done for us at the Cross, and maintained in that capacity (Lk. 9:23; I Cor. 1:17-18, 23; 2:2).

THE BAPTISM WITH THE HOLY SPIRIT

Under the New Covenant, what Jesus did at the Cross, which was to atone for all sin, past, present and future, at least for all who will believe, made it possible for the Holy Spirit to come into the hearts and lives of all Believers, there to abide permanently.

Whenever the believing sinner comes to Christ, upon conversion, immediately the Holy Spirit takes up His abode in the heart and life of the individual (I Cor. 3:16). Then the Believer has the privilege of asking for, and receiving, the Baptism with the Holy Spirit, evidenced with speaking in other Tongues (Acts 2:4).

Before the Cross the Holy Spirit was greatly limited as to what He could do for and with Believers. But, since the Cross, with all sin atoned, He makes His abode with all Believers, and does so forever, helping us as we live this life and run this race, so to speak (Jn. 14:16-17).

THE DISPENSATION OF RIGHTEOUSNESS

• The Dispensation of Righteousness: this period of time

will last for 1,000 years and is characterized in the Word of God in the Twentieth Chapter of Revelation. However, even though most every Prophet of the Old Testament spoke of this coming grand time, the Prophet Isaiah had more to say than all. Some of his statements are found in Chapter 2 of his great Book, plus Chapters 4, 9, 11, 12, 14, to name a few. The Earth at that time, with Jesus reigning personally from Jerusalem, will experience prosperity and freedom as it has never known before. At that time Satan will be locked in the bottomless pit along with all fallen Angels and demon spirits. At that time, as well, *"The Earth shall be full of the Knowledge of the Lord, as the waters cover the sea"* (Isa. 11:9). Then every Saint of God who has ever lived will rule and reign with Christ, having Glorified Bodies, which will be eternal.

THE PERFECT AGE TO COME

• The Perfect Age to come: this period will last forever and forever and is portrayed in Chapters 21 and 22 of the great Book of Revelation. The Lord will renovate the heavens and the Earth with fire, cleansing them, with Him then transferring His headquarters from Heaven to Earth, where it will remain forever. While it is very, very difficult to select any one of several Scriptures from these two Chapters to explain that great time, perhaps the following will help. John wrote:

NO MORE CURSE

"And there shall be no more curse *(a curse was placed on the Earth at the Fall; it is being said here that there will be no more curse because there will be no more sin)*: but the Throne of God and of the Lamb shall be in it *(the authority of rulership will be as great with God the Son as it is with God the Father; in fact, by the use of the word 'Lamb,' we are made to realize that all of this is made possible because of what Jesus did at the Cross)*; and His servants shall serve Him *(the idea is that every Believer in the Perfect age will so love the Lord and the Lamb that they will gladly 'serve Him')*:

HIS FACE AND HIS NAME

"**And they shall see His face** *(shows intimate relationship)*; **and His Name** *shall be* **in their foreheads** *(refers to ownership; we were bought 'with a price,' and that price was the Blood of the Lamb)*.

"**And there shall be no night there** *(this speaks of the New Jerusalem only, for night and day will be in the balance of the Earth forever)*; **and they need no candle, neither light of the sun; for the Lord God gives them light** *(presents the Source of this Light)*: **and they shall reign forever and ever.** *(It has never been known for servants to 'reign' like kings; however, these servants shall!)*" (**Rev. 22:3-5**).

THE CHURCH AGE

The Dispensation of Grace could be referred to as the Dispensation of the Church. In fact, the Church began on the Day of Pentecost nearly 2,000 years ago.

At the time of this writing (2009), the Church is approximately 1,976 years old, assuming that Christ died and rose from the dead in A.D. 33. This means, as is obvious, that the Church has been in existence for nearly 2,000 years.

EVERY 1,000 YEARS OR 2,000 YEARS

• From the time of Adam and Eve to the time of Abraham was a time frame of approximately 2,000 years. At that time God gave the meaning of Justification by Faith to the Patriarch, which was one of the greatest moments in history.

• From the time of Abraham to the time of David was a

time frame of approximately 1,000 years. It was to David that the Lord gave the Promise that the Redeemer would come through his family, hence, our Lord being referred to as *"the Son of David."*

• From the time of David to Christ was a time frame of approximately 1,000 years.

• From the time of Christ to this present time, as stated, is a time frame of nearly 2,000 years.

If these time frames mean anything at all, this tells us that the Rapture of the Church is very, very near.

"We praise You, O God,
"For the Son of Your love,
"For Jesus Who died,
"And is now gone above."

"We praise You, O God,
"For Your Spirit of Light,
"Who has shown us our Saviour,
"And scattered our night."

"All glory and praise,
"To the Lamb that was slain,
"Who has borne all our sins,
"And has cleansed every stain."

"Revive us again,
"Fill each heart with Your love;
"May each soul be rekindled,
"With fire from above."

"Hallelujah! Thine the Glory,
"Hallelujah! Amen;
"Hallelujah! Thine the Glory;
"Revive us again."

CHAPTER ONE

What Is The Rapture Of The Church?

QUESTION:

WHAT IS THE RAPTURE OF THE CHURCH?

ANSWER:

The following are some of the questions we will address in this Chapter regarding the tremendously important event of the Rapture of the Church. They are:
• What is the Rapture?
• When will the Rapture occur?
• What are the qualifications for being ready for the Rapture?
• What will happen on Earth with every Believer gone?
• Will all babies and all little children go in the Rapture?
• What do the words *"caught up"* mean, which are found in I Thessalonians 4:17?
• What is the difference in the Rapture and the Second Coming?
• Why is the Rapture so important to the Church?
• Will the Holy Spirit be taken out of the world at the Rapture?
• What is the meaning of the words *"Shout," "Voice,"* and *"Trumpet,"* found in I Thessalonians 4:16?

THE APOSTLE PAUL

It was to Paul that the meaning of the New Covenant was given (Gal. 1:12). Included in the meaning of the New Covenant is the great Doctrine of the Rapture of the Church.
It is believed that I Thessalonians was the very first Epistle written by the Apostle. If that is the case, he included this great Doctrine in this first Epistle, which was not known or understood under the Old Covenant. Before the Cross, due to the fact that the blood of bulls and goats could not take away sins, there was no point in the Doctrine being addressed. The

reason being, when Saints died before the Cross, they didn't go to Heaven, but rather, to Abraham's bosom, which was Paradise (Lk. 16:22). In fact, Paul mentioned the fact of the *"Resurrection of the dead"* not being fully understood during that time (Heb. 6:1-2). Under the Old Covenant, and even before that Covenant was given, the Patriarchs and the Prophets knew there would be a Resurrection of the dead, but of that great Doctrine they had precious little understanding.

I AM THE RESURRECTION, AND THE LIFE

The Cross of Christ and the Resurrection of our Lord are what make the coming Resurrection of all Saints possible. Paul also said:

"But now is Christ risen from the dead *(so says the Holy Spirit)*, **and** become the Firstfruits of them who slept. *(The Resurrection of Christ guarantees the Resurrection of all Saints)*" **(I Cor. 15:20).**

THE RAISING OF LAZARUS

That the Resurrection, i.e., *"the Rapture,"* is wrapped up in Jesus, is beautifully illustrated by the statement of our Lord to Martha as it regards the raising of her brother from the dead. The Scripture says:

"Then when Jesus came, He found that he *(Lazarus)* had *lain* in the grave four days already *(on the fourth day of death, decomposition begins to set in; so there was no doubt about the death of this man)*.

"Now Bethany was near unto Jerusalem, about fifteen furlongs off *(about two miles from Jerusalem)*:

"And many of the Jews came to Martha and Mary, to comfort them concerning their brother *(this shows that the family could well have been one of some wealth, position, and importance)*.

"Then Martha, as soon as she heard that Jesus was coming, went and met Him *(implies that Jesus, upon coming close to Bethany, stopped short of coming into the town; knowing the animosity against Him, He did not desire to attract any undue disturbance, especially at this time; evidently He had sent someone to their home to inform them He had arrived, with information as to where He was)*: **but Mary sat** *still* **in the house** *(someone had to be in the house to meet the people who came to pay their respects)*.

MARTHA

"Then said Martha unto Jesus, Lord, if You had been here, my brother had not died *(evidently she does not seem to think of Jesus as raising her brother from the dead)*.

"But I know, that even now, whatsoever You will ask of God, God will give *it* **You** *(the terminology used by Martha shows it was still unclear to her exactly Who Jesus was)*.

"Jesus said unto her, your brother shall rise again *(very plainly, Jesus tells her what is about to happen; but in her doubt, she misunderstands)*.

"Martha said unto Him, I know that he shall rise again in the Resurrection at the last day *(proclaims what she had probably learned at the feet of Jesus [Dan. 12:2, 13; Jn. 6:39-40, 44, 54; 12:48])*.

"Jesus said unto her, I am the Resurrection, and the Life *(in effect He is saying, 'Martha, look at Me, you are looking at the Resurrection and the Life'; this shows that 'Resurrection' and 'Life' are not mere doctrines, but in reality, a Person, the Lord Jesus Christ)*: **he who believes in Me, though he were dead, yet shall he live** *(speaks of* *the coming Resurrection of Life, when all the Sainted dead will rise [I Thess. 4:13-18])*:

DO YOU BELIEVE THIS?

    "And whosoever lives and believes in Me shall never die *('whoever believes in Me will live Eternally')*. **Do you believe this?** *(The Resurrection is the end of death; consequently death has no more to do with the Redeemed; it has done all it can do; it is finished! The Redeemed live in the imparted life that put an end to it; for them, the old life, its death and judgment no longer exist.)*
    "She said unto Him, Yes, Lord: I believe that You are the Christ, the Son of God, which should come into the world. *(Proclaims her belief in the Lord in a different light than she had known Him previously; she now believes that Jesus is God!)*" **(Jn. 11:17-27).**

**THE RAISING OF LAZARUS FROM THE DEAD,
A TYPE OF THE RAPTURE**

    Jesus now comes to the tomb of Lazarus, who had died some four days earlier, and the Scripture says:

    "Then they took away the stone *from the place* **where the dead was laid. And Jesus lifted up** *His* **Eyes, and said, Father, I thank You that You have heard Me** *(proclaims this as a thanksgiving for that which had already been prayed and heard)*.
    "And I knew that You hear Me always *(this speaks of relationship beyond our comprehension)*: **but because of the people which stand by I said** *it*, **that they may believe that You have sent Me** *(the people heard Him pray to the Father, and now they will see the Father answer His prayer; consequently, the proof of Who He is will be undeniable)*.

LAZARUS, COME FORTH

"And when He thus had spoken, He cried with a loud voice, Lazarus, come forth *(constitutes a Command, and from the Creator of the Ages; considering that He is the Resurrection and the Life, had He not called Lazarus by name, all the other Sainted dead would have come forth as well!)*.

"And he who was dead came forth *(constitutes the greatest Miracle in human history)*, bound hand and foot with graveclothes *(his legs were, no doubt, bound separately with him able to walk, but with some difficulty)*: and his face was bound about with a napkin *(concerns a cloth which had been tied over his face, but which he had probably partially removed)*. Jesus said unto them, Loose him, and let him go. *(Refers, as is obvious, to this burial shroud being taken off his body; Lazarus had been called up from Paradise where he had been for the past four days; one can only surmise as to what happened when the Voice of Jesus rang out in that place concerning Lazarus)*" **(Jn. 11:41-44)**.

THE FACT OF THE RAPTURE

Before we address the questions, we will give the great Scriptural verbiage given by Paul concerning the fact of the Rapture found in I Thessalonians, Chapter 4.

The great Apostle said:

"But I would not have you to be ignorant, Brethren, concerning them which are asleep *(refers to Believers who have died)*, that you sorrow not, even as others which have no hope. *(This concerns those who do not know the Lord who will have no part in the First Resurrection of Life and, therefore, no hope for Heaven.)*

"For if we believe that Jesus died and rose again

(the very Foundation of Christianity is the Death and Resurrection of Christ; it is the proof of life after death in a glorified state for all Saints in that life, which, incidentally, will never end), **even so them also which sleep in Jesus will God bring with Him.** *(This refers to the Rapture of the Church, or the Resurrection of all Believers, with both phrases meaning the same thing, even as Paul describes in I Cor., Chpt. 15. At death, the soul and the spirit of the Child of God instantly go to be with Jesus [Phil. 1:23], while the physical body goes back to dust. At the Rapture, God will replace what was the physical body with a Glorified Body, united with the soul and the spirit. In fact, the soul and the spirit of each individual will accompany the Lord down close to this Earth to be united with a Glorified Body, which will then make the Believer whole.)*

THE WORD OF THE LORD

"For this we say unto you by the Word of the Lord *(presents the Doctrine of the Rapture of the Church as the 'Word of the Lord')*, **that we which are alive *and* remain unto the Coming of the Lord** *(all Believers who are alive at the Rapture)* **shall not prevent them which are asleep.** *(This refers to the fact that the living Saints will not precede or go before the dead Saints.)*

THE SHOUT, THE VOICE, AND THE TRUMP

"For the Lord Himself shall descend from Heaven with a shout *(refers to 'the same Jesus' which the Angels proclaimed in Acts 1:11)*, **with the voice of the Archangel** *(refers to Michael, the only one referred to as such [Jude, Vs. 9])*, **and with the Trump of God** *(doesn't exactly say God will personally blow this Trumpet, but that it definitely does belong to Him, whoever does signal the blast)*: **and the dead in Christ shall rise first** *(the criteria* *for being ready for the Rapture is to be 'in Christ,' which means that all who are truly Born-Again will definitely go in the Rapture)*:

TO MEET THE LORD IN THE AIR

"Then we which are alive *and* remain shall be caught up *(Raptured)* **together with them** *(the Resurrected dead)* **in the clouds** *(clouds of Saints, not clouds as we normally think of such)*, **to meet the Lord in the air** *(the Greek word for 'air' is 'aer,' and refers to the lower atmosphere or from about 6,000 feet down; so, the Lord will come at least within 6,000 feet of the Earth, perhaps even lower, with all the Saints meeting Him there; but He, at that time, will not come all the way to the Earth, that awaiting the Second Coming, which will be seven or more years later)*: **and so shall we ever be with the Lord.** *(This presents the greatest meeting humanity will have ever known.)*

"Wherefore comfort one another with these words. *(This pertains to the future of the Child of God, which is Glorious indeed!)*" **(I Thess. 4:13-18).**

WHAT IS THE RAPTURE?

The Rapture of the Church, as the term is commonly used, refers to the catching away from this Earth to the Lord Jesus Christ and then to Heaven, of every Saint of God who has ever lived, all the way back to Adam and Eve. It will also include every Saint of God who will be alive on Earth at that particular time. It will take place, *"in a moment, in the twinkling of an eye"* **(I Cor. 15:52).**

Incidentally, the two words, *"Rapture"* **and** *"Resurrection,"* **both portray the same event. So, if one believes in the Resurrection, then one at the same time believes in the Rapture. While some may argue the time of this coming event, they cannot Scripturally argue the fact of this event. Paul goes into**

great detail concerning the great Doctrine of the Resurrection. In I Thessalonians 4:13-18, he proclaims by the guidance of the Holy Spirit the fact of the Resurrection. In I Corinthians, Chapter 15, he gives us the manner of the Resurrection.

Jesus addressed this as well. He said:

JESUS

"**Verily, verily, I say unto you** *(always signals a statement of the highest authority, and proclaims Jesus as that Authority)*, **The hour is coming, and now is, when the dead shall hear the Voice of the Son of God: and they who hear shall live** *(has a double meaning:*

• *It refers to people being Saved, thereby, coming from spiritual death to Spiritual Life.*

• *It refers to the coming Resurrection of Life, when all Saints will be resurrected.)*

"**For as the Father has Life in Himself** *(refers to God as the Eternal Fountain of Life, the Source Ultimate)*; **so has He given to the Son to have Life in Himself** *(Jesus saying that He is not merely a participator in this 'Life,' but in fact is, as well, the Source of Life and, in Truth, the Ultimate Source exactly as the Father; consequently, He again claims Deity)*;

JESUS IS THE JUDGE

"**And has given Him Authority to execute judgment also** *(this speaks of 'The Judgment Seat of Christ,' which will be for all Believers and, as well, the 'Great White Throne Judgment,' which will be for all the unsaved)*, **because He is the Son of Man** *(refers to Him paying the price on Calvary's Cross, and by the merit of such, He will also be the 'Judge')*.

"**Marvel not at this** *(these statements, as given by Christ, left the religious leaders of Israel speechless)*:

for the hour is coming, in the which all who are in the graves shall hear His Voice *(speaks of the Resurrection of Life and the Resurrection of Damnation; again, these statements proclaim Christ as the Lord of both life and death)*,

THE RESURRECTION OF LIFE

"And shall come forth *(portrays both Resurrections, as we shall see, and according to His 'Voice')*; they who have done good, unto the Resurrection of Life *(pertains to the First Resurrection, or as commonly referred, 'the Rapture' [I Thess. 4:13-18])*;

THE RESURRECTION OF DAMNATION

"And they who have done evil, unto the Resurrection of Damnation. *(This last Resurrection will take place approximately a thousand years after the First Resurrection of Life [Dan. 12:2; Rev., Chpt. 20])*" **(Jn. 5:25-29).**

Let me again emphasize the fact that both the Rapture and the Resurrection are two words for the same event. For those who claim they don't believe in the Rapture, whether they realize it or not, they are saying they don't believe in a Resurrection, and I don't think they mean to say that.

WHEN WILL THE RAPTURE OCCUR?

We are given no date, or anything that resembles such, in the Word of God as to the time of the Rapture. In fact, our Lord said the following:

The Disciples asked Him, *"Lord, will You at this time restore again the Kingdom to Israel?"*

Even though this question has nothing to do with the Rapture, still, the answer of our Lord will throw some light on the subject. He said:

"... It is not for you to know the times or the seasons, which the Father has put in His Own power. *(The Master is saying that it is not the business of the followers of Christ to know this information, but rather to 'occupy till I come' [Lk. 19:13])*" **(Acts 1:7).**

We've already addressed this, however, we do know that at approximately every 1,000 year interval or 2,000 year interval, the Lord does something special. The Church Age has lasted now for nearly 2,000 years. If nothing else, that tells us that the Rapture will take place very soon.

We do know from the Word of God that the Great Tribulation cannot come about until the Rapture takes place. Paul said concerning this, and I quote from THE EXPOSITOR'S STUDY BIBLE:

AND THEN SHALL THAT WICKED BE REVEALED

"And now you know what withholds *(speaks of the Church)* that he might be revealed in his time. *(This speaks of the Antichrist who will be revealed or made known after the Rapture of the Church.)*

"For the mystery of iniquity does already work *(concerns false teaching by false teachers)*: only he *(the Church)* who now lets *(who now hinders evil)* **will let** *(will continue to hinder)*, until he *(the Church)* be taken out of the way. *(The pronoun 'he' confuses some people. In Verses 4 and 6, the pronoun 'He' refers to the Antichrist, while in Verse 7, 'he' refers to the Church.)*

"And then *(after the Rapture of the Church)* shall that Wicked *(the Antichrist)* be revealed *(proving conclusively that the Rapture takes place before the Great Tribulation [Mat. 24:21])*, whom the Lord shall consume with the spirit of His Mouth *(should have been translated, 'the Breath of His Mouth' [Isa. 11:4])*, and shall destroy with the brightness of His Coming. *(Both phrases refer to the*

Second Coming)" (II Thess. 2:6-8).

WILL THE GREAT TRIBULATION BEGIN IMMEDIATELY AFTER THE RAPTURE?

The Great Tribulation probably will not begin immediately after the Rapture. In fact, it would not be unscriptural to say that the possibility exists that several years could pass between the Rapture of the Church and the advent of the Antichrist, which will signal the beginning of the Great Tribulation. But then again, it is possible that the Great Tribulation could begin very shortly after the Rapture. The Scripture gives no indication either way.

WHAT ARE THE QUALIFICATIONS FOR BEING READY FOR THE RAPTURE?

There is only one qualification for being ready for the Rapture and that is to be *"Born-Again,"* i.e., *"to be in Christ."* The Scripture says, *". . . and the dead in Christ shall rise first"* (I Thess. 4:16).

There is no such thing as a partial justification. One is either totally justified or not justified at all. While some Christians most definitely are closer to the Lord than others, still, all will go. Yet, there are millions in churches who think they are Born-Again, when, in reality, they aren't. In fact, in the United States alone, I am told that approximately one hundred million people claim to be Born-Again. I would to God that were so, but I'm certain that it's not. As to exactly how many are truly Saved in this particular country, only the Lord knows, as He is the only One Who knows regarding the entirety of His Body, and wherever in the world they might be.

LUKEWARM

The Holy Spirit likens those who were once Saved but now

construed as *"lukewarm,"* as being labeled by the Lord as lost. Jesus said:

"I know your works, that you are neither cold nor hot: I would you were cold or hot.

"So then because you are lukewarm, and neither cold nor hot, I will spew you out of My Mouth" (Rev. 3:15-16).

A FORM OF GODLINESS

Paul addressed those who were religious, but who were not Saved, regardless of what they claimed, as *"having a form of Godliness, but denying the power thereof."* He then said, *"from such turn away"* (II Tim. 3:5).

Regrettably and sadly, millions fit this description.

THOSE WHO HAVE DEPARTED FROM THE FAITH

To *"depart from the Faith"* means that they have once been in the Faith. The Faith speaks of Christ and the Cross. In other words, the Cross of Christ is the Object of one's Faith, if such a person is right with God. When people leave the Cross and go to other things, which millions are now doing, the Scripture says of them:

"Now the **Spirit** *(Holy Spirit)* **speaks expressly** *(pointedly),* **that in the latter times** *(the times in which we now live, the last of the last days, which begin the fulfillment of Endtime Prophecies)* **some shall depart from the Faith** *(anytime Paul uses the term 'the Faith,' in short, he is referring to the Cross; so, we are told here that some will depart from the Cross as the means of Salvation and Victory),* **giving heed to seducing spirits** *(evil spirits, i.e., 'religious spirits,' making something seem like what it isn't),* **and doctrines of devils.** *(Should have been translated, 'doctrines of demons'; the 'seducing spirits' entice Believers away from the true Faith, causing them to believe* *'doctrines inspired by demon spirits')"* **(I Tim. 4:1).**

Needless to say, such individuals, as with the lukewarm and as with those who have a form of Godliness, are labeled by the Lord as unsaved, despite their claims, and will not go in the Rapture.

Regrettably and sadly, there is less true Gospel of Jesus Christ being preached presently than at any time since the Reformation. As a result, fewer people are being Born-Again. Fewer Believers are being baptized with the Holy Spirit. Fewer lives are being changed.

THE CROSS OF CHRIST

Paul said:

"**We preach Christ Crucified** *(this is the Foundation of the Word of God and, thereby, of Salvation)*, **unto the Jews a stumblingblock** *(the Cross was the stumblingblock)*, **and unto the Greeks foolishness.** *(Both found it difficult to accept as God a dead Man hanging on a Cross, for such Christ was to them)"* **(I Cor. 1:23).**

The great Apostle is here plainly stating that the Message of *"Christ Crucified"* was not a popular message. It was not popular among the Jews, and for all the obvious reasons, and neither was it popular with the Greeks, i.e., *"Gentiles."* Nevertheless, the great Apostle said this is what must be preached, Christ and Him Crucified, and nothing else.

Why?

The only means of Salvation for the sinner is what Jesus did for sinners at the Cross. The only means of Sanctification for the Saint, i.e., how we live for God, is what Jesus did for us at the Cross. So, if any preacher preaches anything else other than *"Christ and Him Crucified,"* whatever it is he is preaching, and ever how good it might sound to the carnal ear, it will affect no positive results. Concerning this, Paul was a whole lot stronger than I am. He said:

LET HIM BE ACCURSED

"But though we *(Paul and his associates)*, or an Angel from Heaven, preach any other gospel unto you than that which we have preached unto you *(Jesus Christ and Him Crucified)*, let him be accursed. *(Eternally condemned; the Holy Spirit speaks this through Paul, making this very serious. 'Accursed' means to be 'eternally condemned,' which means the loss of the soul)*" (Gal. 1:8).

To be sure, most of the so-called gospel that's going out presently is certainly not *"Christ and Him Crucified."*

WHAT WILL HAPPEN ON EARTH WITH EVERY BELIEVER GONE?

When the Believers are gone from the Earth, the Wrath of God is going to be poured out on this world which has forgotten the Lord and spurned His Mercy and Grace, and done so days without number. John wrote:

"For the great day of His wrath is come *(the 'Great Day' is the coming Great Tribulation, which will last for seven years)*; and who shall be able to stand? *(This refers to the fact that man has set himself against God ever since the Fall. Now man will see exactly how powerful God actually is)*" (Rev. 6:17).

One of the many reasons we know that Believers will not have to go through the Great Tribulation, as some claim, is because the Scripture plainly says:

"For God has not appointed us to wrath *(has not*

appointed Believers to go through the Great Tribulation)*, **but to obtain Salvation by our Lord Jesus Christ** *(again, pertains to the Rapture of the Church)*,

"**Who died for us, that, whether we wake or sleep, we should live together with Him** *(again, the Rapture, all made possible by the Cross)*.

"**Wherefore comfort yourselves together** *(it refers to comfort in view of the coming Rapture and the escape from wrath, which will be poured out upon the world in the coming Great Tribulation)*, **and edify one another, even as also you do.** *(This refers to cheering and strengthening one another)*" **(I Thess. 5:9-11).**

FOR CLEANSING AND PURIFICATION?

Some claim that Believers will have to go through the Great Tribulation in order to be cleansed and purified. The following should be noted:
• What about all the Believers who have lived and died before the coming time of the Great Tribulation? They did not go through the Wrath of God in order to be cleansed and purified.
• Those who claim that Believers will have to go through the Great Tribulation in order to be cleansed and purified are making a mockery of the Cross of Christ. It is the Blood, the precious Blood of the Lord Jesus Christ, which cleanses from all sin (I Jn. 1:7). To claim that something has to be added to that is a gross sin, as should be overly obvious.

The Church, and we speak of those who are truly Born-Again, serves as a restraining force against evil in this world, and has been doing so since its inception on the Day of Pentecost. Even in America, think about what would happen to this country if every Born-Again Believer were suddenly removed. The true Body of Christ is the restraining force against evil all over the world. The following should be noted:
• Much Bible, much freedom!
• A little Bible, a little freedom!

• No Bible, no freedom!

When all Believers are taken out at the Rapture, this world is not going to be a very pleasant place in which to live, especially considering that the Wrath of God is now going to be poured out, as well, and over the entirety of the Earth.

WILL ALL BABIES AND ALL LITTLE CHILDREN BELOW THE AGE OF ACCOUNTABILITY GO IN THE RAPTURE?

For certain all these will be included in the Rapture whose Mother or Dad or both belong to the Lord. Concerning this, the Scripture says:

"For the unbelieving husband is Sanctified by the wife, and the unbelieving wife is Sanctified by the husband *(means that the Believer, by virtue of being one flesh with his or her unbelieving spouse, is not considered living in an unlawful relationship; 'Sanctified' means that God looks at the home as a Christian home and marriage, even though one or the other partner is unsaved)*: else were your children unclean; but now are they holy. *(Looked at by the Lord as being born in a Christian home, despite the fact that either the Mother or Dad is unsaved)*" (I Cor. 7:14).

UNCLEAN

The latter part of this Verse says, *"else were your children unclean,"* which means that children in a home with both parents unsaved, and we speak of those below the age of accountability, are looked at by the Lord as unclean!

What does that mean?

It means that if the Rapture takes place, they will not go in the Rapture, despite the fact of being children below the age of accountability. This does not mean they are eternally lost, for at any time upon reaching the age of accountability, where they have the capacity to reason and make decisions, they can accept the Lord and be Saved.

WHAT IS THE AGE OF ACCOUNTABILITY?

The age of accountability varies with different children in different homes. If little children are raised in Christian homes, meaning that they are exposed to the Word of God even on a daily basis, such children might very well reach the age of accountability at the tender age of six. Raised in a home that doesn't know God, the children might be as old as eight or ten.

If I remember my age correctly, my parents came to the Lord when I was five years old. I don't recall the Lord dealing with me about Salvation until I was eight years of age. Strangely enough, I was Saved while standing in front of a moving picture theater on a Saturday afternoon, waiting to go into the movie. Standing in line with the children, waiting for the ticket window to open, the Lord spoke to my heart and said, *"Do not go in this place, give your heart to Me, for you are a chosen vessel to be used exclusively in My Service."*

When the Lord said that to me, it startled me greatly. Even though I was only eight years of age, I knew it was the Lord, and of that I had no doubt.

I made no move, meaning that I did nothing. The Lord spoke to me again, basically saying the same thing.

About that time, the ticket window opened and the kids were buying their tickets and going into the movie house. I remember laying my quarter on the counter in order to buy a ticket with the Voice of the Lord still ringing in my heart and ears. The spool of tickets jammed with the attendant then becoming occupied with that. I'll always believe that the Lord jammed that spool of tickets in order that He could move upon me again, which He did.

I grabbed my quarter and left and went down to the corner drugstore where I bought an ice-cream cone.

I remember coming out of the drugstore, standing on the corner with the ice-cream cone, and, all of a sudden, I felt it. It was like 50 pounds had lifted off my shoulders. I knew I was Saved.

If I had not said *"yes"* to the Lord at that time, from that moment when the Lord first spoke to me, I would have been responsible for my soul. In other words, had I been killed in a car wreck or died in some way, even at the tender age of eight, I would have died eternally lost. But, thank the Lord, I said an eternal *"yes"* to the Lord Jesus Christ, and the Lord wondrously Saved me.

FAMILY WORSHIP CENTER'S SALVATION STATION

Salvation Station is the name of our children's group at Family Worship Center. We have, we think, one of the finest Children's Pastors in the country. It is quite common in the Campmeetings and the Children's Camps for boys and girls to lie flat on their backs on the floor, speaking with other Tongues, as the Spirit of God gives the utterance. That and that alone is the only answer for juvenile delinquency.

Our Lord said a long time ago, *"Suffer the little children to come unto Me, and forbid them not: for of such is the Kingdom of God"* (Mk. 10:14).

Then the Scripture says:

"Verily I say unto you, Whosoever shall not receive the Kingdom of God as a little child *(the simplicity of the little child is the model and the rule for everyone who desires, by the Grace of Christ, to obtain the Kingdom of Heaven)*, he shall not enter therein *(presents a double negative in the Greek, and consequently, presents an emphatic denial)*.

"And He took them up in His Arms, put *His* hands upon them, and blessed them. *(He blessed them fervently)*" (Mk. 10:15-16).

WHAT DO THE WORDS *"CAUGHT UP"* FROM I THESSALONIANS 4:17 MEAN?

The words *"caught up"* in the Greek are *"harpazo,"* and actually have several meanings. They are:
• It means *"to carry off by force."* This means that Satan and his demons will not be able to stop this departure, with the Lord using whatever force is necessary against the powers of darkness in order to accomplish this task.
• The word means *"to snatch out or away."* This means it will be done instantly.
• The word also means *"to seize and carry off speedily."* It is used of Divine Power transferring a person marvelously and swiftly from one place to another.
It is believed by some scholars that Heaven is beyond the furthest star. It has taken the light of some stars five hundred million years to reach this Earth, traveling 186,000 miles per second. So, that means that if Believers would travel at the speed of light to Heaven, it would take five hundred million years to reach Heaven, which we know is not the case. The idea is that Christians with Glorified Bodies will travel with the speed of thought. In other words, wherever one wants to be, irrespective of the distance, there they will be. One might say, *"One moment on Earth, the next moment in Heaven."*
• The last meaning is *"to claim for one's self eagerly."* The idea is, the Lord Jesus Christ as the Bridegroom, Who comes from Heaven, will claim His Bride, the Church. He will eagerly take us with Him to Glory.

WHAT IS THE DIFFERENCE IN THE RAPTURE AND THE SECOND COMING?

• The Rapture will take place seven or more years before the Second Coming (II Thess. 2:7-8).
• The Rapture will take place before the Great Tribulation and the Second Coming will take place at the end of the

Great Tribulation (II Thess. 2:6-8).

• At the Rapture our Lord will come for His Saints, while at the Second Coming, He will come <u>with</u> His Saints (I Thess. 4:13-18; Rev. 19).

• At the Rapture our Lord will not come all the way to the Earth, while at the Second Coming, our Lord most definitely will come all the way to the Earth, namely the Mount of Olivet (I Thess. 4:13-18; Zech. 14:4).

• At the Rapture our Lord will not fight Satan and his demon spirits, etc. At the Second Coming our Lord will cast the Evil One, along with all his demon spirits and fallen angels, into the bottomless pit (Rev. 19).

• At the Rapture all Believers, those who have passed on and those who are alive, will receive Glorified Bodies. At the Second Coming all Believers will already have Glorified Bodies (I Cor. 15:51-55).

• At the Rapture of the Church all the Saints will go to Heaven with Christ, while at the Second Coming, all Believers will come from Heaven with Christ to the Earth (I Thess. 4:13-18; Rev. 19).

• The Rapture and the Second Coming are not two parts of one coming, but rather, two different Comings (I Thess. 4:13-18; Zech. 14:4-21; Rev. 19).

• At the Rapture no one but the Saints of God will see the Lord Jesus Christ, while at the Second Coming, every eye shall see Him (Rev. 17).

• There are no Biblical signs to be fulfilled before the Rapture of the Church, while there are many signs to be fulfilled before the Second Coming (II Thess. 2:6-8).

• While at the Rapture, no mention is made as to the mode of transportation; at the Second Coming every Saint will be riding white spirit horses (Rev. 19:14).

WHY IS THE RAPTURE SO IMPORTANT TO THE CHURCH?

The Rapture is important to the Church for many and

varied reasons!

• At the Rapture all Saints, both those who had passed on and those who are alive, will receive Glorified Bodies (I Cor. 15:51-55).

• The Rapture will take every Saint of God to Heaven, where every Believer will receive a reward (I Cor. 3:8).

• The Rapture will take all Believers away from the Wrath of God that is to be poured out on this Earth during the time of the Great Tribulation, which will follow the Rapture (I Thess. 5:9-11).

• Due to apostasy, some have stated that, as the Second Coming will save the Earth, likewise, the Rapture will save the Church (I Thess. 4:13-18).

• The Rapture of the Church will open the door for the Antichrist to make his debut (II Thess. 2:6-8).

WILL THE HOLY SPIRIT BE TAKEN OUT OF THE WORLD AT THE RAPTURE OF THE CHURCH?

No! The Holy Spirit will not be taken out of the world at the Rapture of the Church.

I realize that some teach this, but it's not correct. The Holy Spirit is God and, as such, He is everywhere.

Peter plainly states that the Holy Spirit will be in the world during the Great Tribulation and working mightily. The Scripture says:

"And it shall come to pass in the last days, saith **God** *(proclaims these 'last days' as beginning on the Day of Pentecost and continuing through the coming Great Tribulation)*, **I will pour out of My Spirit upon all flesh** *(speaks of all people everywhere and, therefore, not limited to some particular geographical location; as well, it is not limited respecting race, color, or creed)*; **and your sons and your daughters shall Prophesy** *(includes both genders)*, **and your young men shall see visions, and** your old men shall dream dreams *(all given by the Holy Spirit; the Hebrew language insinuates, 'both your young men and old men shall see visions, and both your old men and young men shall dream dreams'; it applies to both genders as well)*:

I WILL POUR OUT IN THOSE DAYS OF MY SPIRIT

"And on My servants and on My handmaidens I will pour out in those days of My Spirit *(is meant purposely to address two classes of people who have been given very little status in the past, slaves and women)*; and they shall Prophesy *(pertains to one of the 'Gifts of the Spirit' [I Cor. 12:8-10])*:

"And I will show wonders in Heaven above, and signs in the Earth beneath; blood, and fire, and vapor of smoke *(pertains to the fact that these 'days of My Spirit' will cover the entirety of the Church Age, even into the coming Great Tribulation; that time limit has now been nearly two thousand years)*:

"The sun shall be turned into darkness, and the moon into blood *(not meant to be literal, but rather that the moon will look blood red because of atmospheric conditions)*, before that great and notable Day of the Lord come *(the Second Coming)*:

"And it shall come to pass, *that* whosoever shall call on the Name of the Lord shall be Saved *(Joel 2:30-32; presents one of the most glorious statements ever made; it includes both Jews and Gentiles equally)*" **(Acts 2:17-21).**

WHAT IS THE MEANING OF *"SHOUT," "VOICE,"* AND *"TRUMPET,"* OF I THESSALONIANS 4:16?

• The *"Shout"* will come from the Lord Jesus Christ, and it will be a *"Victory shout."*

• The *"Voice"* of the Archangel speaks of Michael. Considering that He is the protector of Israel, the *"Voice"* will signal His coming to their defense.

• The *"Trump"* of God pertains to the following:

In Old Testament times the blast of the Trumpet signaled either the fact that all able-bodied men were to gather for a great festival or war. This Trump will signal both, war made on the Antichrist and his army, and then followed by a great festival upon his defeat.

Incidentally, this is the *"Trump of God."* However, as to who will originate the blast, we aren't exactly told.

"Whom have I, Lord, in Heaven but Thee?
"None but Thee! None but Thee!
"And this my song through life shall be:
"Christ for me! Christ for me!
"He has for me the winepress trod,
"He has redeemed me 'by His Blood.'
"And reconciled my soul to God:
"Christ for me! Christ for me!"

"I envy not the rich their joys:
"Christ for me! Christ for me!
"I covet not Earth's glittering toys:
"Christ for me! Christ for me!
"Earth can no lasting bliss bestow,
"Fading is stamped on all below;
"Mine is a joy no end can know:
"Christ for me! Christ for me!"

"Though with the poor be cast my lot:
"Christ for me! Christ for me!
"He knows best, I murmur not:
"Christ for me! Christ for me!
"Though 'vine' and 'fig-tree' blight assail,
"The labor of the olive fail,

"And death o'er flock and herd prevail,
"Christ for me! Christ for me!"

"Though I am now on hostile ground,
"Christ for me! Christ for me!
"And sin beset me all around,
"Christ for me! Christ for me!
"Let Earth her fiercest battles wage,
"And foes against my soul engage,
"Strong in His strength I scorn their rage:
"Christ for me! Christ for me!"

"And when my life draws to its close,
"Christ for me! Christ for me!
"Safe in His arms I shall repose,
"Christ for me! Christ for me!
"When sharpest pains my frame pervade,
"And all the powers of nature fade,
"Still will I sing through death's cold shade,
"Christ for me! Christ for me!"

CHAPTER TWO

When Will The Antichrist Be Revealed?

QUESTION:

WHEN WILL THE ANTICHRIST BE REVEALED?

ANSWER:

After the Rapture of the Church.

We know from the Word of God that the Antichrist will not be revealed until after the Rapture of the Church; however, the Scripture is silent as to how long. In fact, for certain events to be brought into place for the Antichrist to make his debut, which we will address momentarily, several things have to happen. So, it could well be several years from the time of the Rapture until the Antichrist is revealed. Concerning this, the Apostle Paul deals with the Second Coming and in that explanation gives us information concerning the Antichrist, in effect, that the Antichrist must make his debut before the Second Coming can take place. It will be during the Battle of Armageddon.

There were some people even during the time of Paul who were claiming that the Second Coming was about to take place at any time. Remember, Paul is here speaking of the Second Coming and not the Rapture, even though the Rapture will as well be addressed in his explanation. Concerning this he says:

THE DAY OF THE LORD

"Now we beseech you, Brethren, by the coming of our Lord Jesus Christ *(refers to both the Rapture and the Second Coming)*, **and** *by* our gathering together unto Him *(this phrase refers strictly to the Rapture)*,

"That you be not soon shaken in mind, or be troubled *(false doctrine does this)*, **neither by spirit** *(messages in Tongues and Interpretation, which purport to be of the Lord, but really were not)*, **nor by word** *(pertaining to* *those who claimed to have a Word from the Lord)*, **nor by letter as from us** *(someone had written a letter claiming certain prophetic things, and evidently had signed Paul's name to it, which means it was a forgery)*, **as that the Day of Christ is at hand** *(should have been translated, 'the Day of the Lord,' because this is how the best manuscripts read; the 'Day of the Lord' refers to all events after the Rapture; some were claiming, even in Paul's day, that the Second Coming was about to take place, which, of course, was wrong)*.

THE DEPARTURE

"Let no man deceive you by any means *(in other words, don't listen to that which is Scripturally incorrect)***: for** *that day shall not come*, **except there come a falling away first** *(should have been translated, 'for that day shall not come, except there come a departure first'; this speaks of the Rapture, which, in essence, says the Second Coming cannot take place until certain things happen)*, **and that man of sin be revealed, the son of perdition** *(this speaks of the Antichrist, who must come upon the world scene before the Second Coming)***;**

"Who opposes and exalts himself above all that is called God *(pertains to his declaration of himself as Deity)*, **or that is worshipped** *(the Antichrist will put down all religions, at least in the area which he controls, making himself alone the object of worship)***; so that he as God sits in the Temple of God** *(refers to the Jewish Temple, which will be rebuilt in Jerusalem; the Antichrist will take over the Temple, making it his religious headquarters)*, **showing himself that he is God** *(This proclaims his announcement of Deity as it regards himself)*.

"Don't you remember, that, when I was yet with you, I told you these things? *(So, there was no excuse for the Thessalonians to be drawn away by false doctrine.)*

THE RAPTURE OF THE CHURCH

"**And now you know what withholds** *(speaks of the Church)* **that he might be revealed in his time.** *(This speaks of the Antichrist who will be revealed or made known after the Rapture of the Church.)*
"**For the mystery of iniquity does already work** *(concerns false teaching by false teachers)*: **only he** *(the Church)* **who now lets** *(who now hinders evil)* ***will let*** *(will continue to hinder)*, **until he** *(the Church)* **be taken out of the way.** *(The pronoun 'he' confuses some people. In Verses 4 and 6, the pronoun 'he' refers to the Antichrist, while in Verse 7, 'he' refers to the Church.)*

THE ANTICHRIST WILL THEN BE REVEALED

"**And then** *(after the Rapture of the Church)* **shall that Wicked** *(the Antichrist)* **be revealed** *(proving conclusively that the Rapture takes place before the Great Tribulation [Mat. 24:21])*, **whom the Lord shall consume with the spirit of His Mouth** *(should have been translated, 'the Breath of His Mouth' [Isa. 11:4])*, **and shall destroy with the brightness of His Coming** *(both phrases refer to the Second Coming)*:

THE ANTICHRIST

"***Even him*** *(the Antichrist)* **whose coming is after the working of Satan** *(means that Satan is the sponsor of the Antichrist)* **with all power and signs and lying wonders** *(proclaims the fact that the Antichrist's rise to power, at least in the beginning, will be very religious)*,
"**And with all deceivableness of unrighteousness in them who perish** *(refers to the fact that 'all lying powers and lying signs and lying wonders' will be used to deceive the world)*; **because they received not the love**

of the Truth, that they might be Saved *(they rejected Christ and the Cross)*.

A STRONG DELUSION

"And for this cause *(the rejection of Christ and the Cross)* God shall send them strong delusion *(if one doesn't want 'the Truth,' God will see to it one receives a 'delusion')*, that they should believe a lie *(should have been translated, 'that they should believe the lie'; the Greek Text has the definite article 'the lie,' which refers to a specific lie, that 'lie' pertains to anything that leads a person away from the Cross)*:

"That they all might be damned who believe not the Truth *(who would not accept the Cross)*, but had pleasure in unrighteousness. *(The Greek has the definite article, which actually says, 'the unrighteousness,' specifying a particular unrighteousness; it is really referring to the results of rejection of the Cross of Christ)*" (II Thess. 2:1-12).

A good portion of this quoted from II Thessalonians, Chapter 2, is also given in the preceding Chapter; however, inasmuch as these particular prophetic happenings are at times studied separately, I felt it necessary that it be given again. It plainly tells us three things. They are:
• The Rapture of the Church will take place first.
• After the Rapture of the Church, the Antichrist, at a point in time, will then be revealed.
• After the Rapture and the Antichrist being revealed, which includes his effort to take over the world and to destroy the Jews, then the Second Coming will take place.
This is what the Holy Spirit through Paul is telling us.

HOW WILL THE ANTICHRIST MAKE HIS DEBUT?

That's an interesting question!

We know the Antichrist will burst upon the world scene by making peace between the Palestinians, i.e., the Muslim world, and the Jews, which the brightest minds in America have never been able to accomplish. However, the great question is, how will he do this? He will even make it possible for Israel to build her Temple. In fact, we are told that the plans have actually already been drawn for that. How will he be able to persuade the Muslims to allow Israel to build their Temple on the very sight of the Dome of the Rock, the third most holy place, so-called, in Islam?

Some have claimed that Israel will rebuild the Temple somewhere else in the city or even beside the Dome of the Rock; however, I personally do not think there is even a remote chance of that.

We aren't speaking here of just another building site. We are speaking here of the place where God told David that the Temple would be built, which was the threshing floor of Araunah, what is now referred to as the Temple Mount (II Sam. 24:16-25; II Chron. 3:1).

As well, it is believed that the Holy of Holies in the Temple sat over the very spot where Abraham was to offer Isaac, but the Lord intervened by substituting a ram. The Bible says that:

> ". . . Abraham called the name of that place Jehovah-jireh *(meaning 'the Lord will provide')*: as it is said to this day, In the Mount of the Lord it shall be seen *(should read, 'In this Mount Jehovah shall be seen'; this was fulfilled in II Sam. 24:25; I Chron. 21:26; II Chron. 7:1-3)*" (Gen. 22:9-14).

At any rate, there is no way that Israel will build this Temple in that coming day anywhere else than the original Temple site.

The question begs to be answered as to how the Antichrist will pull this off.

Daniel tells us when this will happen, but not exactly how. The great Prophet-Statesman said:

"And he *(the Antichrist)* shall confirm the covenant with many for one week: and in the midst of the week he shall cause the sacrifice and the oblation to cease, and for the overspreading of abominations he shall make it desolate, even until the consummation, and that determined shall be poured upon the desolate. *('And he shall confirm,' refers to the Antichrist. The phrase, 'and in the midst of the week,' refers to three and a half years, at which time the Antichrist will show his true colors and stop the Sacrifices in the newly-built Temple. At that time, he will actually invade Israel, with her suffering her first defeat since her formation as a nation in 1948.*

"'Even until the consummation,' means until the end of the seven-year Great Tribulation period. The phrase, 'and that determined shall be poured upon the desolate,' refers to all the Prophecies being fulfilled regarding the great suffering that Israel will go through the last three and a half years of the Great Tribulation [Mat. 24:21-22])" (Dan. 9:27).

The *"week,"* as Daniel here uses the word, stands for a week of years, or seven years.

THE ATTENTION OF THE WORLD

As we have stated, getting the Muslims to agree to a seven-year pact with Israel, guaranteeing her safety and security and, above all, agreeing to allow the Dome of the Rock to be torn down and the Jewish Temple to be built in its place, will most definitely grab the attention of the world. How in the world will he do this? How can he get these enemies, whose hatred goes back to the time of Abraham, to agree on anything? Five American Presidents have failed in this effort, and Obama will fail also. But yet, the Antichrist will succeed in doing what no one else has been able to do. Two things will then happen:

• The Antichrist will instantly grab the attention of the

world by accomplishing this tremendous feat, which no one else has been able to do. In fact, the world will then breathe a sigh of relief, heralding him as the man of peace, with Israel actually accepting him as her Messiah. His face will be on every television screen in the world, the headlines of every newspaper, and the major magazines heralding his ability. He is the man of the hour. John the Beloved said that he will make his entrance as a lamb, which we will address momentarily.

• Signing the seven-year non-aggression pact between Israel and the Muslim world will begin the seven-year Great Tribulation referred to by Christ (Mat. 24:21).

However, the question still looms large, how will he do this? Daniel gives us a hint. He said:

DECEIT

"And through his policy also he shall cause craft to prosper in his hand; and he shall magnify himself in his heart, and by peace shall destroy many: he shall also stand up against the Prince of princes; but he shall be broken without hand. *(The word 'craft' in the Hebrew is 'mirmah,' meaning 'deceit.' The Antichrist will be the greatest deceiver of all [II Thess. 2:8-12; Rev. 13:14; 19:20]. The last phrase, 'he shall stand up against the Prince of princes,' refers to his war against Christ, which will culminate with the Battle of Armageddon [Joel, Chpt. 3; Zech., Chpt. 14; Rev. 16:13-16; 19:11-21])"* **(Dan. 8:25).**

It is commonly known that the Muslims are looking for a Messiah as well. Actually, the present figurehead in Iran is Ahmadinejad. He has made several statements about wiping Israel off the face of the Earth, etc. According to the Koran, a catastrophe in the world will occur, which will then bring to the fore the Muslim Messiah, who will solve the problems of the world ,and then catapult Islam to its place of world dominance, or so they say.

So, the reason the Muslim world will throw in their lot with this man, who, incidentally, will be a Jew, thinking he is their Messiah, while Israel thinks the same thing, could very well be because of the following:

THE MASTER STROKE

Even though the Bible does not portray the following, and for all the obvious reasons, still, this could very well be the way and the means this man of sin will carry out his evil design.

He will hold secret meetings with the Muslims, in effect, telling them that if they will go along with him in signing this seven-year non-aggression pact with Israel, even agreeing to the Dome of the Rock being torn down and the Jewish Temple built in its place, he will lure the Jews into a false security, with the Apostle Paul prophesying that they will then proclaim *"peace and safety."* He will then turn on Israel and destroy them. This could very well be the *"how"* all of this takes place. One thing is certain:

The Antichrist most definitely will turn on Israel at the mid-point of this seven-year non-aggression timeframe ,and, at that time, were it not for particular events that will take place, he would destroy them. Actually, Israel at that time will suffer her first military defeat since becoming a nation in 1948.

The Muslims will find that the promises of the man of sin are no more positive for them than they have been for Israel. The Antichrist will turn on the Muslims also. In fact, he will oppose every religion in the world, actually setting himself up as god. If Israel desired, they could see his opposition to every religion, in fact, eliminating all other religions except himself, or at least trying to, if they only believed the Bible. It's all there; however, they don't believe the Bible ,so they too will be lured into the trap set by the man of sin.

WHO WILL THE ANTICHRIST BE?

First of all, he will be a Jew. Israel would not accept a

Gentile as her Messiah, as should be obvious. Furthermore, Daniel said, and regarding this very thing, *"neither shall he regard the God of his fathers."* This means that he will not regard the God of *"Abraham, Isaac, and Jacob"* (Dan. 11:37). Inasmuch as the Holy Spirit referred to this as *"his fathers,"* this lets us know that he is a Jew. He will no doubt be extremely charismatic, brilliant, intelligent, etc.; however, that will not be the secret of his power, which we will address momentarily.

FROM WHERE WILL THE ANTICHRIST COME?

While he will be a Jew, he will not originate from Israel, at least as far as is known. Daniel, in essence, tells us where he will come from and the manner in which it will happen in the spirit world. Actually, the Visions given to Daniel as it regards the rise of the Antichrist, which is even yet to come, cover a timeframe of some 2,500 years. We will go to the first Vision the great Prophet-Statesman had, at least as it regards the Antichrist. The Scripture says:

DANIEL'S VISION OF THE FOUR WINDS
AND THE FOUR BEASTS

"In the first year of Belshazzar King of Babylon Daniel had a dream and Visions of his head upon his bed: then he wrote the dream, and told the sum of the matters. *(Chapters 7 through 12, sometimes called The Second Book of Daniel, are mainly occupied with the predictions of the 'fourth beast,' which pertain to the Endtime.)*

"Daniel spoke and said, I saw in my Vision by night, and, behold, the four winds of the heaven strove upon the great sea. *('The four winds of the heaven,' refers to wars, strife, and judgments from God [Jer. 25:32-33; Rev. 7:1-3]. 'Strove upon the great sea,' refers to large numbers of people [Rev. 13:1; 17:1, 15]).*

"And four great beasts came up from the sea, diverse

one from another. *('Beasts' in symbolic Passages repre-sent kingdoms [Rev. 17:8-11] and their rulers, and more than all, the fallen angels behind these kingdoms [Rev. 11:7; 13:18; 17:8]. As stated, 'the sea' has reference to great numbers of people, i.e., 'came up from the people.')*

THE FIRST BEAST, A LION:
BABYLON

"The first was like a lion, and had eagle's wings: I beheld till the wings thereof were plucked, and it was lifted up from the Earth, and made stand upon the feet as a man, and a man's heart was given to it. *('The first was like a lion,' refers to the Babylonian Empire. The 'eagle's wings' symbolize the rapid pace with which the Babylonian Empire conquered its enemies and gained its ascendancy. The phrase, 'I beheld till the wings thereof were plucked,' pertains to the rapid expansion of this Empire, until Nebuchadnezzar went insane as a result of pride [Dan. 4:25-26]).*

THE SECOND BEAST, A BEAR:
MEDO-PERSIA

"And behold another beast, a second, like to a bear, and it raised up itself on one side, and it had three ribs in the mouth of it between the teeth of it: and they said thus unto it, Arise, devour much flesh. *(On the statue of Chapter 2 of the Book of Daniel, the Medo-Persian Empire was represented by a breastplate of silver. The statue as seen in Nebuchadnezzar's dream represented these king-doms as man sees them. The dream given to Daniel repre-sents these kingdoms as God sees them, i.e., 'ferocious.'*
"The term, 'raised up itself on one side,' simply means that the strength of the Persians ultimately was greater than the Medes. The three ribs in the mouth of it between

the teeth refer to the bear devouring much flesh. It symbolized the conquest of Babylon, Lydia, and Egypt.)

THE THIRD BEAST, A LEOPARD:
GRECIA

"After this I beheld, and lo another, like a leopard, which had upon the back of it four wings of a fowl; the beast had also four heads; and dominion was given to it. *(This short description defines the Grecian Empire under Alexander the Great as a 'leopard.' This Empire would come to the fore about 200 years from Daniel's day. The 'four wings of a fowl' symbolized swiftness out of proportion to normal conquests.*

"The 'four heads' symbolized the breakup of this Empire after the death of Alexander at 32 years of age. Heads always symbolize kingdoms in Bible Prophecy. Those four divisions were Greece, Thrace, Syria, and Egypt.)

THE FOURTH BEAST, NON-DESCRIPT:
ROMAN EMPIRE

"After this I saw in the night Visions, and behold a fourth beast, dreadful and terrible, and strong exceedingly; and it had great iron teeth: it devoured and broke in pieces, and stamped the residue with the feet of it; and it was diverse from all the beasts that were before it; and it had ten horns. *(This beast represents the Roman Empire, which was the strongest and most powerful of all. It lasted for nearly a thousand years.*

"The phrase, 'and it had ten horns,' speaks of that which was a part of this beast, and for a particular reason. But, it had nothing to do with the conquests of the original Roman Empire. These 'ten horns' portray ten kingdoms which will arise in the latter days, in fact, in the very near future. These ten nations will persecute Israel.)

THE TEN HORNS AND THE *"LITTLE HORN"*: REVISED ROME AND REVIVED GRECIA

"I considered the horns, and, behold, there came up among them another little horn, before whom there were threeofthefirsthornspluckedupbytheroots: and, behold, in this horn were eyes like the eyes of a man, and a mouth speaking great things. *(At first, Daniel did not understand the horns. Even though the Roman Empire has come and gone, still, the 'ten horns' have not yet risen to power; however, the breakup of the former Soviet Union is the beginning of the fulfillment of this Passage. If one is to notice, the 'ten horns' were a part of the non-descript beast, which has to do with the territory which the old Roman Empire controlled.*

" 'There came up among them another little horn,' means this one came up after the 'ten horns' were fully grown. The 'little horn' is the Antichrist.

"Three of the horns will be plucked by the 'little horn,' meaning that he will defeat these countries in battle, with the others then submitting to him. This will take place in the first half of the Great Tribulation.)

THE JUDGMENT

"I beheld till the thrones were cast down, and the Ancient of Days did sit, Whose garment was white as snow, and the hair of His head like the pure wool: His throne was like the fiery flame, and His wheels as burning fire. *(The phrase, 'I beheld till the thrones were cast down,' speaks of all the Empires, even from Babylon straight through to the Antichrist. All of them have already been 'cast down' with the exception of the 'ten horns' and the 'little horn.' However, as surely as the others were cast down, these two kingdoms also will be cast down.*

" 'And the Ancient of Days did sit,' refers to God the Father and His Dominion. His Kingdom will remain!)

"A fiery stream issued and came forth from before Him: thousand thousands ministered unto Him, and ten thousand times ten thousand stood before Him: the judgment was set, and the books were opened. *(In the Hebrew, the number is 'chiliads of chiliads.' It is a Hebraism meaning 'countless numbers.' 'The judgment was set, and the books were opened,' has to do with the judgment of the nations, which will take place at the beginning of the Millennial Reign.)*

THE *"LITTLE HORN"* DESTROYED

"I beheld then because of the voice of the great words which the horn spoke: I beheld even till the beast was slain, and his body destroyed, and given to the burning flame. *('The great words which the horn spoke' speak of great opposition against God. At the Second Coming of Christ, the Antichrist will be killed and cast into Hell.)*

THE BEASTS PRECEDING THE RULE OF THE *"LITTLE HORN"*

"As concerning the rest of the beasts, they had their dominion taken away: yet their lives were prolonged for a season and time. *('As concerning the rest of the beasts,' refers to the kingdoms preceding the little horn, beginning back with the Babylonian Empire. Even though these Empires have long since passed away, still, Gentiles rule the world; this is referred to as the 'Times of the Gentiles' [Lk. 21:24]. The 'prolonging' will continue until the Second Coming.)*

THE SECOND ADVENT OF THE MESSIAH

"I saw in the night Visions, and, behold, One like the Son of Man came with the clouds of Heaven, and came to the Ancient of Days, and they brought Him near before

Him. *(This 'One like the Son of Man' is 'The Lord Jesus Christ.' We have here the Trinity represented: God the Father, i.e., 'the Ancient of Days,' 'the Son of Man,' Who, as stated, is Jesus Christ, and 'the Holy Spirit,' Who inspired this.)*

"**And there was given Him dominion, and glory, and a kingdom, that all people, nations, and languages, should serve Him: His dominion is an everlasting dominion, which shall not pass away, and His kingdom that which shall not be destroyed.** *(This Verse corresponds with 2:35. This Kingdom of Righteousness will begin immediately after the Second Coming, with Christ as its Supreme and Eternal Head.)*

THE INTERPRETATION OF THE VISION

"**I Daniel was grieved in my spirit in the midst of my body, and the Visions of my head troubled me.**

"**I came near unto one of them who stood by, and asked him the truth of all this. So he told me, and made me know the interpretation of the things.** *(The phrase, 'One of them who stood by,' refers to the countless numbers who are standing before the Throne of God. Quite possibly, this was Gabriel; however, we have no proof.)*

"**These great beasts, which are four, are four kings, which shall arise out of the Earth.** *(The 'four kings' are, as stated, Babylon, Medo-Persia, Greece, and Rome. 'Which shall arise out of the Earth,' simply means that they are of the people, of man, and, therefore, not of God. The Kingdom of Verse 14 is of God and from God, and consequently, will last forever.)*

SAINTS OF THE MOST HIGH

"**But the Saints of the Most High shall take the kingdom, and possess the kingdom forever, even forever and ever.** *('The Saints' in this Passage refer to Israel,* which will be restored and become the leading nation in the world under Christ.)

THE FOURTH BEAST

"**Then I would know the truth of the fourth beast, which was diverse from all the others, exceeding dreadful, whose teeth were of iron, and his nails of brass; which devoured, broke in pieces, and stamped the residue with his feet** *(the 'fourth beast,' as stated, is a symbol of the old Roman Empire, the fourth of four kingdoms in succession. It is mentioned by name only in the New Testament [Jn. 11:48; Acts 2:10; 16:21].*

"'And his nails of brass,' presents something added, which is not mentioned in the description given in Verses 7 and 8. They symbolize the Grecian Empire element of the image of Dan. 2:39, 45.

"This means that the Antichrist will have characteristics of both the Roman Empire and the ancient Grecian Empire);

THE TEN HORNS

"**And of the ten horns that were in his head, and of the other which came up, and before whom three fell; even of that horn that had eyes, and a mouth that spoke very great things, whose look was more stout than his fellows.** *(The 'other which came up' is the same as the 'little horn' of Verse 8, and is the Antichrist, who will come on the world scene shortly after the Rapture of the Church [II Thess. 2:7-8])*.

"**I beheld, and the same horn made war with the Saints, and prevailed against them** *(the 'Saints' mentioned here are not the Church, but rather Israel. The 'war' spoken of here concerns the Antichrist signing a seven-year non-aggression pact with Israel, and then breaking it at approximately the midpoint, then declaring war on Israel)*;

THE ANCIENT OF DAYS

"Until the Ancient of Days came, and judgment was given to the Saints of the Most High; and the time came that the Saints possessed the kingdom. *('Until the Ancient of Days came,' refers back to Verses 9, 13, and 14. It does not actually mean that God the Father will come to planet Earth at this time, but instead that He will direct the proceedings from His Throne.*

"*'And the time came that the Saints possessed the kingdom,' refers to the Second Coming of the Lord, when Israel will then accept Christ as Saviour, Lord, and Messiah, and will be restored and brought back to her rightful place and position).*

THE FOURTH BEAST

"Thus he said, The fourth beast shall be the fourth kingdom upon Earth, which shall be diverse from all kingdoms, and shall devour the whole Earth, and shall tread it down, and break it in pieces. *(The Angel Gabriel speaks in Verses 17 and 18 in answer to Daniel's request; then Daniel asks more questions in Verses 19 through 22. Gabriel now picks up the dialogue and continues with the explanation through Verse 27.*

"*'And shall devour the whole Earth, and shall tread it down, and break it in pieces,' refers to the ferocity and the total power of the Roman Empire. It ruled the world not too much short of a thousand years.)*

THE TEN HORNS

"And the ten horns out of this kingdom are ten kings that shall arise: and another shall rise after them; and he shall be diverse from the first, and he shall subdue three kings. *(Some teach that the ten toes and ten horns of*

Daniel, Chapters 2 and 7, are ten barbarous tribes which overran the old Roman Empire between A.D. 351-474. However, this is error because of the following:

"The God of Heaven is to set up a Kingdom on Earth 'in the days of these kings' [2:44-45; Rev. 19:11-20:7]. It should be obvious to all that the Lord did not set up such a kingdom in A.D. 351-474. In fact, He has not yet done so; therefore, it is obvious that the 'ten horns' representing ten nations are yet future.)

THE ANTICHRIST

"And he shall speak great words against the Most High, and shall wear out the Saints of the Most High, and think to change times and laws: and they shall be given into his hand until a time and times and the dividing of time. *('And he shall speak great words against the Most High,' is used several times by the Holy Spirit in various ways, drawing our attention to the blasphemy of the Antichrist.*

"The phrase, 'And they shall be given into his hand until a time and times and the dividing of time,' refers to Israel being defeated and being greatly persecuted for a period of three and a half years.)

THE JUDGMENT

"But the Judgment shall sit, and they shall take away his dominion, to consume and to destroy it unto the end. *(The Angel refers back to Verse 10. 'But the Judgment shall sit,' refers to the Throne of God and the Judgment passed upon the Antichrist by that Heavenly Court.)*

AN EVERLASTING KINGDOM

"And the kingdom and dominion, and the greatness

of the kingdom under the whole heaven, shall be given
to the people of the Saints of the Most High, Whose
Kingdom is an Everlasting Kingdom, and all domin-
ions shall serve and obey Him. *('The greatness of the
kingdom under the whole heaven,' refers to the entirety of
the Earth, with Christ Jesus reigning supreme.)*

"Hitherto is the end of the matter. As for me Daniel,
my cogitations much troubled me, and my countenance
changed in me: but I kept the matter in my heart. *(This
Verse indicates that Daniel, despite the interpretation of
the Angel, still did not fully comprehend the extent of his
Vision.)*" **(Dan. 7:1-28).**

THE FIRST CLUE

Daniel said, *"I considered the horns, and, behold, there came
up among them another little horn"* (Dan. 7:8).

This tells us first of all that the *"little horn"* is the Antichrist.
It also tells us that he will come up among the *"ten horns,"*
which are in the old Roman Empire territory. So, this tells us
that the Antichrist will not come from America, the Far East,
etc., but rather, somewhere from among the territory once controlled by the Roman Empire. That territory included North
Africa, the Middle East, as far east as Armenia, and all of
Western Europe. One can easily look at a modern map and
ascertain the countries which presently occupy that territory.

In the second Vision given to Daniel, at least as it regards
the rise of the Antichrist, we will find that the area from
which the Antichrist will come will now be narrowed down
even more.

DANIEL'S VISION OF THE RAM AND HE GOAT:
THE TIME OF THE VISION

"In the third year of the reign of king Belshazzar a
Vision appeared unto me, even unto me Daniel, after

that which appeared unto me at the first. *(The phrase,
'In the third year of the reign of king Belshazzar,' means
that this Vision was given some two years after the Vision
of Chapter 7. Consequently, this was not long before
the overthrow of the Babylonian Empire, as described in
Chapter 5. So, chronologically, both Chapters 7 and 8
preceded Chapter 6.)*

"And I saw in a Vision; and it came to pass, when I
saw, that I was at Shushan in the palace, which is in the
province of Elam; and I saw in a Vision, and I was by
the river of Ulai.** *('Shushan' was the chief city of Persia.)*

THE RAM: MEDO-PERSIA

"Then I lifted up my eyes, and saw, and, behold,
there stood before the river a ram which had two horns:
and the two horns were high; but one was higher than
the other, and the higher came up last. *('A ram which
had two horns,' symbolized the Medo-Persian Empire,
ruled by two kings, Darius of the Medes and Cyrus of Persia. 'And the two horns were high,' spoke of their power,
which was great enough to overthrow the mighty Babylonian Empire, to which they had been subject for many
years. The phrase, 'but one was higher than the other,
and the higher came up last,' pertains to Persia developing
after the Median Empire, but ultimately growing into the
stronger of the two.)*

"I saw the ram pushing westward, and northward,
and southward; so that no beasts might stand before
him, neither was there any that could deliver out of
his hand; but he did according to his will, and became
great. *(The 'ram' is used here by the Holy Spirit as symbolic of the Empire of the Medes and the Persians. 'I saw
the ram pushing westward,' refers to an event of the recent
past, the taking of Babylon. 'And northward,' refers to
Lydia, while 'southward,' refers to Egypt.)*

THE HE-GOAT: GRECIA

"And as I was considering, behold, an he goat came
from the west on the face of the whole Earth, and
touched not the ground: and the goat had a notable
horn between his eyes. *(In Nebuchadnezzar's dream, the
Grecian Empire is represented by the 'belly and thighs
of brass.' In Daniel's first Vision in Chapter 7, a 'leopard with four wings and also four heads' symbolized this
Empire. In this Vision, it is symbolized by an 'he goat.'*

*"The phrase, 'and touched not the ground,' refers to the
speed of Alexander's conquests, which were symbolized in
the first Vision by a leopard with four wings. In thirteen
years, he conquered the whole known world. The 'notable
horn' refers to its first king, Alexander the Great.)*

WAR: MEDO-PERSIA AND GRECIA

"And he came to the ram that had two horns, which
I had seen standing before the river, and ran unto him
in the fury of his power. *('The fury of his power,' portrays
the speed of his conquests and the ferociousness of his
attack, plus military strategy that completely overwhelmed
the much larger force of the Medes and the Persians.)*

"And I saw him come close unto the ram, and he
was moved with choler against him, and smote the ram,
and broke his two horns: and there was no power in the
ram to stand before him, but he cast him down to the
ground, and stamped upon him: and there was none
who could deliver the ram out of his hand. *(As Daniel
sees this, of course, it is yet future. The word 'choler' means
that Alexander was greatly angry at the Medo-Persians.)*

THE FOUR HORNS

"Therefore the he goat waxed very great: and when

he was strong, the great horn was broken; and for it came up four notable ones toward the four winds of heaven. *('And when he was strong, the great horn was broken,' refers to the untimely death of Alexander the Great in 323 B.C., when he was at the apex of his strength. He was 32 years old when he died.*

" 'And for it came up four notable ones toward the four winds of heaven,' is referring to his kingdom being split into four parts upon his death.)

THE *"LITTLE HORN"*: ANTICHRIST

"And out of one of them came forth a little horn, which waxed exceeding great, toward the south, and toward the east, and toward the pleasant land. *('And out of one of them came forth a little horn,' refers to the future Antichrist coming out of one of these four divisions of the old Grecian Empire. 'Toward the south' refers to Egypt; 'toward the east' refers to Syria, Iraq, and Iran; 'toward the pleasant land' refers to Israel. From this area, the Antichrist will make his bid for world dominion.)*

THE MANNER OF THE ANTICHRIST

"And it waxed great, even to the host of heaven; and it cast down some of the host and of the stars to the ground, and stamped upon them. *('And it waxed great, even to the host of heaven,' refers to the 'little horn' [Antichrist] breaking his seven-year Covenant with Israel, which Daniel speaks of in a future Vision [9:27], actually declaring war on Israel at that time, seeking to destroy her. This is symbolized by the phrase, 'and it [little horn] cast down some of the host and of the stars to the ground, and stamped upon them,' referring to Israel being defeated at that time, which is yet future.)*

THE ACTION OF THE ANTICHRIST

"Yea, he magnified himself even to the prince of the host, and by him the daily sacrifice was taken away, and the place of his sanctuary was cast down. *('Yea, he magnified himself even to the prince of the host,' refers to the Antichrist usurping authority over the High Priest of Israel. These Verses actually speak of the war which will be instituted by the Antichrist when he breaks his seven-year Covenant with Israel and other countries, actually invading the 'pleasant land.' He will defeat Israel and stop the daily sacrifices, which will have been reinstituted by Israel after a lapse of approximately 2,000 years. This tells us that the Jewish Temple is going to be rebuilt.)*

THE PROSPERITY OF THE ANTICHRIST

"And an host was given him against the daily sacrifice by reason of transgression, and it cast down the truth to the ground; and it practiced, and prospered. *('By reason of transgression,' refers to the Antichrist breaking his seven-year Covenant with Israel, therefore, committing 'transgression.' As stated, he will then stop the 'daily sacrifice.' 'And it practiced, and prospered,' refers to the fact that much of the world will applaud him in these actions.)*

SAINTS IN HEAVEN QUESTIONING THE VISION

"Then I heard one Saint speaking, and another Saint said unto that certain Saint which spoke, How long shall be the Vision concerning the daily sacrifice, and the transgression of desolation, to give both the Sanctuary and the host to be trodden underfoot? *(These are 'Saints' in Heaven; Daniel overheard their conversation, but had no identification as to who they were. The 'Sanctuary' spoken of here is the rebuilt Temple. The 'Host to be trodden underfoot,' refers to the worshippers, with their worship stopped, as well as the High Priest and associating Priests abruptly stopping their duties, if not being killed. This is when the Antichrist invades Israel in the middle of the seven-year tribulation period [9:27].)*

"**And he said unto me, Unto two thousand and three hundred days; then shall the Sanctuary be cleansed.** *(This Verse makes reference to the 2,300 evenings and mornings [Verses 11-13, 26], as there are two sacrifices a day. Cutting that in half, which has reference to the number of days, the number is 1,150 [in Daniel's day, the years were counted as 360 days long, instead of our present method of using 365 days]. Hence, the three years, two months, and ten days are the whole and actual length of the doing away of the daily sacrifices in the Temple before they are offered again by the Jews when the Sanctuary is cleansed of the abomination of desolation. Jesus mentioned this [Mat. 24:15-16]).*

THE INTERPRETATION; ANGELIC INTERPRETERS

"**And it came to pass, when I, even I Daniel, had seen the Vision, and sought for the meaning, then, behold, there stood before me as the appearance of a man.** *(This is actually the mighty Angel, 'Gabriel,' who stands in the Presence of God [Lk. 1:19]).*

"**And I heard a man's voice between the banks of Ulai, which called, and said, Gabriel, make this man to understand the Vision.** *(It is not known whether the 'man's voice' spoken of here refers to an Angel or a redeemed man. At any rate, he will inform 'Gabriel' that he is to 'make Daniel to understand the Vision.')*

TIME OF FULFILLMENT

"**So he came near where I stood: and when he came, I was afraid, and fell upon my face: but he said unto**

me, Understand, O son of man: for at the time of the
end shall be the Vision. *('For at the time of the end shall
be the Vision,' refers to the Endtime, namely the very days
in which we now live, extending into the immediate future.)*

"Now as he was speaking with me, I was in a deep
sleep on my face toward the ground: but he touched
me, and set me upright. *('My face toward the ground,' is
not by accident! Daniel senses his tremendous unworthi-
ness, especially in such Presence.)*

"And he said, Behold, I will make you know what
shall be in the last end of the indignation: for at the
time appointed the end shall be. *('What shall be in the
last end of the indignation,' concerns God's past, present,
and future indignation against Israel. To that indignation,
He has set an appointed limit. However, the far greater
part of the 'indignation' spoken of here concerns the 'last
end,' i.e., the last days, the Great Tribulation.)*

THE RAM: MEDO-PERSIA

"The ram which you saw having two horns are the
kings of Media and Persia. *(Daniel served in this Empire
for a number of years before his death.)*

THE HE-GOAT: GRECIA

"And the rough goat is the king of Grecia: and the
great horn that is between his eyes is the first king. *(The
'great horn' is Alexander the Great.)*

THE FOUR HORNS: GREECE, TURKEY, SYRIA, AND EGYPT

"Now that being broken, whereas four stood up
for it, four kingdoms shall stand up out of the nation,
but not in his power. *('That being broken,' refers to the*

'great horn, 'symbolizing the death of Alexander the Great. 'Whereas four stood up for it, ' refers to four generals who took the empire after the death of Alexander, dividing it up among themselves. 'But not in his power, ' means that Alexander did not designate these kingdoms to them, because he was dead.)

THE *"LITTLE HORN"*

"And in the latter time of their kingdom, when the transgressors are come to the full, a king of fierce countenance, and understanding dark sentences, shall stand up. *('And in the latter time of their kingdom, 'pertains to the coming of the Antichrist. 'When the transgressors are come to the full, ' refers to the nation of Israel reaching the climax of her guilt by accepting the Antichrist instead of Christ, as predicted by the Lord Himself [Jn. 5:43]. 'A king of fierce countenance, and understanding dark sentences, shall stand up, ' proclaims the Antichrist having a majestic presence and superhuman knowledge, which is actually inspired of Satan.)*

THE *"LITTLE HORN'S"* POWER AND WAR ON THE SAINTS

"And his power shall be mighty, but not by his own power: and he shall destroy wonderfully, and shall prosper, and practice, and shall destroy the mighty and the holy people. *('And he shall destroy wonderfully, 'refers to Rev. 6:4-8. 'And shall prosper, and practice, 'means that his efforts will be extremely successful. 'And shall destroy the mighty and the holy people, ' refers to Israel.)*

HIS EXALTATION AND WAR WITH THE MESSIAH

"And through his policy also he shall cause craft to

prosper in his hand; and he shall magnify himself in his heart, and by peace shall destroy many: he shall also stand up against the Prince of princes; but he shall be broken without hand. *(The word 'craft' in the Hebrew is 'mirmah,' meaning 'deceit.' The Antichrist will be the greatest deceiver of all [II Thess. 2:8-12; Rev. 13:14; 19:20]. The last phrase, 'he shall stand up against the Prince of princes,' refers to his war against Christ, which will culminate with the Battle of Armageddon [Joel, Chpt. 3; Zech., Chpt. 14; Rev. 16:13-16; 19:11-21]).*

THE TIME OF THE VISION

"And the Vision of the evening and the morning which was told is true: wherefore shut thou up the Vision; for it shall be for many days. *('For it shall be for many days,' signifies that the Vision from Daniel's day would be a long time in coming to fulfillment. Actually, it has not yet been fulfilled, but it most definitely shall be in the near future.)*
"And I Daniel fainted, and was sick certain days; afterward I rose up, and did the king's business; and I was astonished at the Vision, but none understood it. *('But none understood it,' refers to the fact that the comprehension of events in the distant future was difficult. Presently, in the light of the history of many of these things, especially considering that they are beginning now to come to pass, our understanding of those things which the Angel Gabriel intended is being enlightened!)"* **(Dan. 8:1-27).**

THE AREA IS NARROWED DOWN EVEN FURTHER

Daniel said, *"Therefore the he goat waxed very great: and when he was strong, the great horn was broken; and for it came up four notable ones toward the four winds of heaven.*
"And out of one of them came forth a little horn, which waxed exceeding great, toward the south, and toward the east,

and toward the pleasant land" (Dan. 8:8-9).

From the Vision of the Seventh Chapter that placed the Antichrist coming from the old Roman Empire territory, we now have him coming from one of the divisions of the Grecian Empire, which took place when Alexander died.

This Vision places the Antichrist coming from the area occupied by Seleucus, one of Alexander's generals. It comprised the countries of modern Syria, Israel, Lebanon, Iraq, Iran and Afghanistan, and even the western part of Pakistan. So, the Antichrist, we know from what Daniel said, will come from one of these countries.

THE LAST DAYS

Now we come to the last Vision given to Daniel, which will pinpoint the location of the rise of the Antichrist. In other words, he will tell us the exact area of the world from which the man of sin will make his debut. The great Prophet-Statesman said:

"And some of them of understanding shall fall, to try them, and to purge, and to make them white, even to the time of the end: because it is yet for a time appointed. *(With this Verse begins the account of the Endtime, which will continue through the Twelfth Chapter. Therefore, the entirety of the time, now totaling nearly 2,000 years, is omitted in Scripture, which includes the entirety of the Church Age, because Gabriel told Daniel, 'These Prophecies only pertain to "your people," and more particularly, "in the latter days"' [Dan. 10:14]).*

THE EXALTATION OF SELF

"And the king shall do according to his will; and he shall exalt himself, and magnify himself above every god, and shall speak marvelous things against the God of gods, and shall prosper till the indignation be

accomplished: for that that is determined shall be done.
('And the king shall do according to his will,' refers to the Antichrist, who will pretty much have his way until the Second Advent of Christ. 'And magnify himself above every god,' actually refers to him deifying himself [II Thess. 2:4]. At this time, and according to 9:27, he will take over the newly-built Temple in Jerusalem, do away with the Jewish Sacrifices, which have not long since begun, and will set up an image of himself [Rev. 13:15].

" 'And shall speak marvelous things against the God of gods,' means that he will literally declare war on Christ. His campaign of declaring himself 'god' will, of necessity, demand that he blaspheme the True God as no one has ever blasphemed.

" 'And shall prosper till the indignation be accomplished,' means that much of the world will accept his claims, joining with him in their hatred of the God of the Bible.)

THE GOD OF HIS FATHERS

"Neither shall he regard the God of his fathers, nor the desire of women, nor regard any god: for he shall magnify himself above all. *('Neither shall he regard the God of his fathers,' no doubt refers to him being a Jew. He will not regard the God of 'Abraham, Isaac, and Jacob.'*

" 'Nor the desire of women,' probably refers to him turning against the Catholic Church and, thereby, the Virgin Mary.

" 'Nor regard any god: for he shall magnify himself above all,' refers to all the religions of the world, all of which will be outlawed, at least where he has control, demanding that worship be centered up on him.)

THE GOD OF FORCES

"But in his estate shall he honor the god of forces:

and a god whom his fathers knew not shall he honor with gold, and silver, and with precious stones, and pleasant things. *('And a god whom his fathers knew not shall he honor,' refers to a 'strange god,' mentioned in the next Verse, who is actually the fallen Angel who empowered Alexander the Great. He is called 'the Prince of Grecia,' which does not refer to a mortal, but instead, a fallen Angel [Dan. 10:20]. This 'god,' his fathers 'Abraham, Isaac, and Jacob,' did not know.)*

A STRANGE GOD

"Thus shall he do in the most strongholds with a strange god, whom he shall acknowledge and increase with glory: and he shall cause them to rule over many, and shall divide the land for gain. *('Thus shall he do in the most strongholds,' refers to the great financial centers of the world, which will be characterized by rebuilt Babylon. This 'strange god,' as stated, is a fallen Angel; therefore, he will probably think he is giving praise and glory to himself, when, in reality, he is actually honoring this 'fallen Angel.*

" 'And he shall cause them to rule over many,' refers to the many nations he will conquer because of the great power given to him by this fallen Angel, instigated by Satan.)

WAR

"And at the time of the end shall the king of the south *(Egypt)* **push at him: and the king of the north** *(the Antichrist, Syria)* **shall come against him like a whirlwind, with chariots, and with horsemen, and with many ships; and he shall enter into the countries, and shall overflow and pass over.** *(The phrase, 'And at the time of the end,' refers to the time of the fulfillment of these Prophecies, which, in fact, is just ahead. It is* *known that 'the king of the south' refers to Egypt, because that's who is referred to at the beginning of this Chapter, which speaks of the breakup of the Grecian Empire. As well, 'the king of the north' proves that the Antichrist will come from the Syrian division of the breakup of the Grecian Empire. So, the Antichrist will more than likely be a Syrian Jew.)*

ISRAEL

"He shall enter also into the glorious land *(into Israel)***, and many countries shall be overthrown** *(those in the Middle East)***: but these shall escape out of his hand, even Edom, and Moab, and the chief of the children of Ammon.** *(Edom, Moab, and Ammon comprise modern Jordan. His entering into the 'glorious land' refers to his invasion of Israel at the midpoint of his seven-year non-aggression pact with them, therefore, breaking his Covenant [Dan. 9:27].*

"The countries listed comprise modern Jordan, where ancient Petra is located, to which Israel will flee upon the Antichrist 'entering into the Glorious Land' [Rev. 12:6]).

SATANIC POWER

"He shall stretch forth his hand also upon the countries: and the land of Egypt shall not escape. *('Egypt' refers to 'the king of the south' of Verse 40, as stated.)*

"But he shall have power over the treasures of gold and of silver, and over all the precious things of Egypt: and the Libyans and the Ethiopians shall be at his steps. *(The 'precious things of Egypt' no doubt refer to the ancient mysteries of Egypt, regarding the tombs, the pyramids, etc. He will no doubt claim to unlock many of these mysteries; he very well could do so, regarding the supernatural power given to him by the powers of darkness.)*

TIDINGS OUT OF THE EAST AND
OUT OF THE NORTH

"But tidings out of the east and out of the north shall
trouble him: therefore he shall go forth with great fury
to destroy, and utterly to make away many. *(After the
Antichrist breaks his covenant with Israel, actually 'entering into the Glorious Land,' he will be prevented from further destroying her by the 'tidings out of the east and out of
the north' that 'shall trouble him.' No doubt, these will be
nations, probably led by Russia [north], Japan, and China
[east], forming a union against him, but which will have
no success.)*

THE DEFEAT OF THE ANTICHRIST

"And he shall plant the tabernacles of his palace
between the seas in the glorious Holy Mountain; yet he
shall come to his end, and none shall help him. *('And
he shall plant the tabernacles of his palace,' refers to his
taking over the newly-built Temple and stopping the Sacrifices, as prophesied in 8:9-12.*
*"The phrase, 'Between the seas in the glorious Holy
Mountain,' refers to the Dead Sea and the Mediterranean
Sea. The 'glorious Holy Mountain' is Mount Moriah,
where the Temple is located.*
*"'Yet he shall come to his end, and none shall help
him,' is tied to the first part of this Verse, which speaks of
him desecrating the Temple. This ensures his destruction
by the Lord, which will take place at the Second Coming.)*"
(Dan. 11:35-45).

THE EXACT LOCATION OF THE ANTICHRIST

In the account of the three Visions given to Daniel by the
Lord concerning the Antichrist, we now have it narrowed

down to a particular area.

• The first Vision contained the information that the Antichrist would come from the old Roman Empire territory. This area spanned North Africa, the Middle East, and Western Europe, plus part of Eastern Europe (Dan. 7:7-8).

• The second Vision narrows it down to the area of the conquests of Alexander the Great. Whenever Alexander died, his kingdom was divided among four of his generals. The Scripture says, *"And out of one of them came forth a little horn,"* which refers to the Antichrist (Dan. 8:9). So, the location is brought down from the entire area of the old Roman Empire territory to a part of the area conquered by Alexander the Great. It is the area granted to Seleucus, one of his Generals. It was the northern part, which included Israel, Lebanon, Syria, Iraq, Iran, Afghanistan, and even a part of Pakistan. So, the Antichrist will come from one of these countries.

• In the third Vision given to Daniel, the area of the Antichrist will be narrowed down to *"the king of the north"* (Dan. 11:40). What does that mean?

First of all, phrases such as *"king of the south,"* and *"king of the north,"* etc., refer to the area south or north of Israel. Egypt is south of Israel, while Syria is north of Israel. Israel is always the focal point.

So, the Antichrist will come from Syria and will, no doubt, be a Syrian Jew. This *"little horn,"* which refers to the Antichrist, this *"king of the north,"* will subdue Egypt plus, no doubt, Iraq and Iran, as well as Afghanistan, which is *"toward the east"* — east of Israel.

All of this means that the *"king of the north"* is not from America or from Russia, as some preachers have claimed. As well, we must not think of these things in terms of the present. Where this man is from has little bearing on anything. He will become great and powerful with an attempt to take over the entirety of the world, and because Satan will invest more in him than he has any other man in human history. However, the Antichrist will find to his dismay that ever how great and powerful he might be, he will be no match for the Lord Jesus Christ.

WHY WILL ISRAEL ACCEPT THE ANTICHRIST?

Jesus predicted that Israel would accept the *"man of sin"* as their Messiah. He said concerning this:

"I am come in My Father's Name, and you receive Me not *(proclaims that the real reason they did not receive Him is because they did not know the Father, despite their claims)*: if another shall come in his own name, him you will receive. *(Actually speaks of the coming Antichrist, as well as all other false Messiahs; shortly after the Rapture of the Church, Israel will receive a false Messiah, claiming that he is the one for whom they have long looked; they will find, to their dismay, how wrong they are!)*" (Jn. 5:43).

REJECTION OF THE TRUE MESSIAH

Having rejected Jesus Christ and even having crucified Him Who was the true Messiah; the spiritual impetus of the Jewish people is to accept that which is false. When a person leaves God, he ceases to know and understand, at least as one should, right from wrong, good from bad. In fact, oftentimes the good to them seems bad, as the bad seems good, etc. For one to be without God is one thing, but for the Jewish people to have purposely publicly rejected Him is something else altogether.

Israel will accept the Antichrist primarily because she has rejected the true Christ. Rejection of that which is right opens the door for the wrong to be admitted.

Years ago in a Message aired over television, I made the statement, or words to this effect, that Israel has suffered down through the centuries because of her rejection of Jesus Christ. Israel said at the trial of our Lord, *"We have no king but Caesar"* (Jn. 19:15), and they have found that Caesar has been a hard taskmaster. They then said, *"His blood be on us, and on our children"* (Mat. 27:25). They have reaped that bitter statement from then until now.

In making that statement, it angered some Jewish leaders across the nation. They wrote me complaining.

They said, *"How can you claim that God has punished the Jewish people all of these centuries because of statements made at the trial of Christ?"*

I answered saying, *"I did not say that God is punishing Jewish people, or anyone else for that matter."* I went on to say how that God loves the Jewish people the same as He loves anyone else. In fact, He has made great promises to the Jewish people, which will be fulfilled in totality.

I then said, *"The Jewish people took themselves out from under the protective Hand of God when they made those statements at the trial of Christ, and did so purposely."* I then added, *"It's not God who is punishing them, it is Satan. They stated they wanted Caesar, and that's what they have gotten. They stated that they wanted the Blood of the Lord Jesus Christ to be upon them and their children. That's exactly what they got."*

They wrote a rebuttal in a particular magazine concerning my answer, that is, if you would call it a rebuttal. They stated that I had answered theologically. The truth is that they could not deny my answer.

That goes not only for the Jewish people, but for anyone on the face of the Earth. When people purposely take themselves out from under the protective Hand of the Lord, in essence, they then place themselves, and again, purposely, under the hand of Satan. To be sure, Satan *"steals, kills and destroys"* (Jn. 10:10).

They will accept the Antichrist primarily because they have rejected the true Christ. However, due to the Antichrist having been able to guarantee their protection for some seven years, and their having been allowed to build their Temple on the Temple mount in place of the Dome of the Rock, all of that will sway them mightily. Their reasoning will be, *"The brightest minds in America couldn't bring this about, but this man could and did.*" So, in the natural, the Jewish people will think, and because of these great strides that have been made, that surely this is the one for whom they have so long looked. Therefore, at that time, Israel will herald *"the son of perdition"* as their Messiah.

HOW IS IT THAT THE ANTICHRIST WILL BE SO SUCCESSFUL?

He will be successful simply because Satan will invest more in this man than he ever has in anyone before him. In a sense, the Antichrist will be the one, at least in the thinking of Satan, to defeat the Lord Jesus Christ. He will attempt to do this by causing the Word of God to fall to the ground. He will choose all the many promises made by God to the Jewish people as the means for him to carry this out. If he can destroy the Jewish people and take over the land of Israel completely and in totality, then he will have succeeded, and Satan will then be god.

It must be understood that Satan doesn't care any more for the Antichrist than do Bible Believers. Satan is a past master at using whomever he so desires and then, when he is through with them, casting them aside as a piece of cheap goods. In fact, that is his forte. To be sure, the Antichrist is not going to succeed; however, he will come close, and would succeed were it not for the Second Coming of the Lord.

Concerning this, the Scripture says:

"And they worshipped the dragon which gave power unto the beast *(refers to the fact that men worship power)*: and they worshipped the beast *(Antichrist)*, saying, Who *is* like unto the beast? Who is able to make war with him?" (Rev. 13:4).

The Scripture then says, *"And there was given unto him a*

mouth speaking great things and blasphemies" (Rev. 13:5).

WILL THE ANTICHRIST TAKE OVER
THE WHOLE WORLD?

No! However, that will be his goal and he will come close to succeeding.

The Scripture says:

"He shall enter also into the glorious land *(into Israel)*, and many countries shall be overthrown *(those in the Middle East)*: but these shall escape out of his hand, even Edom, and Moab, and the chief of the children of Ammon. *(The countries listed comprise modern Jordan, where ancient Petra is located, to which Israel will flee upon the Antichrist 'entering into the Glorious Land')*" **(Dan. 11:41).**

So, even in the Middle East where he will reign supreme, we find here that Jordan will not come under the control of the Antichrist. No doubt, the Lord will engineer this thing, due to the fact that it is to Jordan to where Israel will flee when the Antichrist declares war on her in the middle of the Great Tribulation.

Also, the Scripture tells us, *"but tidings out of the east and out of the north shall trouble him: therefore he shall go forth with great fury to destroy, and utterly to make away many"* (Dan. 11:44).

If he controlled the entirety of the world, these nations would not be able to rise up against him. While it is true that he will conquer them, still, he will not rule the entirety of the world.

There are several Scriptures which some have taken to mean that the entirety of the world will come under the domain of the Antichrist; however, let's make the statement again. While that will definitely be his ambition, and while he definitely will be well on his way to accomplishing the task, still, he will not completely succeed. Let's look at some of these Scriptures.

• *"And the great dragon was cast out, that old serpent, called the Devil, and Satan, which deceives the whole world: he was cast out into the Earth, and his Angels were cast out with him"* (Rev. 12:9).

The statement, *"which deceives the whole world,"* is something that has been done from the very beginning, continues to be done presently, and will be done in the future, at least until Jesus comes back. No doubt, during the coming Great Tribulation, the deceptive power of Satan will be greater than ever, due to the fact that the true Church has been raptured away, which proved a deterrent against evil.

• *"And I saw one of his heads as it were wounded to death; and his deadly wound was healed: and all the world wondered after the beast"* (Rev. 13:3).

The word *"wondered"* means, *"to admire, to have in admiration, to marvel, to wonder."*

Most definitely this will happen all over the world, but that doesn't mean that the Antichrist will have the entirety of the world under his thumb, so to speak.

• *"And it was given unto him to make war with the Saints, and to overcome them: and power was given him over all kindreds, and tongues, and nations"* (Rev. 13:7). This speaks of the areas over which he has control.

• *"And all who dwell upon the Earth shall worship him, whose names are not written in the Book of Life of the Lamb slain from the foundation of the world"* (Rev. 13:8).

The emphasis is on the word *"worship."* It means that those who conclude the Antichrist to be *"God,"* which, no doubt, hundreds of millions will, shall *"worship him."* However, such is not speaking of the dominion of nations, but rather, the worship by individuals.

• *"For they are the spirits of devils, working miracles, which go forth unto the kings of the Earth and of the whole world, to gather them to the battle of that Great Day of God Almighty"* (Rev. 16:14).

As is obvious here, these are nations the Antichrist doesn't control but whose help he will seek. If he controlled these nations, whatever they might be, he wouldn't have to seek their help but would automatically demand it.

It is definitely true that the Antichrist will affect the entirety of the world, which includes every nation on the face of the Earth. In fact, there will, no doubt, be millions in these respective nations who will actually worship him as God. However, the truth is, and as stated, while his ambition will be to take over the entirety of the world, and while he will be steadily working toward that conclusion, in fact, he will be stopped by the Second Coming before he succeeds.

WILL AMERICA BE RULED BY THE ANTICHRIST?

As we have given the information in this Chapter respecting the domain of the Antichrist, we find that he will rule all of the Middle East with the exception of the little country of Jordan and, as well, he will no doubt control some of the countries in Europe. Also, according to Daniel 11:44, he will defeat in battle some of the countries of the north and the east, which could very well be Russia and China, etc.

John wrote and said, *"And the fifth Angel poured out his Vial upon the seat of the beast; and his kingdom was full of darkness; and they gnawed their tongues for pain"* (Rev. 16:10).

The implication is that, while the Antichrist has a kingdom, it is only a part of this Earth and not the entirety of the world. If he controlled the entirety of the world, the words *"his kingdom"* would not be mentioned in that capacity.

While America, as no doubt every other nation in the world, will be greatly influenced by the Antichrist, i.e., *"the beast,"* still, there is no indication that the Antichrist will control America or any other nations in this hemisphere, for that matter. But, again we emphasize that most definitely the Antichrist will hold great sway in America, plus every other country in the world, but dominating the entirety of the world, the Scripture doesn't teach such.

WHAT DOES THE NUMBER 666 MEAN?

The number *"666"* will be one of the identification marks of the Beast with the other being his name. John wrote about this, saying:

"And he caused all, both small and great, rich and poor, free and bond, to receive a mark in their right hand, or in their foreheads *('all' represents only those in his domain, not the entirety of the world; this domain will include virtually the entirety of the area of the old Roman Empire, which includes North Africa, the Middle East, and most of modern Europe; this will be a literal mark)*:

"And that no man might buy or sell, save he who had the mark *(we are told in Verses 11 through 13 that the seduction of the Antichrist will be religious; now we are told in Verses 16 and 17 it will be economic)*, or the name of the beast, or the number of his name. *(The thought is that either the 'name' of the beast or his 'number' will be required as a brand or mark upon all.)*

"Here is wisdom *(this is the Wisdom of God)*. Let him who has understanding count the number of the beast *(the idea is that it is the number of a man, not of God, which means he will give account to Jehovah, Whom he has repeatedly blasphemed)*: for it is the number of a man; and his number *is* six hundred three score *and* six. *(It is the number of a man, not a kingdom, not a religion, not a dispensation, but a man. The number will be 666.)*" **(Rev. 13:16-18).**

THE KEY

The key to the number *"666"* is the phrase, *"the number of a man." "Six"* is man's number, while *"seven"* is God's number. Seven is the number of totality, completion, universality, and perfection, while six is the number of incompletion and imperfection. The number itself states the fact that man cannot rise to the status of Godhood and, in fact, never will. As well, all that man does, at least that which is done without the Lord, is always incomplete, unfinished, or it is totally wrong. Everything that God does is perfect.

Man was created on the sixth day (Gen. 1:26-31).

All of this means that irrespective of the claims of the Antichrist, irrespective of his boasts, still, he is but a man with all of man's imperfections. Using a play on words, man has ever tried to catapult himself from *"six"* to *"seven,"* but always without success.

HIS NUMBER AND HIS NAME

Over the area of the world controlled by the Antichrist, he will force everyone who follows him to have a little mark placed on themselves, either *"666,"* or his name, which could very well be *"Gog"* (Ezek. 38:2, 14). For those in his domain who will not take his mark, they will not be able to buy food or engage in transactions in any way or manner. Consequently, no doubt many in *"his kingdom"* will die because of this.

THOSE WHO WOULDN'T TAKE THE MARK

John wrote and said:

"And I saw another sign in Heaven, great and marvelous, seven Angels having the seven last plagues *(proclaims the concluding Judgments upon the territory of the Antichrist, which will be the worst)*; for in them is filled up the Wrath of God *(should have been translated, 'anger of God')*.

"And I saw as it were a sea of glass mingled with fire *(is that which is immediately before the Throne of God and mentioned in Rev. 4:6)*: and them who had gotten the victory over the beast, and over his image, and over his mark, *and* over the number of his name *(this group was murdered by the Antichrist)*, stand on the sea of glass, having the harps of God *(presents a picture of peace and tranquility)*.

THE SONG OF THE LAMB

"**And they sing the song of Moses the servant of God** *(is the song given to us in Deut. 32:1-43; it is recorded that Moses wrote this song and taught it to the people [Deut. 31:22]),* **and the song of the Lamb** *(this is the second song, and begins with the Crucifixion, which was absolutely necessary if man were to be redeemed, and closes with Jesus Christ as 'King of kings, Lord of lords'),* **saying, Great and marvelous** *are* **Your works, Lord God Almighty** *(refers to Christ; while all His Works are 'great and marvelous,' what He did at the Cross presents itself as the greatest work of all);* **just and true** *are* **Your ways, Thou King of Saints.** *(Christ is our King by virtue of what He did at the Cross, and our Faith in that Finished Work.)*

YOU ONLY ARE HOLY

"**Who shall not fear You, O Lord, and glorify Your Name?** *(This leaps ahead to the Millennial Reign. At that time, every human being on the face of the Earth will fear the Lord, and will glorify His Name as well.)* **For** *You* **only** *are* **Holy** *(speaks of the origination of Holiness, and that this Holiness can be given to Believers by virtue of what Christ did at the Cross):* **for all nations shall come and worship before You** *(refers to the Millennial Reign);* **for Your Judgments are made manifest.** *(Refers to the fact that the Judgment of God will be poured out upon the Antichrist during the Battle of Armageddon, where he will be defeated along with the entirety of his Army)*" **(Rev. 15:1-4).**

REIGNING WITH CHRIST

John then wrote:

"And I saw Thrones, and they sat upon them, and judgment was given unto them *(refers to the 24 Elders who represent the entire Plan of God, which pertains to the Redeemed of all ages; we aren't told who these men are)*: and I *saw* the souls of them who were beheaded for the witness of Jesus, and for the Word of God, and which had not worshipped the Beast, neither his image, neither had received *his* mark upon their foreheads, or in their hands *(categorizes the Tribulation Saints Who gave their lives for the cause of Christ; the idea is that these will be included in the first Resurrection of Life, and will enjoy all its privileges)*; and they lived and reigned with Christ a thousand years. *(This is the Kingdom Age)*" **(Rev. 20:4).**

THOSE WHO TAKE THE MARK OF THE BEAST

It should be clearly understood that those who take the mark of the beast during the Great Tribulation will doom themselves, in essence, blaspheming the Holy Spirit. This means that once this mark is taken, they cannot be Saved, and there is no evidence that they will even desire to be Saved. Again we state, the mark of the beast will be demanded by the Antichrist as it regards his followers, with him killing all who will not take the mark. And yet, this is only the area of the world in which he has dominion. As stated, that will be the Middle East with the country of Jordan seemingly not coming under his sway. As well, he will rule most, if not all, of western Europe and even some of eastern Europe. His rule and reign could also very well extend to Russia and even to China and possibly Japan. At any rate, the area of his control, with every effort being made to take over the entirety of the world, will be substantial, to say the least.

Concerning those who are in his domain, John wrote of the warning given by the Angel. He said:

"And the third Angel followed them, saying with a loud voice *(presents the last of this Heavenly trio)*, If any man worship the beast and his image, and receive *his* mark in his forehead, or in his hand *(proclaims a warning of unprecedented proportion; this is a declaration that every single individual is responsible)*,

"The same shall drink of the wine of the Wrath of God, which is poured out without mixture *(there will be no Mercy in this Judgment)* into the cup of His indignation *(when the cup gets full, the Judgment of God will commence; this 'cup' is not only full, but is running over with evil)*; and he shall be tormented with fire and brimstone *(refers to everyone who receives the mark of the beast, and speaks of Eternal Hell)* in the Presence of the Holy Angels, and in the Presence of the Lamb *(refers to the Great White Throne Judgment [Rev. 20:11-15])*:

THE SMOKE OF THEIR TORMENT

"And the smoke of their torment ascended up forever and ever *(refers to the fact that a conscious existence will be forever)*: and they have no rest day nor night *(refers to an unbroken continuance of torment)*, who worship the beast and his image, and whosoever receives the mark of his name. *(All who take the Mark of the Beast in the coming Great Tribulation will, in essence, be, as stated, blaspheming the Holy Spirit, for which there is no forgiveness)*" **(Rev. 14:9-11).**

JUDGMENT ON THOSE WHO RECEIVE THE MARK

Of course, some would surmise that surely these particular people in the domain of the Antichrist in the coming Great Tribulation can read the Bible, which speaks of their doom if they take this mark. They can read it and, no doubt, some of them will; however, the fact is, they simply will not believe what they read, even as most of the world doesn't believe the Bible at the present time.

John went on to say:

"And the first *(Angel)* went, and poured out his Vial upon the Earth *(constitutes the first plague)*; and there fell a noisome and grievous sore upon the men which had the mark of the beast, and *upon* them which worshipped his image. *(This proves that these plagues will be poured out only on the kingdom of the beast)*" **(Rev. 16:2).**

ETERNAL HELL

As we have stated, for those who take the mark of the beast, they have doomed themselves, and eternally.
John said:

"And the beast was taken, and with him the false prophet who wrought miracles before him *(refers to both of them falling in the Battle of Armageddon)*, with which he deceived them who had received the mark of the beast, and them who worshipped his image *(pertains to Satan's chief weapon, which is deception)*. These both were cast alive into a Lake of Fire burning with brimstone *(thus is the destiny of the Antichrist and the False Prophet, and all who follow them)*" **(Rev. 19:20).**

WHEN WILL THE MARK OF THE BEAST
BE INTRODUCED?

Every indication is that it will not be introduced by the Antichrist until the midpoint of the Great Tribulation. The first part of that trying time, which will last for three and a half years, the Antichrist will put on a front of peace to the world. And then he will turn on Israel and would destroy her at that time were it not for other events which demand his immediate attention (Dan. 11:44). However, then he will tighten his grip over the domain that he controls and introduce the mark with all of his followers compelled to take it. For those who will not take this mark, they will be killed, which will, no doubt, include possibly millions.

There is no evidence that America will be subjected to such, although the Antichrist most definitely will have great sway in this country, plus every country of the world. As we have stated, his ambition will be to take over the entirety of the world ,and he will be well on his way toward success., In fact, he would succeed but for the Second Coming of the Lord.

WILL THE ANTICHRIST HAVE A NAME?

Of course he will, even as everyone has a name.

There is a good possibility that his name will be *"Gog"* (Ezek. 38:2-3, 14, 18; 39:1, 11).

The name *"Gog"* is very close to the title *"God,"* which, in essence, the Antichrist will claim himself to be.

Yet, there is no record that he will refer to himself as the *"Christ,"* which actually means *"the anointed!"* The reason is simple; he will be filled with the deadliest hate against the name and offices of the Lord Jesus Christ, the exalted King of Glory. However, every evidence is that he will set himself up as a *"pseudochrist,"* which tries to fill the role of Christ without taking His Name.

The term *"antichristos,"* actually denies that there is a Christ. The term *"Pseudochrist,"* claims to be Christ.

While the Antichrist will not take the name of Christ, and for the reasons stated, still, every evidence is that he will try to imitate the true Christ, hence, a *"Pseudochrist."* He will claim to be the world's saviour, claiming to make this world a paradise instead of a shadowy, uncertain heaven.

Concerning this, Wuest says:

"It will follow, therefore, that however he will not assume the name of Christ, and so will not, in the letter be a 'Pseudochristos,' yet, usurping to himself Christ's offices, presenting himself to the world as the true center of its hopes, as the satisfier of all

its needs and healer of all its hurts, he, 'Gog' as his servants may very well call him, will in fact take up and absorb into himself all names and forms of blasphemy." As stated, he will be the great *"Pseudochristos"* and the *"antichristos"* all wrapped into one.

ETERNAL HELL

Yet, the final result of the man of sin, the son of perdition, the Antichrist, will be as follows:

"And I saw the beast *(John saw the Antichrist leading this mighty army; this is the 'man of sin' mentioned by Paul in II Thess., Chpt. 2)*, and the kings of the Earth, and their armies *(refers to all the Antichrist could get to join him; it includes the 'kings of the East' of Rev. 16:12)*, gathered together to make war against Him Who sat on the horse, and against His army *(refers to Christ and the great army of Heaven which is with Him; as stated, this is the Battle of Armageddon [Ezek., Chpts. 38-39])*.

THE LAKE OF FIRE

"And the beast was taken, and with him the false prophet who wrought miracles before him *(refers to both of them falling in the Battle of Armageddon)*, with which he deceived them who had received the mark of the beast, and them who worshipped his image *(pertains to Satan's chief weapon, which is deception)*. These both were cast alive into a Lake of Fire burning with brimstone *(thus is the destiny of the Antichrist and the false prophet, and all who follow them)*.

"And the remnant were slain with the sword of Him Who sat upon the horse, which *sword* proceeded out of His mouth *(the Lord Jesus will speak the word in the Battle of Armageddon, and whatever He speaks will take place)*: and all the fowls were filled with their flesh.

(This proclaims the end of this conflict. The Antichrist and his hoards will announce to the world what they are going to do regarding Israel, but the end result will be buzzards gorging on their flesh)" **(Rev. 19:19-21).**

"Safe in the arms of Jesus,
"Safe on His gentle breast,
"There, by His love overshaded,
"Sweetly my soul does rest."

"Hark! 'tis the voice of Angels,
"Borne in a song to me,
"Over the fields of glory,
"Over the jasper sea."

"Safe in the arms of Jesus,
"Safe from corroding care,
"Safe from the world's temptations,
"Sin cannot harm me there."

"Free from the blight of sorrow,
"Free from my doubts and fears;
"Only a few more trials,
"Only a few more tears."

"Jesus my heart's dear Refuge,
"Jesus has died for me;
"Firm on the Rock of Ages,
"Ever my trust shall be."

"Here let me wait with patience,
"Wait till the night is o'er,
"Wait till I see the morning,
"Break on the golden shore."

CHAPTER THREE

What Is The Great Tribulation?

QUESTION:

WHAT IS THE GREAT TRIBULATION?

ANSWER:

In this Chapter we will deal with the following questions regarding the Great Tribulation. They are:
- **What is the Great Tribulation?**
- **When will it occur?**
- **Will the Great Tribulation be worldwide?**
- **What are the Seals, Trumpets, and Vials of that particular time?**
- **Was the Book of Revelation fulfilled in A.D. 70 as claimed by some?**
- **Why will there be a Great Tribulation?**
- **What role will the Church play in this event?**
- **Will there be people Saved in the Great Tribulation?**
- **What is the purpose of the Great Tribulation?**
- **Why will the Wrath of God be poured out at this time?**

Concerning this coming time, Jesus said the following:

THE ABOMINATION OF DESOLATION

"**When you therefore shall see the abomination of desolation, spoken of by Daniel the Prophet, stand in the Holy Place** *(speaks of the Antichrist invading Israel, and taking over the Temple)*, **whoso reads, let him understand:** *(reads it in the Word of God [Dan. 8:9-14; 9:27; 11:45; 12:1, 7, 11]).*

"**Then let them which be in Judaea flee into the mountains** *(when the Antichrist invades Israel at the mid-point of the Great Tribulation)*:

A SOMBER WARNING

"**Let him which is on the housetop not come down to**

take anything out of his house *(houses are flat on top in that part of the world; during the summer, people often sleep on top of the house; speaks of the necessity of haste)*:

"Neither let him which is in the field return back to take his clothes.

"And woe unto them who are with child, and to them who give suck in those days! *(The necessity of fleeing at this time will be so urgent that it will be difficult for pregnant women and mothers with little babies.)*

"But pray ye that your flight be not in the winter *(bad weather)*, neither on the Sabbath Day *(concerns the strict religious observance of the Sabbath, doesn't permit travel)*:

THE GREAT TRIBULATION

"For then shall be great tribulation *(the last three and one half years)*, such as was not since the beginning of the world to this time, no, nor ever shall be *(the worst the world has ever known, and will be so bad that it will never be repeated)*.

"And except those days should be shortened, there should no flesh be saved *(refers to Israel coming close to extinction)*: but for the elect's *(Israel's)* sake those days shall be shortened *(By the Second Coming)*" (Mat. 24:15-22).

WHAT IS THE GREAT TRIBULATION?

This time of terrible Tribulation which is coming upon this Earth, and in the very near future, is commonly referred to in Biblical terms as *"Daniel's seventieth week."*

This concerns a Vision experienced by Daniel where the Angel Gabriel gave him information as it regards the future of Israel, and especially the last days, in fact, the days that Israel must face in the very near future. I quote verbatim from THE

EXPOSITOR'S STUDY BIBLE.

THE ANGEL GABRIEL

"And while I was speaking, and praying, and con-
fessing my sin and the sin of my people Israel, and presenting my supplication before the LORD my God for
the holy mountain of my God *(Daniel declared that Jerusalem has been called by God's Name, and has been chosen by God. Actually, it will be the capital of His Eternal
Kingdom on Earth [Ps. 2:6; 48:2; 87:2; 102:16; 132:13;
Isa. 2:2-4; Ezek., Chpt. 48; Zech., Chpt. 14])*;
"Yea, while I was speaking in prayer, even the man
Gabriel, whom I had seen in the Vision at the beginning, being caused to fly swiftly, touched me about the
time of the evening oblation. *(Once again, 'Gabriel' is
sent to Daniel's side. The phrase, 'about the time of the
evening Oblation,' referred to 3 p.m., which was the time
of the evening Sacrifice; however, this does not imply that
those Offerings were made in Babylon, but simply that,
through the nearly seventy years that had intervened since
the fall of Jerusalem, the sacred hour had been kept in
remembrance, and possibly as one consecrated to prayer.)*

TO GIVE DANIEL UNDERSTANDING

"And he informed me, and talked with me, and
said, O Daniel, I am now come forth to give you skill
and understanding. *('To give you skill and understanding,' refers to the future of Israel and last-day events.)*
"At the beginning of your supplications the commandment came forth, and I am come to show you; for
you are greatly beloved: therefore understand the matter, and consider the Vision. *(The study of Bible Prophecy was not for Daniel a mere intellectual entertainment,
but moral and spiritual nourishment.)*

70 WEEKS OF YEARS – 490 YEARS

"**Seventy weeks are determined upon your people and upon your holy city, to finish the transgression, and to make an end of sins, and to make reconciliation for iniquity, and to bring in everlasting righteousness, and to seal up the Vision and Prophecy, and to anoint the Most Holy.** *('Seventy weeks are determined upon your people,' actually means seventy sevens, which translates into 490 years. This period of time has to do with 'your people' and 'your holy city' referring to the Jews and Jerusalem. The Second Coming of Christ and their acceptance of Him will 'finish the transgression.'*

" 'To make reconciliation [atonement] for iniquity,' refers to the fact that Israel will not only accept Christ at the Second Coming, but will also accept what He did for us at Calvary. One can well imagine this moment, for they are the ones who crucified Christ.

"The phrase, 'to anoint the Most Holy,' has to do with the building of the Millennial Temple, even as described by Ezekiel in Chapters 40 through 48 of his Book.)

483 YEARS

"**Know therefore and understand, that from the going forth of the Commandment to restore and to build Jerusalem unto the Messiah the Prince shall be seven weeks, and threescore and two weeks: the street shall be built again, and the wall, even in troublous times.** *(If one is to notice in this Scripture, the 'seventy weeks' of years is broken up into two periods. One 'shall be seven weeks' [49 years] and the other will be 'threescore and two weeks' [434 years], totaling 483 years. 'That from the going forth of the Commandment to restore and rebuild Jerusalem,' is the beginning of this 490-year period. However, from that time until it was actually finished was some*

141 years. Actually, the clock stopped and started several times, so to speak, in this 141-year period, totaling some 49 years when work was truly in progress, comprising the first seven weeks of years [49 years].

THE 434 YEARS

"The second block of time started at the end of the 49 years and ended with the Crucifixion of the Lord Jesus Christ, which was 434 years. Combining, as stated, the 49 years with the 434 years brings the total to 483 years.

"The third block of time, which we will study in the last Verse, will be the last week of years, totaling seven years, which will make up the Great Tribulation period, concluding Daniel's Prophecy of seventy weeks of years. This last seven years comprising the Great Tribulation is yet future.

"Again, it must be remembered that these 490 years did not run consecutively. There were stoppages, as stated, in the first 49 years; then there has been a huge halt of nearly 2,000 years from the time that Christ was crucified, which has not concluded yet. In other words, the last week of years [seven years], as stated, is yet to come.)

THE CRUCIFIXION OF CHRIST

"And after threescore and two weeks shall Messiah be cut off, but not for Himself; and the people of the prince who shall come shall destroy the city and the Sanctuary; and the end thereof shall be with a flood, and unto the end of the war desolations are determined. *(The phrase, 'And after threescore and two weeks shall Messiah be cut off,' gives us the exact time, even the very year, that the Messiah would be crucified. The words, 'cut off,' refer to His Crucifixion.*

" 'But not for Himself,' refers to Jesus dying for mankind

and taking upon Himself the penalty for mankind. In other words, He did not die for crimes He had committed, but rather, for the crimes mankind had committed.

" 'And the people of the prince who shall come shall destroy the City and the Sanctuary,' refers to the Romans, who fulfilled this Prophecy in A.D. 70; however, the 'prince,' as used here, actually refers to the Antichrist, who has not yet come, but will come from among the ten kingdoms yet to be formed inside the old Roman Empire territory. The next Verse proves this.)

THE ANTICHRIST WILL BREAK HIS SEVEN-YEAR COVENANT WITH ISRAEL

"And he shall confirm the covenant with many for one week: and in the midst of the week he shall cause the sacrifice and the oblation to cease, and for the overspreading of abominations he shall make it desolate, even until the consummation, and that determined shall be poured upon the desolate. *('And he shall confirm,' refers to the Antichrist. The phrase, 'and in the midst of the week,' refers to three and a half years, at which time the Antichrist will show his true colors and stop the Sacrifices in the newly-built Temple. At that time, he will actually invade Israel, with her suffering her first defeat since her formation as a nation in 1948.*

" 'Even until the consummation,' means until the end of the seven-year Great Tribulation Period. The phrase, 'and that determined shall be poured upon the desolate,' refers to all the Prophecies being fulfilled regarding the great suffering that Israel will go through the last three and a half years of the Great Tribulation [Mat. 24:21-22])" (Dan. 9:20-27).

The Great Tribulation, among other things, is the fulfillment of the great Prophecy given by Daniel some 2,500 years ago. As stated, it is Daniel's seventieth week.

IN THE SPIRIT WORLD

We learn from the great Book of Daniel in the Old Testament and from the Book of Revelation in the New Testament that events on Earth, events of note we should say, are all orchestrated by the Lord of Glory.

In the Old Testament the Lord dealt with nations as they impacted Israel. There is very little evidence that the Lord directed situations as it regarded nations which had no contact with Israel. While the Lord, of course, looks out over the entirety of the world, and for all time, still, it is obvious that His major concern on Earth during that time period was Israel and how she was impacted by other nations. While the Prophets of Israel knew this, of course, the Gentile nations had no idea as to what was happening.

As it regards the New Testament and the Church, understanding that the Church is scattered all over the world, still, the Lord most definitely is directing events on Earth as it pertains to the fulfillment of Bible Prophecy in regard to the last days. If it is to be noticed in the Book of Acts, which is an account of the Early Church, the Lord mentioned Rome only as Rome impacted the Church. In fact, the most prosperous time for Rome, in all of its approximate 1,000 year reign on Earth, was the approximate 100 years from the time of the Day of Pentecost until the Apostles, and they who knew them, passed away. Regrettably, the Church began to apostatize after that and Rome at the time began to suffer terrible decline.

JUDGMENT MUST FIRST BEGIN AT THE HOUSE OF GOD

Peter said:

"For the time *is come* that judgment must begin at the House of God *(Judgment always begins with*

*Believers, and pertains to their Faith, whether in the Cross
or otherwise; the Cross alone is spared Judgment, for there
Jesus was judged in our place)*: **and if *it* first *begin* at us,
what shall the end *be* of them who obey not the Gospel
of God?** *(If God will Judge His Own, how much more
will He Judge the unredeemed? The Cross alone stays the
Judgment of God. Let that ever be understood.)*

"And if the Righteous scarcely be saved *(can be
Saved only by trusting Christ and the Cross, and nothing
else)*, **where shall the ungodly and the sinner appear?**
*(If the great Sacrifice of Christ is rejected and spurned,
where does that leave those who do such a thing? There is
no hope for their Salvation)"* **(I Pet. 4:17-18).**

As the Body of Christ in this nation and, in fact, in any and
every nation of the world, is either weak or strong, spiritually
speaking, so goes the nation.

Where there are precious few Believers in some nations of
the world, those nations are actually ruled by demon spirits,
which causes all type of pain and suffering.

SODOM AND GOMORRAH

It doesn't take many true Believers in any place to make a
great difference. Ever how large Sodom and Gomorrah were,
we aren't told, but, no doubt, these places carried at least several thousands of population.

In essence, the Lord told Abraham that if there were but
ten righteous in the twin cities of Sodom and Gomorrah, the
cities would be spared (Gen. 18:32). Regrettably, there were
not ten righteous in the twin cities, and they were destroyed.

However, from this we see the impact that even a small
number of righteous individuals can have on any given place.

Concerning Believers, Jesus said:

"You are the salt *(preservative)* **of the earth: but if the**

salt have lost his savour, wherewith shall it be salted? it is thenceforth good for nothing, but to be cast out, and to be trodden under foot of men *('Salt' is a Type of the Word of God; the professing Believer who no longer holds to the Word is of no use to God or man).*

"You are the Light of the world *(we are a reflector of the light which comes from Christ).* A city that is set on a hill cannot be hid *(proper light will not, and in fact, cannot be hid).*

"Neither do men light a candle, and put it under a bushel, but on a candlestick *(the light is not to be hid)*; and it gives light unto all who are in the house *(that is the purpose of the light).*

"Let your light so shine before men, that they may see your good works *(proper Faith will always produce proper works, but proper works will never produce proper Faith),* and glorify your Father which is in Heaven. *(Proper works will glorify our Heavenly Father, while improper works glorify man)*" (Mat. 5:13-16).

Just before the coming Great Tribulation, the Church is going to be raptured out of this world. The Church, and we speak of those who are truly Blood-bought, is a great hinderer of evil. With it removed, that which hinders evil is removed as well. This will make the world a ready platform for the man of sin, i.e., the Antichrist.

WHEN WILL THE GREAT
TRIBULATION OCCUR?

According to II Thessalonians 2:6-11, it will begin after the Rapture of the Church.

In these Passages, the Apostle Paul proclaims the fact that the true Body of Believers in the world acts as a restraining force against evil, which should be obvious. When the true Body of Christ will be taken out of this world and taken, of course, to be with Christ, Paul said, *"and then shall that Wicked be revealed"* (II Thess. 2:8).

His time will begin when he is able to bring together the leaders of Israel and the leaders of the Muslim-world, thereby, signing a seven-year non-aggression pact, guaranteeing Israel's protection. He will even be able to get the Muslims to agree to dismantle the *"Dome of the Rock,"* the supposed third most sacred place in the world of Islam, allowing Israel to then build her Temple.

Some have claimed that Israel will possibly build her Temple on the Temple Mount near the Dome of the Rock, or else, use the great Synagogue in Jerusalem for this purpose; however, that cannot be. It is for certain that the Temple is going to be rebuilt. Daniel said so. The great Prophet-Statesman said:

"**And he** *(the Antichrist)* **shall confirm the covenant with many for one week** *(a week of years)*: **and in the midst of the week he shall cause the sacrifice and the oblation to cease, and for the overspreading of abominations he shall make it desolate, even until the consummation, and that determined shall be poured upon the desolate.** *('And he shall confirm,' as stated, refers to the Antichrist. The phrase, 'And in the midst of the week,' refers to three and a half years, at which time the Antichrist will show his true colors and stop the Sacrifices in the newly-built Temple. At that time, he will actually invade Israel, with her suffering her first military defeat since her formation as a nation in 1948.*

"*'Even until the consummation,' means until the end of the seven-year Great Tribulation period. The phrase, 'and that determined shall be poured upon the desolate,' refers to all the Prophecies being fulfilled regarding the great suffering that Israel will go through the last three and a half years of the Great Tribulation [Mat. 24:21-22])*"
(Dan. 9:27).

HOW WILL THE ANTICHRIST PERSUADE THE MUSLIMS TO GIVE UP THE TEMPLE MOUNT?

The Antichrist will have the powers of Satan working with him and through him as no human being ever has (Dan. 8:23-25; 11:38-39).

No doubt, and as the Bible bears out, this man will have tremendous persuasive ability; however, that within itself will, no doubt, not be enough to sway the Muslims, considering that they look at the Temple Mount as the third most holy place in Islam. As we have previously stated, they claim that Mohammed went to Heaven on a winged horse from this particular location. Of course, all of that is foolishness, but, still, that's what they believe. So, for them to give up the Temple Mount, there must be something in the works that will carry with it tremendous persuasive power.

WHAT WILL THE MUSLIM WORLD THINK OF THE ANTICHRIST?

As is known, the Muslims are looking for their Messiah, so-called, as well! Considering the following, they may very well think that he is their Messiah. Even though he will be Jewish, which he will have to be for Israel to accept him as their Messiah, which they will do, still, he could very well tell the Muslims that he really isn't Jewish, thereby, playing himself up to them as their Messiah. If that, in fact, would happen, it could only be because of the following:

WHAT THE SCRIPTURE SAYS OF THE MAN OF SIN

"And through his policy also he shall cause craft to prosper in his hand" (Dan. 8:25).

The word *"craft,"* as here used, refers to deceit, in other words, *"the lie."*

He could very well tell the Muslim leaders that if they will go along with him in signing the seven-year treaty, guaranteeing *"peace and safety"* for Israel and, as well, the right for them to demolish the Dome of the Rock and there to build their Temple, that he could promise them the following:

By luring Israel into his trap, claiming to be their Messiah, with them fully accepting him, they will think this is their time of prosperity and glory. All the time he is preparing for war and at the midpoint of the Great Tribulation (three and a half years), he will suddenly, and without warning, declare war on Israel and, in fact, would totally and completely destroy them were it not for an intervention by the Lord (Dan. 11:44).

HE WILL DECEIVE THE MUSLIMS AS WELL!

The truth is that the Antichrist will appreciate the Muslim religion little more than he does Judaism or any other religion in the world, for that matter.

DECLARING HIMSELF TO BE GOD

The Scripture says:

"Neither shall he regard the God of his fathers, nor the desire of women, nor regard any god: for he shall magnify himself above all. *('Neither shall he regard the God of his fathers,' no doubt refers to him being a Jew. He will not regard the God of 'Abraham, Isaac, and Jacob.'*

" 'Nor the desire of women,' probably refers to him turning against the Catholic Church and, thereby, the Virgin Mary.

"As well, some have stated that this phrase, 'nor the desire of women,' means that he will be a homosexual. That could very well be the case.

" 'Nor regard any god: for he shall magnify himself above all,' refers to all the religions of the world, all of which will be outlawed, at least, where he has control, demanding

that worship be centered up on him)" **(Dan. 11:37).**

So, Israel will find that by accepting him as her Messiah, she has sowed to the wind and is now reaping the whirlwind. The Muslim world, also, will find to their dismay that their religion of Islam is being opposed by this son of perdition almost as much as Judaism. The great deceiver is now exacting his due!

WILL THE GREAT TRIBULATION BE WORLDWIDE?

The Great Tribulation most definitely will be worldwide! The greatest concentration of the Judgments of God will be in the Middle East, but considering that the Moon and other planetary bodies will be greatly affected, this will involve the entirety of the world. However, the greater majority of the Judgments of the Lord, which will be cataclysmic to say the least, will be poured out most of all on the *"seat of the Beast."* The Scripture says concerning this:

> **"And the fifth Angel poured out his Vial upon the seat of the beast** *(specifies that its coverage area is 'the seat of the beast'; the core of this could refer to Jerusalem, which is now the religious headquarters of the Antichrist)*; **and his kingdom was full of darkness** *(these plagues are possible to Faith, though not to reason)*; **and they gnawed their tongues for pain** *(refers to the 'boils' described in Verse 2),*
>
> **"And blasphemed the God of Heaven because of their pains and their sores** *(they blamed God for their situation, even though He plainly told them not to take the mark of the beast [14:10])*, **and repented not of their deeds.** *(This presents the fact that the heart of man is so incurably corrupt that even the fiercest Judgments fail to affect its attitude, spirit, or conduct)*" **(Rev. 16:10-11).**

WHAT ARE THE SEALS, TRUMPETS AND VIALS OF THE BOOK OF REVELATION?

There are seven Seals, seven Trumpets, and seven Vials, all pertaining to the Judgment of God poured out on the Earth, but more specifically, on the area of the beast, which, for the most part, is the Middle East.

"Seven thunders" are mentioned as well, but the Scripture says of that:

"And when He had cried, seven thunders uttered their voices. *(We aren't told what these seven thunders stated, or what they meant.)*

"And when the seven thunders had uttered their voices, I was about to write *(proclaims the fact that John wrote all of this down, which refers to the entirety of this Book of Revelation)*: and I heard a voice from Heaven saying unto me, Seal up those things which the seven thunders uttered, and write them not *(John knew what they were, but was forbidden to relate it in the Book. Therefore, speculation is useless.)*" (Rev. 10:3-4).

THE SEVEN SEAL JUDGMENTS

• The first Seal Judgment pertains to the debut of the Antichrist, which will take place at the very beginning of the Great Tribulation. He will come on a white horse, which actually is symbolic, meaning that he claims to be a man of peace but will soon prove to be otherwise.

• The second Seal Judgment pertains to constant war that will cause all types of trouble in the world, finally concluding with the Battle of Armageddon.

• The third Seal Judgment pertains to famine caused by war, which will, no doubt, take the lives of untold millions.

• The fourth Seal Judgment pertains to the untold millions who will die during the seven-year Great Tribulation.

• The fifth Seal Judgment pertains to more Believers who will be killed, and by the Antichrist.

• The sixth Seal Judgment speaks of a gigantic earthquake which will, no doubt, take the lives of many, many people.

• The seventh Seal Judgment as well pertains to another earthquake.

All the Seal Judgments are found in the Sixth Chapter of Revelation and the first five Verses of the Eighth Chapter of Revelation. These Judgments somewhat set the stage for all that is to follow.

THE SEVEN TRUMPET JUDGMENTS

Now we have seven Trumpet Judgments which are about to break upon the Earth. These Judgments will cause all the famines and deaths which will take place at this time. In fact, it is quite possible that well over a billion people could die in this seven-year period.

• The first Trumpet Judgment probably refers to a plague that will come upon the Mediterranean area and will, no doubt, take the lives of many.

• The second Trumpet Judgment probably refers to a gigantic meteorite which will crash into the earth, again in the Mediterranean area.

• The third Trumpet Judgment refers, more than likely, to another meteorite which will affect a third part of the waters of the Mediterranean and, no doubt, streams and lakes that surround that area. These particular waters, and that's quite an area, will be made so bitter that it will bring death to those who drink of this water. More than likely, even water out of wells in this area will be affected thusly.

• The fourth Trumpet Judgment concerns itself with something happening to the planetary bodies. What this will do on Planet Earth, we aren't told; however, one can be certain it will not be something pleasant.

• The fifth Trumpet Judgment concerns the bottomless

pit being opened with millions of demon locusts let out upon the Earth, which will sting like a scorpion. Even though the description is given in this Ninth Chapter of Revelation, still, they will be invisible to the human eye, but their sting most definitely will be felt. One wonders what the prognosis will be as to what is happening at that time.

• The sixth Trumpet Judgment speaks of two hundred million demon horsemen, also, which will be loosed on the world with a third part of humanity in that area dying, which probably will be the Mediterranean area.

• The seventh Trumpet Judgment refers, as well, to a great earthquake.

These seven Trumpet Judgments are found in Revelation 8:7-13; 9:1-21; 11:14-19.

THE SEVEN VIAL JUDGMENTS

We now come to the seven Vial Judgments. Incidentally, with the exception of those Judgments that span the entire seven-year period, these Judgments follow each other in succession.

• The first Vial Judgment pertains to a plague that will come upon individuals, again, more than likely, in the Mediterranean area.

• The second Vial Judgment pertains to the Mediterranean Sea becoming poisoned in some way and, thereby, killing every person who is on ships in the sea.

• The third Vial Judgment speaks of the water surrounding the Mediterranean, referring to rivers and streams, etc., becoming blood. One can well imagine what this will cause!

• The fourth Vial Judgment proclaims the Sun becoming so hot that it will literally *"scorch men with fire."* This will, no doubt, cause many more deaths.

• The fifth Vial Judgment pertains to darkness that will cover the *"seat of the beast,"* which will be the Mediterranean area and somehow will cause great pain.

• The sixth Vial refers to preparation made by demon spirits to get leaders ready for the Battle of Armageddon. It will be Satan's final effort to destroy the Jews.

• The seventh Vial pertains to another great earthquake which again, will, no doubt, result in many, many deaths.

• The Vial Judgments are found in the Sixteenth Chapter of Revelation. All of these Judgments can be wrapped up in the words, *"for the great day of His wrath is come; and who shall be able to stand?"* (Rev. 6:17).

Despite these Judgments, the Scripture is quick to point out that *"they repented not"* (Rev. 9:20-21; 16:9, 11). As should be overly obvious, Planet Earth, during the time of the Great Tribulation and especially the last three and a half years, is not going to be a very pleasant place to be.

SOME SAY THE BOOK OF REVELATION WAS FULFILLED IN A.D. 70

The Second Coming of Christ is the chief theme of the Book of Revelation. In fact, the great Nineteenth Chapter of this Book portrays that coming time as no other place in the Word of God. Now, I think it's obvious that our Lord has not yet come back. When He does, this means that everything leading up to that time has now been fulfilled, but not before!

No, the Book of Revelation wasn't fulfilled in A.D. 70 or any other time, for that matter. In fact, the Church is now living in the Third Chapter of that great Book, with the Message to the church at Laodicea actually being the Message to the modern church. The Rapture is next. Then will begin the events of the Great Tribulation, beginning with the Sixth Chapter of Revelation.

A correct understanding of Endtime events is very necessary as it regards the Work of God. Unfortunately, far too many in the modern church know precious little as to what the Bible says about Endtime events. That is because the pulpit is all but silent as it regards these great Truths.

WHAT IS THE PURPOSE OF
THE GREAT TRIBULATION?

No doubt, the Lord has many purposes and reasons for this coming event. However, the greatest purpose of all is to bring Israel back to God, despite what Israel has done, and I speak of their rejection of the Lord Jesus Christ, their Messiah, and above all, of them crucifying Him.

Paul said of Israel as to why they lost their way. It is a lesson that must not be lost upon the modern church, but yet I'm afraid that it's a lesson that is being lost. The great Apostle said:

ISRAEL

"Brethren, my heart's desire and prayer to God for Israel is, that they might be saved *(Israel, as a nation, wasn't Saved, despite their history; what an indictment!).*

"For I bear them record that they have a zeal of God *(should read, 'for God'; they had a zeal which had to do with God as its object)*, but not according to knowledge *(pertains to the right kind of knowledge).*

GOD'S RIGHTEOUSNESS

"For they being ignorant of God's Righteousness *(spells the story not only of ancient Israel, but almost the entirety of the world, and for all time; 'God's Righteousness' is that which is afforded by Christ, and received by exercising Faith in Him and what He did at the Cross, all on our behalf; Israel's ignorance was willful!)*, and going about to establish their own righteousness *(the case of anyone who attempts to establish Righteousness by any method other than Faith in Christ and the Cross)*, have not submitted themselves unto the Righteousness of God *(God's Righteousness is ensconced in Christ and what He did at the Cross).*

"For Christ *is* the end of the Law for Righteousness *(Christ fulfilled the totality of the Law)* to everyone who believes. *(Faith in Christ guarantees the Righteousness which the Law had, but could not give)*" **(Rom. 10:1-4).**

ONE SALVATION FOR ALL

The Lord, as should here be obvious, doesn't have one Salvation for the Jews and another for the Gentiles. There is only one Salvation, and that is the Salvation which is afforded by the Lord Jesus Christ, made possible by what He did for us at the Cross, and our Faith in that Finished Work. There is no other because there need be no other.

Some would say that if such were the case, then that leaves out Israel because Israel doesn't believe in the Lord Jesus Christ.

However, at the same time, every Jew who does believe in Christ, as few as that might be, plus any Gentile, will be Saved.

It is correct that virtually the entirety of the Jewish people, with a few minor exceptions, have rejected Christ, but, regrettably and sadly, so have almost all Gentiles rejected the Lord Jesus Christ. Concerning Salvation, Jesus said:

THE NARROW WAY AND
THE BROAD WAY

"Enter you in at the straight gate *(this is the Door Who is Jesus [Jn. 10:1])*: for wide *is* the gate, and broad *is* the way, that leads to destruction, and many there be which go in thereat *(proclaims the fact of many and varied religions of the world, which are false, and lead to eternal hellfire)*:

"Because straight *is* the gate, and narrow *is* the way, which leads unto life, and few there be that find it. *(Every contrite heart earnestly desires to be among the 'few'; the requirements are greater, however, than most are willing to accept)*" **(Mat. 7:13-14).**

Why are so many led astray? The major problem is the pulpit, so to speak. For every one true Preacher of the Gospel there must be a hundred who aren't true. Jesus addressed this even as one of the greatest causes of men being lost. He said:

FALSE PROPHETS AND DECEPTION

"Beware of false prophets, which come to you in sheep's clothing, but inwardly they are ravening wolves *('beware of false prophets' is said in the sternest of measures! There will be and are false prophets, and are some of Satan's greatest weapons).*

"You shall know them by their fruits *(this is the test as given by Christ as it regards identification of false prophets and false apostles).* Do men gather grapes of thorns, or figs of thistles? *(It is impossible for false doctrine, generated by false prophets, to bring forth good fruit.)*

BY THEIR FRUITS . . .

"Even so every good tree brings forth good fruit; but a corrupt tree brings forth evil fruit *(the good fruit is Christlikeness, while the evil fruit is self-likeness).*

"A good tree cannot bring forth evil fruit, neither can a corrupt tree bring forth good fruit *(the 'good tree' is the Cross, while the 'corrupt tree' pertains to all of that which is other than the Cross).*

"Every tree that brings not forth good fruit it hewn down, and cast into the fire *(Judgment will ultimately come on all so-called gospel, other than the Cross [Rom. 1:18]).*

"Wherefore by their fruits you shall know them. *(The acid test)*" (Mat. 7:15-20).

THE CRITERIA FOR ACCEPTANCE

Bluntly and plainly our Lord tells us that mere profession of religion will not do. In fact, the world is full of such. He said:

"Not everyone who says unto Me, Lord, Lord, shall enter into the Kingdom of Heaven *(the repetition of the word 'Lord' expresses astonishment, as if to say, 'Are we to be disowned?')*; but he who does the Will of My Father which is in Heaven *(what is the Will of the Father? Verse 24 of this Chapter tells us)*.

"Many will say to Me in that day, Lord, Lord, have we not Prophesied in Your Name? and in Your Name have cast out devils? and in Your Name done many wonderful works? *(These things are not the criteria, but rather Faith in Christ and what Christ has done for us at the Cross [Eph. 2:8-9, 13-18]. The Word of God alone is to be the judge of doctrine.)*

"And then will I profess unto them, I never knew you *(again we say, the criteria alone is Christ and Him Crucified [I Cor. 1:23])*: depart from Me, you who work iniquity. *(We have access to God only through Christ, and access to Christ only through the Cross, and access to the Cross only through a denial of self [Lk. 9:23]; any other Message is judged by God as 'iniquity,' and cannot be a part of Christ [I Cor. 1:17])*" **(Mat. 7:21-23).**

THE WISE MAN AND THE FOOLISH MAN

Jesus had a way of saying things that made complicated subjects into that which was very easy to understand. The following is an explanation of what He has just said about professors of religion:

"Therefore whosoever hears these sayings of Mine, and does them, I will liken him unto a wise man, which built his house upon a rock *(the 'Rock' is Christ Jesus and the Foundation is the Cross [Gal. 1:8-9])*:

"And the rain descended, and the floods came, and

the winds blew, and beat upon that house; and it fell not; for it was founded upon a rock *(the Foundation of our belief system must be Christ and Him Crucified [Gal. 6:14]).*

"And every one who hears these sayings of Mine, and does them not, shall be likened unto a foolish man, which built his house upon the sand *(but for the foundation, this house looked the same as the house that was built upon the rock)*:

GREAT WAS THE FALL OF IT

"And the rain descended, and the floods came, and the winds blew, and beat upon that house; and it fell: and great was the fall of it *(while the sun shines, both houses look good; but, when adversity comes and come it shall, Faith, which is alone in Christ and Him Crucified, will stand [I Cor. 1:18]).*

"And it came to pass, when Jesus had ended these sayings *(ended the Sermon on the Mount)*, the people were astonished at His Doctrine *(this Message proclaimed the True intent of the Law of Moses, and, above all, laid the Foundation for the New Covenant)*:

"For He taught them as *one* having authority *(refers to Divine Authority, which He had by the Power of the Holy Spirit; this Sermon and that of Lk., Chpt. 6 are probably one and the same; the Holy Spirit here lays the emphasis on the heart, while in Luke, emphasis is laid on actions produced by the heart; consequently, the distinction between 'standing' and 'state' is apparent)*, and not as the Scribes. *(Those who claim to be expert in the Law of Moses)*" (Mat. 7:24-29).

THE CROSS OF CHRIST AND SELF-RIGHTEOUSNESS

Any faith system that has as its object anything, and I mean anything, other than the Cross of Christ, always and without exception, leads to self-righteousness. It must be remembered that it was not the drunks or the immoral, as wicked as these sins are, which nailed Christ to the Cross. It was the religious leaders of Israel who did so! They did so from a position of self-righteousness. Their faith was not in God, as they claimed! Had it been solely in God, they would have known and accepted the Lord Jesus Christ, God's Son. They didn't accept Him because they really did not know God, despite all of their religiosity, etc.

How much of the modern church presently has its Faith solely in Christ and the Cross? Of course, the Lord alone knows the answer to that question; however, when we look at the *"fruit,"* which is the criteria, then the answer, at least in general, becomes more obvious.

Israel lost her way because *"she went about trying to establish her own Righteousness."*

Sounds familiar, doesn't it!?

ISRAEL'S PRESENT POSITION

Despite Israel's regathering and being formed as a nation in 1948, which was most definitely a Move of God, still, there is not one iota of spirituality present in Israel. In other words, their darkness is just as deep today as it was when they Crucified Christ.

I had a Jewish lawyer to complain once, stating that whatever happened to Jesus Christ some 2,000 years ago was not the fault of the Jews alive today. I answered him in the affirmative. That is true, however, *"you have no more regard for the Lord Jesus today than did the religious leaders of Israel some 2,000 years ago."*

He had no answer for that, knowing that it was true.

THE GREAT TRIBULATION

So, in order for Israel to be brought back to God, to

acknowledge the Lord Jesus Christ, and above all, to repent of their terrible spiritual condition, it is going to take tribulation worse than the world has ever known before. That's basically what the Great Tribulation is all about, to bring Israel back to God. And that it will do!

Israel will be brought to a place of near annihilation. In other words, what Haman, Herod, and Hitler could not do, the Antichrist will come very near to succeeding. In fact, were it not for the Second Coming of the Lord, he would succeed.

The great Prophet Isaiah was given by the Holy Spirit the prayer that Israel will pray in the midst of the Battle of Armageddon when it looks like all hope is lost. In other words, America then will not come to her rescue. In fact, no nation in the world will come to her rescue. Her back is to the wall, half of Jerusalem has fallen, and it looks like it's all over. But then, Israel will begin to cry to God as she has never cried to Him before. Basically, the great Prophet told us what Israel's prayer will be in that day. He said:

ISRAEL'S CONFESSION OF SIN

"Look down from Heaven, and behold from the habitation of Your holiness and of Your glory: where is Your zeal and Your strength, the sounding of Your bowels and of Your mercies toward me? are they restrained? *(This prayer, in effect, will be prayed by Israel, or rather the believing Remnant of Israel, prior to the Second Coming.*

"The faith, attachment, and anguish of the prayer are most effecting, and are made the more-so by the way in which the Holy Spirit lends Himself to the feelings of a dependent and desolate heart, recalling past blessings, expressing present distress, acknowledging sin and the justice of God's Judicial blinding, but pleading for Deliverance, not because of the Repentance and Faith of the supplicants, but nevertheless required, but because of the election of God and the immutability of His Nature.)

YOU ARE OUR FATHER

"Doubtless You are our Father, though Abraham be ignorant of us, and Israel acknowledge us not: You, O LORD, are our Father, our Redeemer; Your name is from everlasting. *(The Pharisee based his expectation of Salvation upon his relation to Abraham, but the spiritual Israelite bases his upon his relation to God. When facing Christ at His First Advent, they boasted that they were children of Abraham [Jn. 8:39]. Now on the eve of His Second Advent, they boast no more, but rather confess that Abraham would not even own them, i.e., 'be ignorant of us.'*

"They now admit that Israel, i.e., Jacob, would not even 'acknowledge them.'

" 'Doubtless You are our Father,' rather says, 'If You will not be our Father, then we have no Father!' This is the ground of their appeal to God. They acknowledge that their ancient relationship to Abraham and Jacob cannot redeem them. If the Lord does not claim them and redeem them, they are eternally lost!)

WE HAVE ERRED FROM YOUR WAYS

"O LORD, why have You made us to err from Your ways, and hardened our heart from Your fear? Return for Your servant's sake, the tribes of Your inheritance. *(This Verse should read: 'O Jehovah, why have You suffered us to err from Your Ways? And why have You let us harden our hearts to Your fear?' Thus, true Repentance confesses that God justly gives men over to a hardened heart when they resist His Will. At the same time, Faith holds to it that the Tribes of Jacob were God's inheritance and His holy people.*

" 'Hardened our heart from Your fear,' refers to the fact that when men have scornfully and obstinately rejected the

*Grace of God, God withdraws it from them judicially, giv-
ing them up to their wanderings, which makes their heart
incapable of faith.*

*"'Return for Your servants' sake,' speaks of humility,
and no longer of a hardened heart.)*

POSSESSED ONLY FOR A LITTLE WHILE

**"The people of Your holiness have possessed it but
a little while: our adversaries have trodden down Your
Sanctuary.** *(The great 'inheritance' that God gave unto
His People was 'possessed by them only a little while.' As
a result of their sin, 'our adversaries have trodden down
Your Sanctuary.' They are referring to the destruction by
Nebuchadnezzar and by Titus, the Roman General. But
more than all, they are speaking of the Antichrist, whom they
erroneously thought was the Messiah, but who turned on
them and did 'trod down their Sanctuary' [Dan. 9:27]).*

WE ARE YOURS

**"We are Yours: You never bore rule over them;
they were not called by Your name.** *(There is no 'Thine'
[Yours] in the original, and so important a word could not
possibly be supplied from without. Therefore, the transla-
tion should read, 'We are as those over whom You have not
ruled from of old, as those upon whom Your Name has not
been called; i.e., we have lost all our privileges — we have
become in God's sight no better than the heathen — He has
forgotten that we were ever His people')*" **(Isa. 63:15-19).**

And then the great Prophet said:

AN UNCLEAN THING

"But we are all as an unclean thing, and all our

righteousnesses are as filthy rags; and we all do fade as a leaf; and our iniquities, like the wind, have taken us away. *(Here Israel confesses the reason for their desperate condition. At long last, they own up as to exactly what it is, 'our iniquities.'*

" 'But we are all as an unclean thing,' is actually saying before God that they are a spiritual leper. They now recognize that their self-righteousness is no more than 'filthy rags,' which refer to the menstrual flux of a woman regarding her monthly period.

"It is very difficult for men, and especially religious men, to admit to such! Hence, not many religious men are Saved!)

THE CAUSE OF OUR INIQUITIES

"And there is none who calls upon Your name, who stirs up himself to take hold of You: for You have hid Your face from us, and have consumed us, because of our iniquities. *(Once again, Israel admits that it is her 'iniquities' which have brought about the Judgment of God upon her. She has only herself to blame!)*

YOU ARE THE POTTER, WE ARE THE CLAY

"But now, O LORD, You are our Father; we are the clay, and You our Potter; and we all are the work of Your hand. *(In this Passage is the gist of the great Salvation Message of Christianity. Only God can change the shape of the clay, thereby, molding the vessel into the shape and design that is desired, thereby, mending the flaws and weaknesses.)*

DO NOT REMEMBER INIQUITY FOREVER

"Be not wroth very sore, O LORD, neither remember

iniquity forever: behold, see, we beseech You, we are all Your people. *(The appeal here is for God to begin all over again, like the potter with the clay. The idea of the phrase, 'Be not wroth very sore,' refers to the fact that God had become very angry with His People. The reason for that anger was sin on the part of Israel. God cannot abide sin in the lives of His Own People any more than He can in the wicked.)*

JERUSALEM IS A DESOLATION

"Your holy cities are a wilderness. Zion is a wilderness, Jerusalem a desolation. *(As we have stated, the entirety of this prayer of Repentance, which began in the Fifteenth Verse of the previous Chapter, will be prayed by Israel at the end of the Great Tribulation — at the Second Advent of Christ.)*

THE SANCTUARY IS RUINED

"Our holy and our beautiful house, where our fathers praised You, is burned up with fire: and all our pleasant things are laid waste. *(This speaks of the Temple that is yet to be built in Jerusalem. In fact, when the Antichrist turns on Israel, he will make their Temple his religious headquarters, committing every act of vileness that one could think.)*

WILL YOU NOT HELP US?

"Will You refrain Yourself for these things, O LORD? will You hold Your peace, and afflict us very sore? *(Israel first repents of her terrible sins, pleading God's Mercy, Grace, and Love. They then bring to His attention the terrible plight of the 'holy cities,' and of 'Jerusalem.' Last of all, they proclaim to Him the destruction of* *the Temple.*

"They then ask, 'Will You refrain Yourself for these things, O LORD?'

"The answer is certain. He will not refrain Himself! He will not hold His peace!)" **(Isa. 64:6-12).**

WHAT ROLE WILL THE CHURCH PLAY IN THE GREAT TRIBULATION?

None!

The Church will be raptured away before the Great Tribulation begins (II Thess. 2:6-9).

John wrote concerning this coming time:

"For the Great Day of His wrath is come *(the 'Great Day' is the coming Great Tribulation, which will last for seven years)*; **and who shall be able to stand?** *(This refers to the fact that man has set himself against God ever since the Fall. Now man will see exactly how powerful God actually is)"* **(Rev. 6:17).**

But, the Holy Spirit has said, as it regards the Church:

"For God has not appointed us to wrath *(has not appointed Believers to go through the Great Tribulation)*, **but to obtain Salvation by our Lord Jesus Christ** *(again, pertains to the Rapture of the Church)*,

"Who died for us, that, whether we wake or sleep, we should live together with Him *(again, the Rapture, all made possible by the Cross)*.

"Wherefore comfort yourselves together *(it refers to comfort in view of the coming Rapture and the escape from wrath, which will be poured out upon the world in the coming Great Tribulation)*, **and edify one another, even as also you do.** *(This refers to cheering and strengthening one another)"* **(I Thess. 5:9-11).**

THE KEY

We are given the key to understanding the Book of Revelation in the following Verse. Our Lord said, and John wrote it down:

"Write the things which you have seen, and the things which are, and the things which shall be hereafter" (Rev. 1:19).

THE THREE PARTS

This Verse is the key to the understanding of the Book of Revelation. It is broken up into three parts.

• *"Write the things which you have seen,"* presents the first part and concerns itself with the Vision of Christ in the midst of the Candlesticks. It is found in Chapter One of this Book.

• *"And the things which are,"* constitute the second part and concerns the Churches, found in Chapters Two and Three.

• *"And the things which shall be hereafter,"* constitutes the third part and concerns itself with events after the Rapture of the Church, which includes the Great Tribulation and Eternity ever after, and is found in Chapters 4-22.

AFTER THE RAPTURE
OF THE CHURCH

Chapter Three, as stated, concludes the Messages of Christ to the Churches, in essence, the Church Age. John then says:

"After this I looked *(represents the time after the Churches, or in other words, after the Rapture)*, **and, behold, a door** *was* **opened in Heaven** *(gives John the ability to see what is taking place there)*: **and the first voice which I heard** *was* **as it were of a trumpet talking with me** *(is actually the Voice of Jesus, harking back to Rev. 1:10)*; **which said, Come up hither, and I will show you things which must be hereafter.** *(After the Rapture* *of the Church)*" **(Rev. 4:1).**

NO MENTION OF THE CHURCH IN
THE GREAT TRIBULATION

If it is to be noticed, beginning with Chapter Four of the Book of Revelation and continuing through the Twentieth Chapter, there is no mention of the Church on Earth at that time. While there is much mention of Israel, there is no mention of the Church whatsoever, at least, as it regards what is happening on Earth. If the Church has to go through the Great Tribulation, as some teach, it certainly would seem that some attention would be given to this which is so very, very important. No mention is made of it because the Church isn't on Earth, but, rather, with the Lord in Glory at this time.

Chapters Four and Five of the Book of Revelation portray to John the things which are about to happen on Earth, with Chapters Six through Twenty portraying what does happen, which is the Great Tribulation.

If it is to be noticed, in the Message that Jesus gave on the Mount of Olivet a short time before His Crucifixion, with most of it concerning the coming Great Tribulation, He really didn't mention the Church, except in passing. Concerning pointed statements about that terrible event that is soon to come, it was Israel only that was mentioned and the Church not at all. Once again, it is because the Church is with the Lord in Glory. In fact, the Church will be with the Lord when He comes back to this Earth the Second Time, referred to as the Second Coming. He will not come at that time to rescue the Church, but, rather, to rescue Israel.

WILL THERE BE PEOPLE SAVED
IN THE GREAT TRIBULATION?

There will be many Saved during this terrible time. Concerning this, the Scripture says:

"After this I beheld, and, lo, a great multitude *(pertains to martyrs who gave their lives for the Lord Jesus Christ in the Great Tribulation)*, which no man could number *(represents the many, possibly millions, who will be Saved in the Great Tribulation)*, of all nations, and kindreds, and people, and tongues, stood before the Throne, and before the Lamb *(by use of the word 'Lamb,' we know and realize that their sin-stained garments have been washed in the Blood of the Lamb)*, clothed with white robes, and palms in their hands *(could be paraphrased, 'dressed in richest wedding garments of purest, dazzling, white'; these are God's Blood-bought; the palms represent joy [Neh. 8:17])*;

CRYING WITH A LOUD VOICE

"And cried with a loud voice *(proclaims great joy)*, saying, Salvation to our God which sits upon the Throne, and unto the Lamb. *(Once again, we are told here how God has brought about Salvation. It is through what Jesus did at the Cross, and through that means alone.)*

"And all the Angels stood round about the Throne, and *about* the Elders and the four Beasts, and fell before the Throne on their faces, and worshipped God *(this tremendous volume of worship and praise has to do with what Jesus did at the Cross, in His Atoning for all sin by the giving of Himself in Sacrifice)*,

"Saying, Amen *(is the proclamation that God has provided Salvation to humanity through the Work of the Lamb)*: Blessing, and Glory, and Wisdom, and Thanksgiving, and Honor, and Power, and Might, *be* unto our God forever and ever. Amen. *(As the praises to God the Father are sevenfold, they are also sevenfold to God the Son [Rev. 5:12]. This shows that both God and the Lamb are regarded in Heaven as entitled to equal praise.)*

WHO ARE THESE?

"**And one of the Elders answered, saying unto me** *(proclaims one of the 24 addressing questions that are in John's mind, but have not been asked)*, **What are these which are arrayed in white robes?** *(This would be better translated, 'Who are these?')* **and whence came they?** *(Where do they come from?)*

"**And I said unto him, Sir, you know** *(presents reverent regard, but definitely not worship)*. **And he said to me, These are they which came out of great tribulation** *(refers to a specific group)*, **and have washed their robes, and made them white in the Blood of the Lamb.** *(They were Saved by trusting Christ and what He did at the Cross. In the Book of Revelation, the emphasis placed on the Cross is overwhelming.)*

THE LAMB

"**Therefore are they before the Throne of God, and serve Him day and night in His Temple** *(all of this particular group came out of the Great Tribulation)*: **and He Who sits on the Throne shall dwell among them.** *(The One Who sits on the Throne will cast His protecting Tabernacle over all the Saints of God, which, in effect, is His Presence.)*

"**They shall hunger no more, neither thirst anymore; neither shall the sun light on them, nor any heat** *(proclaims a perfect environment).*

"**For the Lamb which is in the midst of the Throne shall feed them** *(not only did the Lamb Save them, but He as well 'shall feed them'; not only does our Salvation come by and through what Jesus did at the Cross, but we 'live' by what Jesus did for us at the Cross as well)*, **and shall lead them unto living fountains of waters** *(symbolic of the Holy Spirit [Jn. 7:37-39])*: **and God shall wipe away** all tears from their eyes. *(All things causing sorrow will be forever gone)*" **(Rev. 7:9-17).**

SALVATION THROUGH CHRIST AND WHAT CHRIST DID AT THE CROSS

It should be understood that there will be millions upon millions of people in churches, and all over the world, for that matter, who think they are Saved, when, in reality, they aren't. As a result, these individuals will not go in the Rapture; however, the moment the Rapture takes place, it will be obvious as to the thoughts of these people. Millions of them will then give their hearts to Christ and will even give up their lives for the Cause of Christ during the coming months, as the Antichrist gathers his sway and influence over the world.

This group is specified in the Word of God under three categories. They are:

THE LUKEWARM

This group comes under the heading of the Laodicean Church. This particular Church characterizes the Church in the last days, which points to the present time. In other words, the Laodicean Church is, sadly and regrettably, the modern church. Our Lord said to this Church:

"And unto the Angel *(Pastor)* of the Church of the Laodiceans write *(this is the 'Apostate Church'; we do not know when it began, but we do know it has begun; it is the last Church addressed by Christ, so that means the Rapture will take place very shortly)*; These things says the Amen, the faithful and true witness *(by contrast to His Church, which is not faithful and true)*, the beginning of the Creation of God *(Jesus is the Creator of all things — Jn. 1:1-3)*;

YOU ARE LUKEWARM

"**I know your works, that you are neither cold nor hot** *(characterizes that which is prevalent at this present time)*: **I would you were cold or hot** *(half measures won't do)*.

"**So then because you are lukewarm, and neither cold nor hot** *(if a person is lukewarm towards something, it means he hasn't rejected it, but at the same time he has by no means accepted it; in the Mind of God, a tepid response is equal to a negative response)*, **I will spue you out of My Mouth.** *(There is no prospect of Repentance here on the part of this Church, or Restoration. In fact, there is Divine rejection.)*

YOU DO NOT KNOW

"**Because you say, I am rich, and increased with goods, and have need of nothing** *(they equated the increase in material goods with spiritual Blessings, which they were not)*; **and knowest not that you are wretched, and miserable, and poor, and blind, and naked** *(the tragedy lay in the fact that while this Church gloated over material wealth, she was unconscious of her spiritual poverty; again indicative of the modern church!)*:

GOLD TRIED IN THE FIRE

"**I counsel you to buy of Me gold tried in the fire, that you may be rich** *(what they needed to 'buy' could not be purchased with money, but only with the precious Blood of Christ, which price has already been paid; but the modern church is not interested!)*; **and white raiment, that you may be clothed, and *that* the shame of your nakedness do not appear** *(refers to Righteousness which is exclusively of Christ, and is gained only by Faith in Christ and the Cross; this tells us that the Laodicean*

Church is extremely self-righteous; not having the Righteousness of Christ, they are 'naked' to the Judgment of God); **and anoint your eyes with eyesalve, that you may see.** *(The modern church is also spiritually blind.)*

REPENT

"As many as I love, I rebuke and chasten *(implies a remnant)***: be zealous therefore, and repent.** *(The modern church desperately needs to repent for its rebellion against God's Divine Order [Christ and the Cross] and for following cunningly devised fables [II Pet. 1:16]).*

"Behold, I stand at the door, and knock *(presents Christ outside the Church)***: if any man hear My voice** *(so much religious racket is going on that it is difficult to 'hear His Voice')***, and open the door** *(Christ is the true Door, which means the Church has erected another door)***, I will come in to him, and will sup with him, and he with Me.** *(Having been rejected by the Church, our Lord now appeals to individuals, and He is still doing so presently.)*

THE OVERCOMER

"To him who overcomes will I grant to sit with Me in My Throne *(the overcomer will gain the prize of the Throne, which can only be done by one ever making the Cross the Object of his Faith)***, even as I also overcame, and am set down with My Father in His Throne.** *(This presents Christ as our Substitute, going before us, and doing for us what we could not do for ourselves.)*

"He who has an ear, let him hear what the Spirit says unto the Churches *(In plain language, the Holy Spirit is saying, 'Come back to Christ and the Cross!')*" **(Rev. 3:14-22).**

In essence, these Passages tell us that the Lord looks at the

lukewarm as *"unsaved."* Regrettably and sadly, millions in the modern church are in this category — lukewarm!

A DEPARTURE FROM THE FAITH

The Apostle Paul said, and regarding this subject:

"**Now the Spirit** *(Holy Spirit)* **speaks expressly** *(pointedly)*, **that in the latter times** *(the times in which we now live, the last of the last days, which begin the fulfillment of Endtime Prophecies)* **some shall depart from the Faith** *(anytime Paul uses the term 'the Faith,' in short, he is referring to the Cross; so, we are told here that some will depart from the Cross as the means of Salvation and Victory)*, **giving heed to seducing spirits** *(evil spirits, i.e., 'religious spirits,' making something seem like what it isn't)*, **and doctrines of devils** *(should have been translated, 'doctrines of demons'; the 'seducing spirits' entice Believers away from the true Faith, causing them to believe 'doctrines inspired by demon spirits')*;
"**Speaking lies in hypocrisy** *(concerns the teachers of these 'doctrines of demons,' which pertain to anything that leads one away from the Cross)*; **having their conscience seared with a hot iron** *(refers to the fact that these deceivers are not acting under delusion, but deliberately and against conscience)*" **(I Tim. 4:1-2).**

Now, it should be obvious from this Text that for someone to depart from something, they must first have the something from which they now depart.

This Passage speaks of individuals who once were truly Saved, who truly knew the Lord, but now have *"departed from the Faith."*

As we said in the notes, when Paul uses the words, *"the Faith,"* he is speaking of Jesus Christ and what our Lord did for us at the Cross. Concerning this, the great Apostle also said:

EXAMINE YOURSELVES

"**Examine yourselves, whether you be in the Faith** *(the words, 'the Faith,' refer to 'Christ and Him Crucified,' with the Cross ever being the Object of our Faith)***; prove your own selves.** *(Make certain your Faith is actually in the Cross, and not other things.)* **Know you not your own selves, how that Jesus Christ is in you** *(which He can only be by our Faith expressed in His Sacrifice)***, except you be reprobates?** *(Rejected)*" **(II Cor. 13:5).**

The Apostle also warned us, and did so of the following:

ENEMIES OF THE CROSS

"**Brethren, be followers together of me** *(be 'fellow-imitators')***, and mark them which walk so as you have us for an example** *(observe intently)***.**

"**(For many walk** *(speaks of those attempting to live for God outside of the Victory and rudiments of the Cross of Christ)***, of whom I have told you often, and now tell you even weeping** *(this is a most serious matter)***, *that they are* the enemies of the Cross of Christ** *(those who do not look exclusively to the Cross of Christ must be labeled 'enemies')***:**

"**Whose end *is* destruction** *(if the Cross is ignored, and continues to be ignored, the loss of the soul is the only ultimate conclusion)***, whose god is their belly** *(refers to those who attempt to pervert the Gospel for their own personal gain)***, and *whose* glory *is* in their shame** *(the material things they seek, God labels as 'shame')***, who mind earthly things.)** *(This means they have no interest in Heavenly things, which signifies they are using the Lord for their own personal gain)*" **(Phil. 3:17-19).**

Regrettably and sadly, most of the modern church has departed from the Cross of Christ. The message that is popular

today is the message of *"ethics"* and *"morality."* While most
certainly good ethics are needed and every Believer wants a
higher degree of morality, still, the preachers promoting this
message are doing so outside of the Cross. In other words,
they are purely and simply, taking the psychological approach,
claiming that what man needs to be, he can effect the change
himself. He cannot! But, because these subjects sound good
to the carnal ear, they are readily accepted. However, the following must ever be understood:

Anything that's outside of the Cross negates the help of the
Holy Spirit, and without the help of the Holy Spirit, nothing is
going to be done, and I mean nothing!

When the Believer places his or her Faith exclusively in
Christ and what Christ has done at the Cross, this guarantees
the help of the Holy Spirit and, to be sure, there is nothing that
He cannot do (Rom. 6:1-14; 8:1-2, 11; I Cor. 1:17-18, 23; 2:2;
Gal., Chpt. 5; 6:14; Eph. 2:13-18; Col. 2:14-15).

A FORM OF GODLINESS BUT DENYING
THE POWER THEREOF

This group, unlike the previous two, has never been Saved.
Unfortunately, millions, in this country alone, fall into this category. They are religious but lost!

The great Apostle also wrote of these. He said:

"This know also, that in the last days *(the days in
which we now live)* perilous times shall come. *(This
speaks of difficult, dangerous times, which Christians living just before the Rapture will encounter.)*

"For men *(those who call themselves Christians)*
shall be lovers of their own selves, covetous, boasters,
proud, blasphemers, disobedient to parents, unthank-
ful, unholy,

"Without natural affection, trucebreakers, false
accusers, incontinent, fierce, despisers of those who

are good,

"Traitors, heady, highminded, lovers of pleasures more than lovers of God *(and remember, this is describing the Endtime Church, which has been totally corrupted [Mat. 13:33; Rev. 3:14-22])*;

FROM SUCH TURN AWAY

"Having a form of Godliness *(refers to all the trappings of Christianity, but without the power)*, but denying the power thereof *(the modern church, for all practical purposes, has denied the Cross; in doing this, they have denied that through which the Holy Spirit works, and in Whom the power resides [Rom. 8:1-2, 11; I Cor. 1:18])*: from such turn away. *(No half measures are to be adopted here. The command is clear! It means to turn away from churches that deny or ignore the Cross.)*

LED AWAY WITH DIVERS LUSTS

"For of this sort are they which creep into houses *(proclaims the methods of false teachers)*, and lead captive silly women laden with sins, led away with divers lusts *(due to Eve succumbing to temptation and deception, women are the easiest prey for these false teachers; the idea is that 'silly women' will support these false teachers, and do so grandly; they are drawn to these false preachers through 'divers lusts')*,

NO KNOWLEDGE OF THE TRUTH

"Ever learning *(proclaims learning that which is wrong)*, and never able to come to the knowledge of the Truth. *(This proclaims the fact that they really do not want the Truth.)*

"Now as Jannes and Jambres withstood Moses

([Ex. 7:11-12], the names of these men are found in the Targum of Jonathan), **so do these also resist the Truth** *(they have been shown the Truth, but have rejected the Truth, which they did purposely; it pertains to a rejection of the Cross of Christ)*: **men of corrupt minds, reprobate concerning the Faith.** *(If it's not 'Christ and Him Crucified,' then it is corrupt and reprobate [I Cor. 2:2])"* **(II Tim. 3:1-8).**

THESE HAVE NEVER BEEN SAVED

As we've already stated, these are individuals who are very religious, but, at the same time, very lost. Regrettably, churches are filled with such. In fact, in most churches presently, a person could not get Saved if he desired to do so. That's how bad the situation actually is.

The modern church has long since substituted humanistic psychology for the Word of God. In the 1700's, the Methodist Church served as a powerful bulwark against evil. In fact, had it not been for the Methodist Church in those times, there is a good possibility that this nation would not now even exist.

In the 1800's, while the Methodists, to a great extent, continued in this capacity, the Baptists, as well, became a strong hindrance of evil.

In the 1900's, the Pentecostals and the Holiness began to step to the forefront in serving as a great hindrance to evil. In fact, the Pentecostal denominations took the Gospel to the furthest corners of the Earth. I know what I'm talking about because I was a part of it, and still am.

Regrettably, virtually the entire church world, at least as far as institutionalized religion is concerned, adopted psychology as the answer to the needs of man, and thereby, forsook the Bible. This goes for the Pentecostals, Holiness, Baptists and Methodists, etc. At the present time, even as I dictate these words (2009), these mighty denominations, spiritually speaking, are little more than a religious shell. In other words, if they went out of business tomorrow, meaning they closed their doors, it would affect the Kingdom of God precious little, if any at all. I realize that these are strong words, but they are the truth.

But, the Lord will never leave Himself without a witness. I firmly believe that at this present time, the Message of the Cross is that which the Spirit is saying to the Churches. To be sure, it's not a new Message, actually originating before the foundation of the world (I Pet. 1:18-21), but I believe the Holy Spirit is emphasizing this great Word today as never before. As stated, it's not a new Message, with its full meaning having been given to the Apostle Paul, which he gave to us in his fourteen Epistles. It is the Word of the Lord (Rom. 6:1-14; 8:1-2, 11; I Cor. 1:17-18, 23; 2:2; Gal. 6:14; Col. 2:14-15).

"There's not a friend like the lowly Jesus,
"No, not one! no, not one!
"None else could heal all our soul's diseases,
"No, not one! no, not one!"

"No friend like Him is so high and holy,
"No, not one! no, not one!
"And yet no friend is so meek and lowly,
"No, not one! no, not one!"

"There's not an hour that He is not near us,
"No, not one! No, not one!
"No night so dark but His Love can cheer us,
"No, not one! No, not one!"

"Did ever Saint find this Friend forsake him?
"No, not one! no, not one!
"Or sinner find that He would not take him?
"No, not one! no, not one!"

"Was e'er a gift like the Saviour given?
"No, not one! no, not one!
"Will He refuse us a home in Heaven?
"No, not one! no, not one!"

CHAPTER FOUR

What Is The Battle Of Armageddon?

QUESTION:

WHAT IS THE BATTLE OF ARMAGEDDON?

ANSWER:

The Battle of Armageddon stands to be the most horrific battle ever fought, resulting in more casualties than any other conflict has ever had. It will be Satan's effort, basically his last, to take over the world and to dethrone God, so to speak. As to how this can be done, considering that the Evil One is but a creature, while God is the Creator, will become more obvious as we go forward.

WHEN WILL THIS BATTLE BE FOUGHT?

The Battle of Armageddon will be fought at the conclusion of the Great Tribulation. The Word of God tells us of the preparations by the Evil One as it regards this Battle.

THE SIXTH VIAL

The Scripture says:

"And the sixth Angel poured out his Vial upon the great river Euphrates; and the water thereof was dried up *(refers to preparations for the coming Battle of Armageddon)*, that the way of the kings of the east might be prepared *(actually says in the Greek, 'the kings of the sunrising'; this will, no doubt, include the armies of China and Japan, plus others which will join the Antichrist in the coming Battle of Armageddon)*.

THREE UNCLEAN SPIRITS

"And I saw three unclean spirits like frogs *(while*

John saw these demon spirits in his Vision, they will be invisible to all others; these invisible creatures are functioning presently on Earth, even as they have since the Fall, and there is only one Power that affects them, and that is the Name of Jesus [Mk. 16:17]) **come out of the mouth of the dragon, and out of the mouth of the beast, and out of the mouth of the false prophet.** *(This concerns the fact that this ungodly trio connives to secure the help of other nations regarding the coming Battle of Armageddon.)*

"For they are the spirits of devils *(refers to a flood of demon spirits working in conjunction with the three unclean spirits)*, **working miracles** *(which will probably be done through the false prophet and others; proclaims the fact that all miracles are not necessarily from God)*, **which go forth unto the kings of the Earth and of the whole world, to gather them to the battle of that Great Day of God Almighty.** *(As is obvious here, there are nations the Antichrist doesn't control, whose help he will seek. But, while he thinks all of this is his plan, 'God Almighty' is actually orchestrating all events. The Antichrist will think to destroy Israel, but God will, in fact, destroy him.)*

CALLED IN THE HEBREW TONGUE ARMAGEDDON

"Behold, I come as a thief *(refers to the fact that the Antichrist has been so successful with his propaganda that very few in the world at that time will actually be expecting Christ to return)*. **Blessed** *is* **he who watches, and keeps his garments** *(points to those on Earth who worship and serve the Lamb, and that they must be constantly vigilant lest their loyalty to Him be diverted through Satanic deception [Mat. 24:43; I Thess. 5:2-4])*, **lest he walk naked, and they see his shame.** *(This refers to being naked to the Judgment of God, and suffering the consequences at the Second Coming, or even before that event.)*

"**And He gathered them together** *(the pronoun 'He' refers to God)* **into a place called in the Hebrew tongue Armageddon.** *(This refers to a literal place where a literal battle will be fought. It is the Mount of Megiddo overlooking the plain of Megiddo west of the Mount, and apparently including the Plain of Esdraelon, i.e., Valley of Megiddo)*" **(Rev. 16:12-16).**

THE BOW WITH NO ARROWS

When the Antichrist makes his debut upon the world, with him gaining phenomenal notoriety after his making possible the nonaggression pact between Israel and the Muslim world, he will have done what no one else in the world, not even the brightest minds in America, have been able to accomplish. As a result, he will be the topic of conversation over every television news network in the world, the subject of every magazine, and the headlines of every newspaper. In fact, Israel will accept him, as we have previously stated, as her Messiah.

He will come as a man of peace. Concerning that, the Scripture says:

"**And I saw when the Lamb opened one of the Seals** *(refers to the Crucified, risen Christ, and is proven by the use of the word 'Lamb')*, **and I heard, as it were the noise of thunder, one of the four Beasts** *(living creatures)* **saying, Come and see.** *(This will follow the Rapture of the Church, but we aren't told exactly how long after the Rapture the Great Tribulation will come. 'Come and see,' says that it is destined and cannot be avoided.)*

"**And I saw, and behold a white horse** *(symbolic; proclaims the Antichrist presenting himself to the world as a prince of peace)*: **and he who sat on him had a bow** *(mentions no arrows; he preaches peace, but is preparing for war, as symbolized by the 'bow')*; **and a crown was given unto him: and he went forth conquering, and**

to conquer. *(The 'crown' represents the fact that he will conquer many countries. At first he does so by peace, but will quickly graduate to war)*" **(Rev. 6:1-2).**

DECEPTION

The Antichrist will lull the entirety of the world into believing that he is a man of peace and, in fact, is the only one who can bring peace to the world. That he will do for a short period of time, and then he will begin to exert his military strength. In fact, he is the very opposite of a man of peace. The Scripture further says concerning him:

THE STRANGE GOD

"But in his estate shall he honor the god of forces; and a god whom his fathers knew not shall he honor with gold, and silver, and with precious stones, and pleasant things. *('And a god whom his fathers knew not shall he honor,' refers to a 'strange god' mentioned in the next Verse, who is actually the fallen Angel who empowered Alexander the Great. He is called 'the Prince of Grecia,' which does not refer to a mortal, but instead, a fallen Angel [Dan. 10:20]. This 'god,' his fathers, Abraham, Isaac, and Jacob did not know.)*

"Thus shall he do in the most strongholds with a strange god, whom he shall acknowledge and increase with glory: and he shall cause them to rule over many, and shall divide the land for gain. *('Thus shall he do in the most strongholds,' refers to the great financial centers of the world, which will be characterized by rebuilt Babylon. This 'strange god,' as stated, is a fallen Angel; therefore, he will probably think he is giving praise and glory to himself, when, in reality, he is actually honoring this 'fallen Angel.'*

" 'And he shall cause them to rule over many,' refers

to the many nations he will conquer because of the great power given to him by this fallen Angel, instigated by Satan)" **(Dan. 11:38-39).**

THE KING OF THE NORTH

When Daniel uses the terms *"king of the north"* and *"king of the south"* in Verse 40, he is speaking to countries which are north or south of Israel. In fact, he is speaking of Syria (king of the north) and Egypt (king of the south).

Many have tried to conclude that the *"king of the north"* is Russia because it is north, etc. While Russia, more than likely, will be involved in trying to oppose the Antichrist and will be defeated by him, the *"king of the north"* is not Russia.

After a short period of time, the Antichrist will begin to exercise his power. The wars which we will now mention probably will take place in the first three and a half years of the Great Tribulation. He will make the world, no doubt, think he's doing it a favor by bringing certain nations into line, the first one seemingly being Egypt. The Scripture says:

"And at the time of the end shall the king of the south *(Egypt)* push at him: and the king of the north *(the Antichrist, Syria)* shall come against him like a whirlwind, with chariots, and with horsemen, and with many ships; and he shall enter into the countries, and shall overflow and pass over. *(The phrase, 'And at the time of the end,' refers to the time of the fulfillment of these Prophecies, which, in fact, is just ahead. It is known that 'the king of the south' refers to Egypt because that's who is referred to at the beginning of this Chapter, which spoke of the breakup of the Grecian Empire. As well, 'the king of the north' proves that the Antichrist will come from the Syrian division of the breakup of the Grecian Empire. So, the Antichrist will more than likely be a Syrian Jew)"* **(Dan. 11:40).**

ATTACK ISRAEL

The attack against Israel will take place at approximately the midpoint of the Great Tribulation. The Scripture says:

"He shall enter also into the glorious land *(into Israel)*, and many countries shall be overthrown *(those in the Middle East)*: but these shall escape out of his hand, even Edom, and Moab, and the chief of the children of Ammon. *(Edom, Moab, and Ammon comprise modern Jordan. His entering into the 'glorious land' refers to his invasion of Israel at the midpoint of his seven-year non-aggression pact with them, therefore, breaking his covenant [Dan. 9:27].*

"*The countries listed comprise modern Jordan, where ancient Petra is located, to which Israel will flee upon the Antichrist 'entering into the Glorious Land' [Rev. 12:6].)*

POWER

"He shall stretch forth his hand also upon the countries: and the land of Egypt shall not escape. *('Egypt' refers to 'the king of the south' of Verse 40, as stated.)*

"But he shall have power over the treasures of gold and of silver, and over all the precious things of Egypt: and the Libyans and the Ethiopians shall be at his steps. *(The 'precious things of Egypt' no doubt refer to the ancient mysteries of Egypt, regarding the tombs, the pyramids, etc. He will no doubt claim to unlock many of these mysteries; he very well could do so, regarding the supernatural power given to him by the powers of darkness.)*

ADVERSARIES TO THE NORTH AND EAST

"But tidings out of the east and out of the north shall trouble him: therefore he shall go forth with great fury

to destroy, and utterly to make away many. *(After the Antichrist breaks his covenant with Israel, actually 'entering into the Glorious Land,' he will be prevented from further destroying her by the 'tidings out of the east and out of the north' that 'shall trouble him.' No doubt, these will be nations, probably led by Russia [north], Japan, and China [east], forming a union against him, but which will have no success)"* **(Dan. 11:41-44).**

WHERE WILL THE BATTLE OF ARMAGEDDON BE FOUGHT?

The Battle of Armageddon will be fought in Israel, more particularly, in the valley of Megiddo. The name *"Armageddon"* used in Revelation 16:16 actually means, *"Mountain of Megiddo."* In fact, the plain of Megiddo, for it is also a valley, has witnessed many important battles. This plain or valley is located about 35 miles southwest of the Sea of Galilee, almost in the middle of Israel.

The area, and I continue to speak of this valley, was basically a swamp when Israel became a nation in 1948; however, the swamp was drained and now bountiful crops are grown there twelve months out of the year. It is beautiful, to say the least! It is about the only part of Israel proper, other than the Sinai, which would be appropriate for tank battles; therefore, this is the place that will be the beginning of this great conflict (Rev. 16:16). As well, the Valley of Megiddo is sometimes referred to as *"the Valley of Jezreel."*

The first recorded battle fought in this valley was one fought by Tuthmosis, III, in 1468 B.C. The last one of any magnitude was fought by Lord Allenby in 1917. There were countless conflicts, as would be obvious, between the Egyptian Tuthmosis and that of the time of Lord Allenby.

Even though Armageddon will begin in the Valley of Megiddo, it will quickly spread to cover almost the entirety of the nation of Israel, even to Jerusalem, and especially to Jerusalem.

WHY IS THE LAND OF ISRAEL SO IMPORTANT?

It is so important because it is the only area on Earth, the land of Israel, to which God has laid claim. In fact, Jerusalem is the only city on Earth where He has chosen to place His Name (Deut. 3:18; Jer. 7:7; II Chron. 6:6; Lev. 25:23).

THE ABRAHAMIC COVENANT

This land, then called the land of Canaan, came to the fore first of all in the command that the Lord gave to Abraham. It is referred to as the *"Abrahamic Covenant."* The Scripture says:

"Now the LORD had said unto Abram *(referring to the Revelation which had been given to the Patriarch a short time before; this Chapter is very important, for it records the first steps of this great Believer in the path of Faith)*, Get thee out of your country *(separation)*, and from your kindred *(separation)*, and from your father's house *(separation)*, unto a land that I will show you *(refers to the fact that Abraham had no choice in the matter; he was to receive his orders from the Lord, and go where those orders led him)*:

A GREAT NATION

"And I will make of you a great Nation *(the Nation which God made of Abraham has changed the world, and exists even unto this hour; in fact, this Nation 'Israel' still has a great part to play, which will take place in the coming Kingdom Age)*, and I will bless you, and make your name great *(according to Scripture, 'to bless' means 'to increase'; the builders of the Tower of Babel sought to 'make us a name,' whereas God took this man, who forsook all, and 'made his name great')*; and you shall be a blessing: *(concerns itself with the greatest blessing of all. It is the glory of Abraham's Faith. God would give this man the meaning of Salvation, which is 'Justification by Faith,' which would come about through the Lord Jesus Christ, and what Christ would do on the Cross. Concerning this, Jesus said of Abraham, 'Your father Abraham rejoiced to see My day: and he saw it, and was glad' [Jn. 8:56]).*

ALL THE FAMILIES OF THE EARTH

"And I will bless them who bless you *(to bless Israel, or any Believer, for that matter, guarantees the Blessings of God)***, and curse him who curses you** *(to curse Israel, or any Believer, guarantees that one will be cursed by God)***: and in you shall all families of the Earth be blessed.** *(It speaks of Israel, which sprang from the loins of Abraham and the womb of Sarah, giving the world the Word of God and, more particularly, bringing the Messiah into the world. Through Christ, every family in the world who desires blessing from God can have that Blessing, i.e., 'Justification by Faith')***" (Gen. 12:1-3).**

THE BOUNDARIES OF THE LAND

The Scripture says:

"In the same day the LORD made a Covenant with Abram *(Abraham)***, saying, Unto your seed have I given this land** *(Promises based on the Precious Blood of Christ are so absolutely sure that Faith can claim them as already possessed; hence, the Believer in the Lord Jesus Christ is neither ashamed nor afraid to say, 'I am Saved')***, from the river of Egypt unto the great river, the river Euphrates.** *(The actual area promised by God to Abraham goes all the way to the Nile River in Egypt, which includes the Sinai, the Arab Peninsula, much of modern Iraq, most of Syria, and all of Lebanon)***" (Gen. 15:18).**

David alone came close to occupying all of this land according to the boundaries that the Lord laid out. To be sure, it most definitely will be occupied by Israel during the coming Kingdom Age, including all of the Arab Peninsula. Israel in that coming day will be almost as large as the modern U.S.A. As well, whereas the Arab Peninsula is now almost all desert, then, and we continue to speak of the Kingdom Age, it will all be a verdant garden.

The present land of Israel has been contested almost from the beginning. The reason is simple!

Satan has done everything within his power to besmirch that which belongs exclusively to the Lord. In fact, the greatest conflict of all has already begun and will conclude with the Battle of Armageddon.

THE MUSLIM WORLD

As a nation, Israel was totally defeated by the Romans in A.D. 70. During that siege of Jerusalem, over a million Jews lost their lives in that conflict, with other hundreds of thousands sold as slaves all over the world of that day. For all practical purposes, at that time, and especially in A.D. 135, Israel was scattered all over the world and effectively ceased to be a nation. Of course, there was always a strong Remnant of Jews that remained in the land and did so continually.

The religion of Islam made its debut in A.D. 622. At that time a man emerged whose message changed the face of the Middle East and affected the history of Judaism and Christianity in a most significant manner. Muhammad, of the tribe of Quraysh in Mecca, claimed to have received a revelation that God (Allah) was *"one"* and that he (Muhammad) was to be Allah's messenger of that truth. After gathering his first converts from among his family members and close friends, Muhammad encountered severe opposition, so much so that he had to flee to the town of Medina. This flight, or *"Hejira"* in Arabic, is now viewed as year one in the Islamic calendar (which, as stated, was A.D. 622).

In Medina, Muhammad encountered a large and influential Jewish community. The influence of Judaism on his teaching must have been significant. For example, during this period Muhammad taught that the faithful should pray facing Jerusalem, as Jewish prayers were always directed there. Only later, after the Jews had rejected his message, did he alter the direction for prayer to Mecca.

MUHAMMAD

Muhammad also taught his followers to fast on the tenth day of Tishri, the same day as the Jewish fast of Yom Kippur. Later, this fast was expanded to include the entire month of Ramadon. As well, Muhammad's followers abstain from pork and circumcise their sons, standard Jewish practices since Biblical days.

Muhammad also accepted the Jewish Prophets Adam, Noah, Abraham, Moses, and David, as well as the *"Prophet"* Jesus, although he strongly rejected His Deity. Muhammad added that he himself was the *"seal of Prophecy"* — God's final messenger. While accepting some of the Scriptures of Jews and Christians, Muhammad's *"revelations,"* embodied in the Koran, became the authoritative *"Scriptures"* for his faithful followers. These followers were called Muslims, from the Arabic word *"Islam,"* meaning *"submission"* to the one God.

Apparently, Muhammad thought that Jews would accept his message of a pure monotheism, but the Rabbis ridiculed his illiteracy and his confusion of Biblical traditions. Furthermore, the Jewish people simply could not accept a non-Israelite as God's *"seal of Prophecy."*

When the Jews of Medina rejected him and his message, Muhammad turned on them with a vengeance. Then followed the expulsion and exile of two Jewish tribes from Medina, as well as the extermination of a third.

Finally, Muhammad and his fanatical adherents massacred

most of the remaining Jews of Northern Arabia and forcibly evicted the rest. The only Jewish community that remained was in Yemen, which continued to 1950, when nearly all the Yemenite Jews were air-lifted to Israel in *"Operation Magic Carpet."*

THE ATTITUDE OF ISLAM TOWARD
THE JEWISH PEOPLE

There is an important contemporary lesson to be learned from this brief historic overview. We cannot fully comprehend the Arab/Israeli conflict unless we understand the attitude of Islam toward the Jewish people. The Land of Israel, or Palestine, as it was called by the Romans and Byzantines, was conquered and ruled by Muslims from the Seventh Century to the Twentieth Century.

The only interruption came when the *"Christian"* crusaders ruled the land for less than a hundred years. Islam finds it unacceptable that this land, originally conquered for Allah by his followers, is now ruled by Jews — a people who are supposed to be inferior and subservient, according to the Koran.

The Muslims find it impossible to acknowledge the historic reality that the Land of Israel, according to the Bible, belongs to the Jews. This is the real key to understanding the impasse that exists in Israel today. The Arab countries, predominantly Muslim, refuse to accept a foreign, Jewish presence in a land that is supposed to be, according to them, a part of the *"world of Islam."*

The modern rise of a more fanatical Islam only heightens the tension for this impasse — an impasse that ultimately can be repaired only by the coming of the Messiah, the Saviour of both Isaac's and Ishmael's sons.

ISAAC OR ISHMAEL?

Respecting what has been said, the impetus behind the Arab and Persian determination to destroy Israel cannot be narrowly defined as a family affair, even though the Arabs and the Israelis are both direct descendants of Abraham, or so it is believed by some (Isaac and Ishmael).

Yes, there was the matter of engendered jealousy over Ishmael being passed over as the recipient of the Abrahamic Covenant. That Blessing and the Promise of perpetual ownership of the Land of Israel fell to Isaac and his heirs, which are the Jews.

"And God said, Sarah your wife shall bear you a son indeed; and you shall call his name Isaac: and I will establish My Covenant with him for an Everlasting Covenant, and with his seed after him" (Gen. 17:19).

But Ishmael was also given the Promise of becoming *"a great nation"* (Gen. 21:18) — a nation so great *"that it shall not be numbered for multitude"* (Gen. 16:10). That Promise has been faithfully fulfilled by God. Tiny Israel floats in the middle of a Sea of Arab nations scattered across a large portion of the globe, but with the greatest concentration in the Middle East.

TWO DIFFERENCES

There are basically two differences between God's Covenant with the Jews and His Covenant with the Ishmaelites. Israel was specifically given the land called Palestine or Israel (Gen. 13:14-17; 17:6-8, 19-21; 28:3-4).

The paramount difference, however, is discovered in these words, as stated:

"And I will bless them who bless you, and curse him who curses you: and in you shall all families of the Earth be blessed" (Gen. 12:3).

The Promise is further defined in Genesis 22:18:

"And in your seed shall all the nations of the Earth be blessed." That *"Seed"* of Blessing delivered to the Gentile nations through the Jewish people — including Arabs — was and is the Messiah.

"Now to Abraham and his Seed were the Promises made. He said not, And to seeds, as of many; but as of One, And to your Seed, which is Christ" (Gal. 3:16).

THE SEED

Jewry's presence and assigned mission are, therefore, uniquely set apart in marked contrast to those described as characteristic of Ishmael's seed and national legacy. The *"Seed"* component in God's program for humanity surpasses every other aspect of history. In addition to being a Saviour of men, Messiah is to be a King. When His Kingdom finally arrives, He will establish and enforce stability. Delivery of the One Who could so bless mankind was the exclusive province of Abraham's Seed through Isaac. The Promise is specific. The Abrahamic Covenant provided:

• A King for the Throne: *"And kings shall come out of you"* (Gen. 17:6).

• A land for the King: *"And I will give unto you, and to your seed after you, the land wherein you are a stranger, all the land of Canaan"* (Gen. 17:8).

• A people for the King: *"And I will be their God"* (Gen. 17:8).

THE BLESSING

Unfortunately, it was the *"Blessing"* aspect of the Covenant that developed the animosity in Esau's posterity because the Blessing fell to Jacob rather than to Esau, who fathered their people. Had the Arabs embraced obediently the Saviour and kingly aspects of the Blessing of the Messiah, history would have taken another course.

These residual resentments became deeply ingrained in the attitudes of the Arabs toward Israel and those resentments spun off in manifold and discernable ways as the centuries passed. Scripture is replete with accounts of the heirs of Ishmael who warred against Israel while growling their determination to *"Come, and let us cut them off from being a nation; that the name of Israel may be no more in remembrance.*

"For they have consulted together with one consent" (Ps. 83:4-5). Their *"one consent"* was the extermination of the nation of Israel.

Since the days of the Psalmist, Arab determination has not wavered; however, the entrance of the new religion, Islam (Seventh Century A.D.), refined and sanctified the rationale. It then became incumbent to subjugate or exterminate Jews *"in God's Name."*

One Islamic leader stated, *"The killing of Jews will continue — killing, killing in God's Name, until they vanish."*

Thus, the Allah discovered by Muhammad was very different from the God found in the Bible. Muhammad's religion, which, in his view, was to replace Judaism and Christianity, would have a new book (the Koran), a new look, and a new center of worship (Mecca).

JIHAD

The word *"Jihad"* is enshrined in the ecstatic vocabulary of the Muslim believer. To kill in the name of Allah in Jihad (holy war) is a privilege. To die in Jihad is to be assured a place in Heaven; consequently, military conquest became a theological pursuit, and conquered people became subjects of Allah.

The religiously fired law of conquest swept Islamic armies into Syria, Israel, Mesopotamia, Egypt, North Africa, and Spain. The advance was finally stopped by Charles Martel, grandfather of Charlemagne, outside Paris in A.D. 732. Later, Muslim hoards encompassed Europe, moving as far west as Austria before being defeated in the late Seventeenth Century.

Subsequently, many of these areas, through erosion or military options, were delivered from Muslim domination. The ultimate affront to Islamic ambitions was the deliverance of Jerusalem from the Muslim Ottoman Turks by the *"Christian"*

British expeditionary force in 1917 and the return of Jewry to the land after 1948.

Symbolically, the modern state of Israel stands as a constant reminder to rabid fundamentalist Muslims of their humiliation before infidels — a condition that can only be remedied through conquest.

RELIGIOUS DOMINANCE

This is a fact of life often misunderstood by those restrained by Western belief and standards, for the issue of land in the Middle East is not primarily a territorial matter. It is a question of religious dominance — the lack of which is intolerable to the Muslim who is taught that Allah is all and is to possess all. This is precisely why the lies of militant Muslim fundamentalists in Iran were viewed with such deep concern — a concern borne out more vividly with every passing day (at that time) by the sight of captive American hostages on the nightly television news broadcast.

An abiding tenet of Islam is that all lands are to be subject to Allah. Therefore, once a territory is taken, it must remain under Muslim domination. If land is lost, Jihad becomes necessary. Any concessions or treaties made with enemies under conditions making it impossible to restore dominion by force are observed only until means are available to remedy the situation.

A NEGOTIATED PEACE?

For this reason, as Arab spokesmen have repeatedly avowed, any negotiated peace agreement with Israel will only provide a staging area from which to pursue total elimination of the Jewish presence from land claimed to be sacred to Allah. Hence, the negotiations and peace treaties with the Palestinians regarding the Gaza Strip, Jericho, and the West Bank should be looked at accordingly. In such a perpetual state of conflict, Israelis know all too well what the Western world must learn or live to regret — survival against the Muslim onslaught means having a superior strength and the will to use it.

MUSLIM EVANGELISM

Make no mistake about it, Muslims are bent on possessing this planet for Allah, either by coercion or persuasion. And while, in the first wave, the swords of Islam were wet with the blood of vanquished *"infidels,"* a great second wave is now moving across the Western world in the form of a Muslim missionary crusade.

Unfortunately, the political leaders in America, and seemingly many religious leaders as well, do not know nor understand the aims of the Muslim religion. They seem to think that we can talk nice to these people, give them that for which they ask, whatever it might be, and the situation will be resolved. They do not seem to realize that it is a religion that we are up against and not merely a political stance. Political directions may change and often do; however, a religion basically does not change.

As it regards Israel, all of this means that the ambition and overriding desire, even a demand, of the Muslim world is that every Jew is dead and every foot of the land of Israel come into Muslim dominance. They will be satisfied with nothing less. Unfortunately, most of the world thinks that the problem in the Middle East is because Israel will not give land to the Palestinians. Nothing could be further from the truth. They are not asking merely for a piece of land, but, rather, all the land.

About the only friend that Israel has in the world is the United States, and it seems that our resolve presently is wavering. If, in fact, that is the case, it's the worst thing that could ever happen to this nation.

THE ROLE OF THE U.S.A.

About 2,500 years ago, the scepter of world power fell from

the trembling hands of the kings of Judah and was picked up by Nebuchadnezzar, the potentate of the mighty Babylonian Empire. Thus, world leadership passed into the hands of Gentile powers. After the Babylonians, it went into the hands of the Medes and the Persians, and then to Greece, and finally to Rome. Israel was destroyed as a nation under the Roman power, becoming a nation once again, only after nearly 2,000 years had passed. Thus, in 1948, the spiritual picture of the entirety of the world changed. Not only was there a mighty moving of the Holy Spirit over basically every nation of the world, but, as well, Israel, once again as a nation, became God's prophetic time clock. In other words, if one wants to know how late it is prophetically speaking, one only need look at Israel.

The scepter of world power then was placed into the hands of the United States, where it remains unto this hour. While that entails much responsibility, still, the greatest responsibility of all, as it regards that place and position, given by God I might quickly add, is the protection of Israel. If we maintain our guarantee of her sovereignty, somehow, the economic problems will be solved; somehow, the social situations will be resolved as well. But, if not. . .?

(Much of the information respecting Islam was derived from articles written by Elwood McQuaid, Editor of *"Israel My Glory"* Magazine, who is with the Organization, *"Friends of Israel Gospel Ministry"*, and also Will Varner, formerly Dean of the Institute of Biblical Studies, who is with *"Friends of Israel Gospel Ministry."*)

WHAT IS THE PURPOSE OF THE BATTLE OF ARMAGEDDON?

In short, the purpose of the Battle of Armageddon is to destroy Israel. When I say destroy Israel, I mean that so many Jews will be killed that it will be impossible for them to form a nation again. That will be the ambition of the Antichrist, and then his goal will be to take the entirety of the land of Israel as his own. One must remember that at this particular time, the Battle of Armageddon, there will be no sanctioned religions on the face of the Earth of any nature, including Islam, with the Antichrist having declared war on all religions, making himself into god. While he will not control the entirety of the world, the part that he does control, which will definitely be the Middle East, the *"worship of the beast"* will be the only worship allowed. As well, he will hold great sway throughout the entirety of the world, with his ambition being to take over the entirety of the world, which he most definitely would do were it not for the Second Coming of the Lord.

WHY IS IT SO IMPORTANT THAT
ISRAEL BE DESTROYED?

Of course, Satan will put it in the heart of the Antichrist to destroy Israel, and for a reason.

Satan has one hope of defeating the Lord, and one hope only. Knowing that Satan is a fallen Angel, therefore, a creature, and that God is the Creator, many may wonder how the Evil One thinks that he can overthrow God, Who has all power.

The way he thinks to do this is to cause the Word of God to fall to the ground. If one word of Prophecy can be proven to be untrue, in other words, if God fails to uphold His Word ,and it proves to be false, then purely and simply, Satan has won the day.

A long time ago, the Evil One said the following:

I WILL . . .

"For you have said in your heart, I will ascend into Heaven, I will exalt my throne above the stars of God: I will sit also upon the mount of the congregation, in the sides of the north:

"I will ascend above the heights of the clouds; I will be like the Most High" (Isa. 14:13-14).

THE GREATEST PROPHECY IN
THE WORD OF GOD?

If the predictions by the Prophets of old concerning the restoration of Israel aren't the greatest Prophecies in the Bible,
they certainly come close. At any rate, this is the most visible
Prophecy, the one that Satan will endeavor to prove untrue.
The Battle of Armageddon will not be his first effort. In fact,
he has contested these people from the very beginning. Considering that even from the beginning most Jews did not live
for God, this gave Satan great latitude to carry out his evil
designs. However, there has always been a Remnant in Israel
who truly loved God and truly lived for God. While it might
be small, nevertheless, it served the purpose. Paul said in relation to this:

"Even so then at this present time (Paul's day) *also there is
a Remnant according to the election of Grace"* (Rom. 11:5).

If the truth be known, there is only a *"Remnant"* in the
modern church who truly knows the Lord and, in fact, a *"small
Remnant."* However, that's not something new, this always
having been the case.

*"Straight is the gate, and narrow is the way, which leads unto
life, and few there be who find it"* (Mat. 7:14).

To quote just one Prophet about the restoration of Israel, it
becomes obvious as to what is being said.

Bluntly and plainly the great Prophet Jeremiah said:

RESTORATION UNDER THE MESSIAH

"And I will gather the Remnant of My Flock out of
all countries whither I have driven them, and will bring
them again to their folds; and they shall be fruitful and
increase. *(Verses 3 through 8 proclaim the re-gathering
of all Israel. In these Verses, the Holy Spirit forges ahead,
even unto the coming Kingdom Age, when these great
Prophecies shall be fulfilled.)*

RIGHTEOUS SHEPHERDS

"And I will set up shepherds over them which shall feed them: and they shall fear no more, nor be dismayed, neither shall they be lacking, says the LORD. *('Shepherds' are the same as the 'Pastors' of Verse 1.)*

THE RIGHTEOUS BRANCH, THE LORD JESUS CHRIST

"Behold, the days come, says the LORD, that I will raise unto David a Righteous Branch, and a King shall reign and prosper, and shall execute judgment and justice in the Earth. *(This 'Righteous Branch' is the Messiah. The justice and benevolence of His Rule here stand in contrast to the injustice and selfishness of that of the four kings who succeeded Godly king Josiah.*

"The beautiful title, 'The Branch,' is given to Him four times in the Old Testament, thus foreshadowing the four Gospels and the necessity that there should be four: the Branch, the King [Matthew]; the Branch, the Servant [Mark]; the Branch, the Man [Luke]; and the Branch, Jehovah [John].)

THE LORD OUR RIGHTEOUSNESS

"In His days Judah shall be saved, and Israel shall dwell safely: and this is His name whereby He shall be called, THE LORD OUR RIGHTEOUSNESS. *('In His days,' refers to the days of the Messiah, which will be the Millennial Reign. 'Judah shall be saved,' is in contrast to Judah now being lost!)*

THE RESTORATION

"Therefore, behold, the days come, says the LORD, that they shall no more say, The LORD lives, which

brought up the Children of Israel out of the land of
Egypt *(during the coming Kingdom Age, the Children of
Israel will then exclaim the great Deliverance by Christ
from the Antichrist)*;

"**But, the LORD lives, which brought up and which
led the seed of the House of Israel out of the north country, and from all countries whither I had driven them;
and they shall dwell in their own land.** *(The 'north country' contains most of the countries where Israel wandered
as outcasts for nearly 2,000 years. At the beginning of the
Kingdom Age, all Jews will come from these countries to
the Land of Israel)*" **(Jer. 23:3-8).**

What I have just given from Jeremiah gives a flavor as to
the scores of like Prophecies given by many Prophets.

The Apostle Paul, under the New Covenant, basically said
the same thing:

LIFE FROM THE DEAD

"**For if the casting away of them *be* the reconciling
of the world** *(refers to the Act of God in setting Israel
aside temporarily as a channel through which to bring the
Good News of Salvation to the world, and in their place
the substitution of the Church)*, **what *shall* the receiving
of them be, but life from the dead?** *(All of this is with a
view to bringing Israel back into fellowship with Himself
and service in the coming Millennium. Their conversion is
likened to a Resurrection)*" **(Rom. 11:15).**

The great Apostle also said:

RESTORATION

"**For I would not, Brethren, that you should be ignorant of this mystery** *(what has happened to Israel)*, **lest**

you should be wise in your own conceits *(the Gentiles were not pulled in because of any merit or Righteousness on their part, but strictly because of the Grace of God)*; that blindness in part is happened to Israel *(is the 'mystery' of which Paul speaks)*, until the fulness of the Gentiles be come in *(refers to the Church; in fact, the Church Age is even now coming to a close)*.

"And so all Israel shall be saved *(when the Church Age ends, and the Second Coming commences; then Israel will accept Christ and be saved)*: as it is written *(Isa. 27:9; 59:20-21)*, There shall come out of Sion the Deliverer *(Jesus Christ will be the Deliverer)*, and shall turn away ungodliness from Jacob *(Christ will deliver Israel from the Antichrist, and more importantly, will deliver them from their sins)*:

"For this *is* My Covenant unto them *(a Promise)*, when I shall take away their sins. *(As stated, it will be done at the Second Coming [Zech. 13:1])*" **(Rom. 11:25-27).**

THE MANNER OF THE RESTORATION

The great Prophet Ezekiel tells us what will happen at the Second Coming when Israel then accepts Christ as her Saviour and her Lord.
He said:

"Therefore say unto the House of Israel, Thus says the Lord GOD; I do not this for your sakes, O House of Israel, but for My Holy Name's sake, which you have profaned among the heathen, whither you went *(This Scripture further reinforces the statement regarding Verse 21, in that the Lord is not doing what He is doing for Israel's sake, but instead 'for His Holy Name's sake.')*

"And I will sanctify My great Name, which was profaned among the heathen, which you have profaned in the midst of them; and the heathen shall know that

I am the LORD, says the Lord GOD, when I shall be sanctified in you before their eyes. *(God's acts of Grace toward guilty men — solely because of His Name as Saviour and not because of any moral excellence in them — are shown in Verses 21 through 23 and 32. The sinner's only claim for Life and Righteousness is the admitting of his sinfulness and not his righteousness, of which he has none.)*

I WILL BRING YOU INTO YOUR OWN LAND

"For I will take you from among the heathen, and gather you out of all countries, and will bring you into your own land. *(This Passage was not fulfilled when the Children of Israel came back from Babylonian captivity, and has not even been fulfilled as of yet! It will be fulfilled immediately after the Second Coming of Christ.)*

THE CLEANSING

"Then will I sprinkle clean water upon you, and you shall be clean: from all your filthiness, and from all your idols, will I cleanse you. *(The word 'then' marks the time for the fulfillment of these Prophecies. Israel, as a nation, will not be won to Christ until the Antichrist is defeated by the Second Coming of Christ. Israel 'then' will accept Christ as Saviour, Lord, and Messiah.)*

A NEW HEART

"A new heart also will I give you, and a new spirit will I put within you: and I will take away the stony heart out of your flesh, and I will give you an heart of flesh. *(This speaks of the New Birth, and totally refutes the claims of those who say that modern Israel will not be restored, and that they have no part or parcel in the Gospel* *program, presently or in the future.)*

A NEW SPIRIT

"**And I will put My Spirit within you, and cause you to walk in My Statutes, and you shall keep My Judgments, and do them.** *('And I will put My Spirit within you,' refers both to regeneration, as carried out by the Holy Spirit at the time of one being Born-Again, and also to the Baptism with the Holy Spirit, which was first evidenced on the Day of Pentecost [Acts 2:1-4]. The entrance of the Holy Spirit is made possible solely by the Cross of Christ [Jn. 14:17], and the 'Statutes' and 'Judgments' fall into the same category. In other words, one can keep those only by and through the Power of the Holy Spirit, Who works exclusively within the framework of the Finished Work of Christ, which demands the constant Faith of the Believer [Rom. 6:3-5; 8:1-2, 11; Lk. 9:23-24]).*

"**And you shall dwell in the land that I gave to your fathers; and you shall be My People, and I will be your God.** *(The conflict regarding the Land of Israel will be solved only when Christ comes back. All hinges on Christ, as all always hinges on Christ)*" (**Ezek. 36:22-28**).

THE EFFORTS OF THE ANTICHRIST

Again we state, we have only given a few of these Prophecies that concern the regathering and the restoration of Israel. Satan, through the Antichrist, hopes to cause these Prophecies to fail, and so he sets out to do that which Haman, Herod and Hitler tried to do but failed, and that is to destroy the entirety of the nation of Israel. In fact, this is why the Battle of Armageddon will be fought. The Antichrist will bring down upon Israel perhaps the mightiest army the world has ever seen. And, to be sure, despite the fact that God will give the army of Israel, as small as it might be, superhuman strength, still, they will be no match for the man of sin.

He will come close to succeeding actually with half of Jeru-salem falling and with the fall of the other half imminent, but he will not succeed because of the Second Coming of the Lord. We will deal with that momentous event, in fact, the most cata-clysmic event the world will have ever known, in that particu-lar Chapter.

WILL AMERICA BE INVOLVED IN THIS BATTLE?

We aren't told in the Scriptures as to exactly what nations will be involved. One thing, however, is clear: it seems that however many nations are present, there will be none which will help Israel. So, while America may not be involved in the battle, every evidence is that she will be neutral, which, as far as God is concerned, presents opposition.

THE DAY OF THE LORD

The Scripture says concerning this coming day:

"**Behold, the Day of the LORD comes, and your spoil shall be divided in the midst of you.** *('Behold, the Day of the Lord comes,' presents this day as beginning with the Second Coming and lasting until the end of the Millennium. At that time, the end of the Millennium, the 'Day of God' begins and will continue through eternity [I Cor. 15:24-28; Eph. 1:10; II Pet. 3:10-13].*

"'And your spoil shall be divided in the midst of you,' concerns the Antichrist coming against Israel [Ezek. 38:11-12]).

ALL NATIONS AGAINST JERUSALEM

"**For I will gather all nations against Jerusalem to battle; and the city shall be taken, and the houses rifled,**

and the women ravished; and half of the city shall go
forth into captivity, and the residue of the people shall
not be cut off from the city. *(The first phrase refers
to the mobilization of the nations to Armageddon [Ezek.,
Chpts. 38-39; Joel, Chpt. 3; Rev. 16:13-16; 19:11-21].*

"*'And the city shall be taken,' actually means that the
Antichrist will prepare to take Jerusalem, with actually
half of it being taken. The phrase, 'and the houses rifled,
and the women ravished,' expresses extreme cruelty practiced by the army of the Antichrist.*

"*'And half of the city shall go forth into captivity,'
means that half of Jerusalem will fall to the advances of
the Antichrist, with the other half fighting furiously to save
themselves, but with futility, other than the Coming of the
Lord. Actually, the phrasing of the sentence structure portrays Israel fighting with a ferocity that knows no bounds,
but yet, not able to stand against the powerful onslaught of
the combined armies of the man of sin.*

"*'And the residue of the people shall not be cut off from
the city,' refers to the army of Israel already cut to pieces,
but determined to defend the city, even house to house,
and, if necessary, to die to the last man)*" **(Zech. 14:1-2).**

SIEGE OF JERUSALEM BY THE ANTICHRIST

"**The burden of the Word of the LORD for Israel,
says the LORD, which stretches forth the heavens, and
lays the foundation of the Earth, and forms the spirit of
man within him.** *(The 'burden' of the first phrase concerns
wholly the future, as the first 'burden' [9:1] concerned
both the present and future. As well, it foretells Israel's
deliverance by Him Whom they rejected and pierced, their
consequent conversion, and Zion's resultant glory.*

"*'Which stretches forth and lays the foundation of the
Earth,' portrays the force of three Hebrew verbs as both
past and present. Immanuel made and maintains all things*

[Col. 1:16]. His Power as Creator and Sustainer assures the fulfillment of His Promises; consequently, the Holy Spirit opens this section proclaiming the certitude of the coming action.

"'And forms the spirit of man within him,' proclaims one of two Hebrew words translated 'spirit' in the Bible. The one is 'spirit' as common to man and the animal creation; the other is an emanation from God possessed only by man, and ever existing, i.e., the Holy Spirit.

"The 'spirit of man within him,' and thus 'formed' by God, proclaims man's spirit as higher than the spirit of animals. In fact, man is in a class by himself, i.e., in the Image of God [Gen. 1:26].)

JERUSALEM A CUP OF TREMBLING

"Behold, I will make Jerusalem a cup of trembling unto all the people round about, when they shall be in the siege both against Judah and against Jerusalem. *(The Holy Spirit uses the word 'Israel' in Verse 1, while using the word 'Judah' in this Verse. Both are interchangeable and mean the same thing.*

"The first phrase pictures this city, Jerusalem, as the focal point of the nations of the world. This will take place in the coming Great Tribulation. 'When they shall be in the siege both against Judah and against Jerusalem,' concerns the Battle of Armageddon.)

JERUSALEM, A BURDENSOME STONE

"And in that day will I make Jerusalem a burdensome stone for all people: all who burden themselves with it shall be cut in pieces, though all the people of the Earth be gathered together against it. *(The first phrase refers to a 'stone' which is difficult to lift or to move. The efforts of the Antichrist to displace it will cause his own* *destruction, for the Stone of Daniel, Chapter 2, will fall upon him from Heaven.*

"'All who burden themselves with it shall be cut in pieces,' concerns any and all nations of the world which join with the Antichrist in his efforts to destroy Jerusalem and Judah at the Battle of Armageddon)" **(Zech. 12:1-3).**

TWO THIRDS OF THE JEWS WILL DIE

The Scripture isn't clear as to the time factor concerning two thirds of the Jews dying; however, most likely it pertains to the last three and a half years of the Great Tribulation and, more particularly, the Battle of Armageddon. The Scripture says:

"And it shall come to pass, that in all the land, says the LORD, two parts therein shall be cut off and die; but the third shall be left therein. *(This Verse pertains to the Great Tribulation, more particularly, the last half of that dreadful time. Zechariah predicts that two-thirds of the population of Israel will die during those last three and a half years, leaving one-third to fight the Antichrist at Armageddon and to make up the nation that will be brought into being at the Second Coming of Christ [Rom. 11:25-29].*

"There are approximately five million Jews in Israel presently. If there are six million at that time, this means that some four million will be killed. Very few times in history has such a large percentage of the population of a nation been destroyed, if ever!)

THEY WILL CALL AND I WILL HEAR

"And I will bring the third part through the fire, and will refine them as silver is refined, and will try them as gold is tried: they shall call on My Name, and I will hear them: I will say, It is My People: and they shall say, The LORD is my God. *(The phrase, 'And I* *will bring the third part through the fire,' refers to those who are left alive after the Battle of Armageddon, who will look upon Him Whom they pierced and repent [12:10-14]. The 'fire' is the Great Tribulation, which Jesus mentioned [Mat. 24:21].*

" 'And will refine them as silver is refined, and will try them as gold is tried,' proclaims the purpose of the coming Great Tribulation. 'They shall call on My Name, and I will hear them,' refers to proper relationship being restored.

" 'I will say, It is My People: and they shall say, The LORD is my God,' pertains to the Remnant who has been 'refined' as silver and 'tried' as gold. These will repent; as a result, they will once again be owned by the Lord, as He says, 'It is My People.' He will do so because they shall say, 'The LORD is my God,' i.e., Jesus Christ is Lord!

"At that time, the Prophecy of Hosea will be fulfilled: 'You shall call Me Ishi; and shall call me no more Baali' [Hos. 2:16]. 'Ishi' means 'My Husband')" **(Zech. 13:8-9).**

THE CHURCH AND AMERICA

The thing that has made this nation great is the hundreds of thousands of Born-Again Believers within its borders. That is what has given this nation the Blessings of God even though the powers that be little recognize such, if at all! However, at the Rapture the Church will be taken out and even though there will possibly be millions Saved in this country immediately after the Rapture, because they know the way, still, the restraining factor provided by the Church that has been Raptured is now gone. Then, evil is going to magnify itself in this nation as never before. In other words, at that coming time, it will be difficult to even recognize America as we know America.

ONE WORLD GOVERNMENT

If it is to be noticed, many politicians, as well as leaders of other nations of the world, along with the Vatican, are calling for a one-world government. It is said that George Bush is a globalist, and so is Obama. This means that every decision that was made, and is being made, is not made with America in mind, but with globalism in mind. They don't have knowledge enough to know, because they don't know the Lord, that America has kept much of the world going, so to speak. If America is dumbed down, until it is little more than a third world country, this doesn't mean that other nations of the world will rise accordingly, but rather, the very opposite.

Yet, all of these things which are presently taking place are bending everything toward the coming man of sin. Regrettably, most of the modern church is preparing to stay in this world instead of leaving this world. No doubt, their wish will be granted, but it won't be what they think.

HOW BAD WILL THE BATTLE OF ARMAGEDDON ACTUALLY BE?

The Scripture gives us a clue as to how bad the Battle of Armageddon will be.

It says:

> "And He Who sat on the cloud thrust in His sickle on the Earth *(refers to Christ, Who will orchestrate this momentous event)*; and the Earth was reaped *(that which takes place on Earth, at least as it regards momentous events, are first of all orchestrated in Heaven)*.
>
> "And another Angel came out of the Temple which is in Heaven *(presents the fifth Angel of this Chapter)*, he also having a sharp sickle *(portrays the fact that Angels will have a great part to play in the coming Battle of Armageddon)*.

THRUST IN YOUR SHARP SICKLE

> "And another Angel came out from the Altar *(is the*

pattern Altar after which the Brazen Altar on Earth was fashioned), **which had power over fire** *(refers to the fire on the Altar)*; **and cried with a loud cry to Him Who had the sharp sickle, saying, Thrust in your sharp sickle, and gather the clusters of the vine of the Earth; for her grapes are fully ripe.** *(The repetitiveness of these statements proclaims the absolute significance of what is about to happen, and that its outcome will affect the Earth greatly.)*

"**And the Angel thrust in his sickle into the Earth, and gathered the vine of the Earth** *(he gathers 'the vine of the Earth' into a place called in the Hebrew tongue, 'Armageddon')*, **and cast** *it* **into the great winepress of the Wrath of God** *(refers to the assembled nations that will gather in the Valley of Jehoshaphat)*.

175 MILES OF BLOOD

"**And the winepress was trodden without the city** *(refers to the actual Battle itself pressing in on Jerusalem, with the intent of completely destroying the city and slaughtering the Jews)*, **and blood came out of the winepress, even unto the horse bridles, by the space of a thousand** *and* **six hundred furlongs.** *(1,600 furlongs is a distance of about 175 miles; the blood, no doubt, will be mixed with water, and in some places will be approximately six feet deep; it is possible that millions will be killed in this Battle)*" **(Rev. 14:16-20).**

THE BATTLE OF ARMAGEDDON FROM THE VIEW OF THE SPIRIT WORLD

Even though the Prophet Zechariah gave us a little information as it regards the Battle of Armageddon from the perspective of nations, it is Ezekiel who takes us behind the scenes from the vantage point of the spirit world and lets us see this conflict from that vantage point. The great Prophet said:

GOG

"And the Word of the LORD came unto me, saying,

"Son of man, set your face against Gog, the land of Magog, the chief prince of Meshech and Tubal, and prophecy against him *('Gog' is another name for the Antichrist)*,

"And say, Thus says the Lord GOD; Behold, I am against you, O Gog, the chief prince of Meshech and Tubal *(for many years, Bible teachers have thought that these Passages referred to Russia, but a closer investigation of the statements prove otherwise; therefore, the phrase 'Behold, I am against you, O Gog,' is not referring to Russia, but instead, to the Antichrist)*;

THE BATTLE OF ARMAGEDDON

"And I will turn you back, and put hooks into your jaws, and will bring you forth, and all your army, horses and horsemen, all of them clothed with all sorts of armour, even a great company with bucklers and shields, all of them handling swords *(this Prophecy refers to the Battle of Armageddon, which will be the second invasion by the Antichrist of Israel, in which he will be totally destroyed. The first invasion will take place in the midst of the Great Tribulation, when the Antichrist will then show his true colors)*:

MANY PEOPLE WITH YOU

"Persia, Ethiopia, and Libya with them; all of them with shield and helmet:

"Gomer, and all his bands; the house of Togarmah

of the north quarters, and all his bands: and many people with you. *(These Passages merely reinforce the statements previously made, that the army of the Antichrist will consist of people from many countries, including Russia.)*

"Be thou prepared, and prepare for yourself, you, and all your company that are assembled unto you, and be thou a guard unto them. *('Be thou prepared,' merely refers to a taunt given by the Holy Spirit to the Antichrist. In other words, 'Prepare yourself to the very best of your ability, and still it will avail you nothing, as you will be totally defeated.')*

IN THE LATTER YEARS

"After many days you shall be visited: in the latter years you shall come into the land that is brought back from the sword, and is gathered out of many people, against the mountains of Israel, which have been always waste: but it is brought forth out of the nations, and they shall dwell safely all of them. *(The two phrases, 'After many days' and 'in the latter years,' refer to this present time and the immediate future; therefore, any claims that this Chapter has already been fulfilled are spurious.*

"'The land that is brought back from the sword,' refers to the many conflicts Israel has had since becoming a nation in 1948.

"'And is gathered out of many people,' refers to the various nations, such as Egypt, Syria, Iraq, etc., which did not desire Israel to become a nation, and which, therefore, greatly opposed her.

"'But it is brought forth out of the nations,' pertains to the United Nations voting that Israel would become a State, with even Russia voting her approval.

"'And they shall dwell safely all of them,' refers to the terrible horror of the Holocaust in World War II, with some 6,000,000 Jews being slaughtered by Hitler, and Israel

then demanding a homeland instead of being scattered all over the world. Their feeling was that if this could be obtained, then they would be 'safe.')

YOU SHALL THINK AN EVIL THOUGHT

"You shall ascend and come like a storm, you shall be like a cloud to cover the land, you, and all your bands, and many people with you. *(As stated, this is the Battle of Armageddon.)*

"Thus says the Lord GOD; It shall also come to pass, that at the same time shall things come into your mind, and you shall think an evil thought *(the 'evil thought' will consist of the plans of the Antichrist, inspired of Satan, to destroy Israel and the Jews. That plan is the Battle of Armageddon!)***:**

COME TO TAKE A SPOIL

"And you shall say, I will go up to the land of unwalled villages; I will go to them who are at rest, who dwell safely, all of them dwelling without walls, and having neither bars nor gates *(the phrases, 'The land of unwalled villages,' 'dwelling without walls,' and 'having neither bars nor gates,' refer to Israel's efforts at mobilization to be rather weak, at least in the mind of the Antichrist)***,**

"To take a spoil, and to take a prey; to turn your hand upon the desolate places that are now inhabited, and upon the people that are gathered out of the nations, which have gotten cattle and goods, who dwell in the midst of the land. *(This is the invasion of Israel by the Antichrist, called the 'Battle of Armageddon,' which will precipitate the Second Coming of the Lord.)*

"Sheba, and Dedan, and the merchants of Tarshish, with all the young lions thereof, shall say unto you, Are you come to take a spoil? have you gathered your

company to take a prey? to carry away silver and gold, to take away cattle and goods, to take a great spoil? *(The questions asked by these particular nations are not meant to proclaim an adversarial position; in fact, they will probably throw in their lot with the Antichrist, hoping to get a part of the 'great spoil.')*

THE ATTACK OF GOG AGAINST ISRAEL

"Therefore, son of man, prophesy and say unto Gog, Thus says the Lord GOD; In that day when My People of Israel dwell safely, shall you not know it? *(The idea of this Verse is: despite the Antichrist invading Israel and defeating her at the midpoint of the Great Tribulation, thereby breaking his seven-year pact, still, due to him having pressing business elsewhere [Dan. 11:44], Israel will then filter back into the land, reoccupying it, and seemingly will dwell safely. This will, no doubt, infuriate the 'man of sin,' and he will set about to handle the situation once and for all!)*

I WILL BRING YOU AGAINST MY LAND

"And you shall come from your place out of the north parts, you, and many people with you, all of them riding upon horses, a great company, and a mighty army *(the 'north parts' do not refer to Russia, as some think, but rather, to Syria. In fact, the Antichrist [Gog] will come from Syria; however, the Syria of Daniel's Prophecies, of which this speaks, included modern Syria, Iraq, and Iran.)*

"And you shall come up against My People of Israel, as a cloud to cover the land; it shall be in the latter days, and I will bring you against My Land, that the heathen may know Me, when I shall be sanctified in you, O Gog, before their eyes. *('In the latter days,' refers to the last of* *the last days, which pertain to the present and near future. In other words, these Prophecies have already begun to come to pass, and, with each passing day, will accelerate their fulfillment.)*

MANY PROPHECIES

"Thus says the Lord GOD; Are you he of whom I have spoken in old time by My Servants the Prophets of Israel, which prophesied in those days many years that I would bring you against them? *(The Lord is actually speaking here of the Prophecies given to Ezekiel, of which this is one, as well as those of Isaiah, Daniel, Zechariah, and others!)*

THE WRATH OF GOD

"And it shall come to pass at the same time when Gog shall come against the land of Israel, says the Lord GOD, that My Fury shall come up in My Face. *(Once again, this is the Battle of Armageddon. 'My Fury shall come up in My Face,' corresponds to the statement of Zechariah [Zech. 14:3]).*

"For in My Jealousy and in the fire of My Wrath have I spoken, Surely in that day there shall be a great shaking in the land of Israel *(the 'great shaking in the Land of Israel' can only transpire in the Battle of Armageddon, and only by the Hand of the Lord)*;

THE SECOND COMING

"So that the fishes of the sea, and the fowls of the Heaven, and the beasts of the field, and all creeping things that creep upon the Earth, and all the men who are upon the face of the Earth, shall shake at My Presence, and the mountains shall be thrown down, and the

steep places shall fall, and every wall shall fall to the ground. *(This Verse pertains to the Second Coming, which will be the most cataclysmic event in human history.)*

FIRE AND BRIMSTONE

"And I will call for a sword against him throughout all My Mountains, says the Lord GOD: every man's sword shall be against his brother. *(This portrays the fact that the Lord has control over all things!)*

"And I will plead against him with pestilence and with blood; and I will rain upon him, and upon his bands, and upon the many people who are with him, an overflowing rain, and great hailstones, fire, and brimstone. *(This Verse proclaims the fact that the Lord will use the elements, over which neither the Antichrist nor any other man has any control.)*

"Thus will I magnify Myself, and sanctify Myself; and I will be known in the eyes of many nations, and they shall know that I am the LORD. *('Thus will I magnify Myself,' has reference to anger held in check for a long time, and then exploding with a fury that defies description.)*

PROPHESY AGAINST GOG

"Therefore, thou son of man, prophesy against Gog, and say, Thus says the Lord GOD; Behold, I am against you, O Gog, the chief prince of Meshech and Tubal *(this Chapter proclaims Gog's defeat by the Lord Jesus Christ. As stated, it is the Battle of Armageddon, as described in Rev. 16:16)*:

"And I will turn you back, and leave but the sixth part of you, and will cause you to come up from the north parts, and will bring you upon the mountains of Israel *(five-sixths of the army of the Antichrist will be killed by the Second Coming of the Lord. 'And will cause you to come up from the north parts,' does not, as previously stated, refer to Russia. It instead refers to the invasion route being the same as it was for the Assyrians, Babylonians, Grecians, and others in the past)*:

YOU SHALL FALL

"And I will smite your bow out of your left hand, and will cause your arrows to fall out of your right hand. *(The Antichrist, called 'Gog,' will think he is fighting Israel only, when, in truth, he is fighting the Lord, a battle he cannot hope to win.)*
"You shall fall upon the mountains of Israel, you, and all your bands, and the people that is with you: I will give you unto the ravenous birds of every sort, and to the beasts of the field to be devoured. *(The idea is that the defeat of the Antichrist and his armies will be so severe that vultures and beasts will feed upon the multitudes of dead bodies littering the 'mountains of Israel.'*
" 'You shall fall,' signifies not only the defeat of the 'man of sin,' but also the collapse of corrupt human society, which includes corrupt human government.)

THEY SHALL KNOW THAT I AM THE LORD

"You shall fall upon the open field: for I have spoken it, says the Lord GOD. *('Open field,' refers to the time of the defeat of the Antichrist. It will be in the very midst of the Battle, with the Antichrist bearing down on Jerusalem, thinking that victory is within his grasp [Zech. 14:1-3]).*
"And I will send a fire on Magog, and among them who dwell carelessly in the isles: and they shall know that I am the LORD. *('Send a fire on Magog,' simply means that the Lord will personally use the elements of the heavens to destroy the vast Gentile armies following the Antichrist.*
" 'And among them who dwell carelessly in the isles,'

pertains to other nations of the world, which, in their minds, are neutral and are simply turning a blind eye to this wholesale slaughter against Israel by the Antichrist.)

THE HOLY ONE OF ISRAEL

"So will I make My Holy Name known in the midst of My People Israel; and I will not let them pollute My Holy Name anymore: and the heathen shall know that I am the LORD, the Holy One in Israel. *(This Verse captures all the Promises made by the Lord to the Patriarchs and Prophets of old!)*

"Behold, it is come, and it is done, says the Lord GOD; this is the day whereof I have spoken. *(This Verse pertains to the coming Great Tribulation, and more especially to these events at the very conclusion of that particular time, including the Battle of Armageddon [Zech. 14:7])*.

BURN WITH FIRE SEVEN YEARS

"And they who dwell in the cities of Israel shall go forth, and shall set on fire and burn the weapons, both the shields and the bucklers, the bows and the arrows, and the handstaves, and the spears, and they shall burn them with fire seven years *(to think of something being burned 'with fire seven years' allows us to know the extent of the destruction)*:

"So that they shall take no wood out of the field, neither cut down any out of the forests; for they shall burn the weapons with fire: and they shall spoil those who spoiled them, and rob those who robbed them, says the Lord GOD.

SEVEN MONTHS TO BURY THE DEAD

"And it shall come to pass in that day, that I will give

unto Gog a place there of graves in Israel, the valley of the passengers on the east of the sea: and it shall stop the noses of the passengers: and there shall they bury Gog and all his multitude: and they shall call it the valley of Hamon-gog. *(No doubt, several millions of men are going to be killed in that which is known as 'the Battle of Armageddon.' Even employing modern equipment to hasten the burial of so many human bodies, still, the stench will 'stop the noses of the passengers.')*

"And seven months shall the House of Israel be burying of them, that they may cleanse the land.

"Yea, all the people of the land shall bury them; and it shall be to them a renown the day that I shall be glorified, says the Lord GOD. *(The Lord links this spectacle to the sanctifying of His Name.)*

TO CLEANSE THE LAND

"And they shall sever out men of continual employment, passing through the land to bury with the passengers those who remain upon the face of the Earth, to cleanse it: after the end of seven months shall they search. *(The Executive Government of Israel will employ and pay the men described in this Verse to collect the human bones, wherever found, and bury them in the huge trench or area of Verse 11. This project, as stated, will require seven months.)*

"And the passengers who pass through the land, when any sees a man's bone, then shall he set up a sign by it, till the buriers have buried it in the valley of Hamon-gog. *(It seems that all the bones will be collected and taken to 'the valley of Hamon-gog,' and there buried. If this is the case, it will be done for a reason, the portraying of such as a monument to Satan's defeat, and the Victory, even the great Victory, of the Lord Jesus Christ.)*

"And also the name of the city shall be Hamonah.

Thus shall they cleanse the land. *(The name 'Hamonah' means 'multitude.' No doubt, it will be a 'city' of graves, housing the silent dead, and not a city of the living.)*

A GREAT SACRIFICE

"And, you son of man, thus says the Lord GOD; Speak unto every feathered fowl, and to every beast of the field, Assemble yourselves, and come; gather yourselves on every side to My Sacrifice that I do sacrifice for you, even a great sacrifice upon the mountains of Israel, that you may eat flesh, and drink blood. *(This is the same command as Rev. 19:17-18, 20).*

"You shall eat the flesh of the mighty, and drink the blood of the princes of the Earth, of rams, of lambs, and of goats, of bullocks, all of them fatlings of Bashan. *(The words, 'The mighty' and 'princes,' signify the military and political elite of the army of the Antichrist. As well, the 'rams, lambs, goats, and bullocks' signify the same!)*

"And you shall eat fat till you be full, and drink blood till you be drunken, of My Sacrifice which I have sacrificed for you. *(The idea is that if they would not accept the Sacrifice of Christ at Calvary, then they would be made a sacrifice, which they were, but which would not Save their souls, but would serve as a part of the salvation of the world.)*

"Thus you shall be filled at My Table with horses and chariots, with mighty men, and with all men of war, says the Lord GOD. *(The Antichrist will think to set a 'table' portraying the defeat of Israel, but instead, he and his army will be the 'table,' i.e., 'My Table,' i.e., the Table of the Lord.)*

THE PURPOSE OF GOD

"And I will set My Glory among the heathen, and

all the heathen shall see My Judgment that I have executed, and My Hand that I have laid upon them. *(The Bible regards as 'the heathen' all who do not accept the Lord Jesus Christ as their Saviour. Therefore, that includes almost all the world.)*

"So the House of Israel shall know that I am the LORD their God from that day and forward. *(Along with 'the heathen' seeing this glorious spectacle, likewise, 'the House of Israel' will now 'know' exactly Who the Messiah is. They will know that the One they rejected and crucified is actually 'the LORD their God.' They will know it 'from that very day and forward.')*

THE SWORD

"And the heathen shall know that the House of Israel went into captivity for their iniquity: because they trespassed against Me, therefore hid I My Face from them, and gave them into the hand of their enemies: so fell they all by the sword. *(The dispersions under the Assyrians and the Romans having been effected by the sword, as well as all who have been exiled through the centuries, and more particularly, the terrible Holocaust of World War II, it can justly be stated: 'they all fell by the sword.'*

" 'They trespassed against Me,' refers to Israel's rebellion from the very beginning, which finally necessitated their destruction and dispersion; however, the crowning 'trespass' of all was their rejection of Christ and His Crucifixion. As a result, they were given over 'into the hand of their enemies,' where they remained for nearly 2,000 years.)

"According to their uncleanness and according to their transgressions have I done unto them, and hid My Face from them. *(As they did not desire Him, He 'hid His Face from them.' This was all He could do! Regrettably, this scenario has not yet ended. Continuing to reject*

Him, Israel will instead accept 'another' as their Messiah [Jn. 5:43]. This will happen in the very near future and will bring Israel yet another Holocaust! [Mat. 24:21-22].

"However, and finally, Israel will come out of the darkness into the light, and will accept Christ as their Saviour and Messiah. The next Passages tell us how!)

THE SALVATION OF ISRAEL

"Therefore thus says the Lord GOD; Now will I bring again the captivity of Jacob, and have mercy upon the whole House of Israel, and will be jealous for My Holy Name *(He will have 'Mercy' because of their Repentance, which will take place at the Second Coming. The phrase, 'And will be jealous for My Holy Name,' is a fearsome statement. 'His Holy Name' stands behind His Word. He is 'Jealous' that His Honor be protected and that every single Prophecy be fulfilled).*

REPENTANCE

"After that they have borne their shame, and all their trespasses whereby they have trespassed against Me, when they dwelt safely in their land, and none made them afraid. *(The idea of this and succeeding Verses is the explanation of the word 'now' in the previous Verse. The 'shame' resulting from the 'trespasses' is now over. 'Now' they can 'dwell safely in their land, and none shall make them afraid.')*

THE SANCTIFICATION OF ISRAEL

"When I have brought them again from the people, and gathered them out of their enemies' lands, and am sanctified in them in the sight of many nations *(this great gathering will take place after the Second Coming* *of Christ, and will include every Jew from every country in the world, who will be brought, and gladly, to Israel. 'And am sanctified in them in the sight of many nations,' refers to His Plan for them finally being realized)*;

THE SPIRIT OF GOD

"**Then shall they know that I am the LORD their God, which caused them to be led into captivity among the heathen: but I have gathered them unto their own land, and have left none of them anymore there.** *(So certain is the future Restoration of Israel that the past tense is used here in predicting it.)*

"**Neither will I hide My Face anymore from them: for I have poured out My Spirit upon the House of Israel, says the Lord GOD.** *(This Passage and many others emphatically state that Israel will never again go astray because of the 'poured out Spirit of God' upon them. This Vision opens and closes with a valley of dry bones. The first Vision saw the resurrection of those bones [Chpt. 37]; in the second part of the Vision, nothing but bones will remain, signifying the catastrophic end of the armies of the Antichrist.*

"*So, these two valleys contrast the one with the other — the one, a testimony to God's Faithfulness and Love; the other, to His Fidelity and Judgment)*" **(Ezek. 38:1-23; 39:1-29).**

"It is Your perfect love that casts out fear,
"I know the voice that speaks the it is I,
"And in these well-known words of heavenly cheer,
"I hear the joy that bids each sorrow fly."

"Your Name is Love! I hear it from the Cross;
"Your Name is Love! I read it on the tomb;
"All meaner love is perishable dross,

"But this shall light me through time's thickest gloom."

"It blesses now, And shall forever bless;
"It Saves me now, And shall forever Save;
"It holds me up in days of helplessness,
"It bears me safely over each swelling wave."

"'Tis what I know of You, My Lord and God,
"That fills my soul with peace, My lips with song:
"You are my health, my joy, my staff, my rod;
"Leaning on You, In weakness I am strong."

CHAPTER FIVE

What Is The Second Coming?

QUESTION:

WHAT IS THE SECOND COMING?

ANSWER:

The Second Coming is the coming of the Lord Jesus Christ in Power and Glory to take command of this world, which He Personally will do so by force. In fact, the Second Coming of the Lord will be the most cataclysmic thing that has ever happened to the human race. There is no way that it can be described by trying to compare it with other things. It is simply indescribable!

Shortly before the Crucifixion our Lord said the following about that coming time:

THE LORD'S COMING WILL BE VERY VISIBLE

The Scripture says:

"**Immediately after the tribulation of those days** *(speaks of the time immediately preceding the Second Coming)* **shall the sun be darkened, and the moon shall not give her light** *(the light of these orbs will be dim by comparison to the light of the Son of God)***, and the stars shall fall from Heaven** *(a display of Heavenly fireworks at the Second Coming)***, and the powers of the Heavens shall be shaken** *(will work with the Son of God against the Antichrist, at the Second Coming)***:**

"**And then shall appear the sign of the Son of Man in Heaven** *(pertains to the Second Coming, which will take place in the midst of these Earth and Heaven shaking events)***: and then shall all the tribes of the Earth mourn** *(concerns all the nations of the world which possibly will see this phenomenon by television)***, and they shall see the Son of Man** *(denotes Christ and His human, Glorified Body)* **coming in the clouds of Heaven with power**

and great glory *(lends credence to the thought that much of the world will see Him by television as He makes His descent)*" **(Mat. 24:29-30).**

THERE WILL BE NO DOUBT AS TO WHO HE IS

When our Lord comes back to this Earth the second time, He will not come back to be spit upon, caricatured, berated, beaten and crucified as He was the first time He came, but rather, He will come *"King of kings and Lord of lords."* In other words, there will be no mistake as to Who He is. No one will have to ask, *"Is this really the Christ?"* It will be obvious as to Who He is.

When He comes back the second time, the very heavens, which includes the untold billions of stars and the very planets themselves, will dance with glee, so to speak, putting on a display like the heavens have never known before and the world has never seen before. Their Creator is coming back to take command!

DANIEL

Some 2,500 years ago, the great Prophet-Statesman Daniel related to king Nebuchadnezzar the dream that God had given the king, but which he could not remember, and, as well, the meaning thereof.

In his dream Nebuchadnezzar saw the statue of a man. The way the form of his statue was given, it portrayed the coming Gentile powers that would greatly persecute Israel, even from Daniel's day unto the time that is immediately ahead of us, which will usher in the Antichrist. Daniel said to the king:

THE GREAT IMAGE

"Thou, O king, saw, and behold a great image. This great image, whose brightness was excellent, stood

before you; and the form thereof was terrible. *(The two words, 'excellent' and 'terrible,' both characterize the history of Gentile powers from the days of Nebuchadnezzar and continuing on to the coming of Christ with His Saints. Excellent and terrible things often exist side by side. When Christ sets up His Millennial Kingdom, only that which is excellent will exist.*

"The 'great image' would portray all the World Empires for the future, at least as they related to Israel.)

THE STONE

"This image's head was of fine gold, his breast and his arms of silver, his belly and his thighs of brass.

"His legs of iron, his feet part of iron and part of clay. *(The Holy Spirit outlines the successive kingdoms by a representation of precious metals, iron, and clay.)*

"You saw till that a Stone was cut out without hands, which smote the image upon his feet that were of iron and clay, and broke them to pieces. *(The 'Stone' is the Lord Jesus Christ, and symbolizes His Second Coming. 'Without hands,' is an expression emphasizing the absence of all human instrumentality and the act of God alone. This destroys the popular belief that Christianity will take over the world, with the Gospel gradually conquering all of mankind.*

"Actually, Bible Christianity ultimately will cover the entirety of the Earth, but only after the Second Coming, even as this Verse proclaims.)

IT FILLED THE WHOLE EARTH

"Then was the iron, the clay, the brass, the silver, and the gold, broken to pieces together, and became like the chaff of the summer threshingfloors; and the wind carried them away, that no place was found for them: and the Stone that smote the image became a great

mountain, and filled the whole Earth. *(This portrays the Second Coming of the Lord and the destruction of all Gentile powers, meaning that never again will Gentile power hold sway, for that time is forever ended.*

"After the Second Coming, Christ will set up His Kingdom of Righteousness, with Israel then being the predominant nation in the world, and remaining that way forever. Hence, the promises made to the Patriarchs and Prophets of old will be fulfilled in totality)" **(Dan. 2:31-35).**

THE ERRONEOUS TEACHING OF KINGDOM NOW

There are some in the modern church who claim that the Book of Daniel and the Book of Revelation have already been fulfilled and was done so in A.D. 70 when Rome destroyed Jerusalem. However, there is one great problem with that teaching.

The Passages they use are always followed by the Second Coming of the Lord. Now, we know that Jesus has not yet returned to this Earth, so that means that this teaching is false.

They claim that Christianity is gradually going to come to terms with all the religions of the world until it finally fills the Earth. When that happens, and it will happen, they say by political power, then they can signal the Lord that it's satisfactory for Him to come back to the Earth.

Our Lord is not waiting on poor, pitiful man for Him to do anything. The timetable of the Lord is not dependant on the church, but is complete within itself. Jesus said concerning this:

"And He said unto them, It is not for you to know the times or the seasons, which the Father has put in His Own power" (Acts 1:7).

The timetable for the Rapture of the Church, the rise of the Antichrist, the coming of the Great Tribulation, the Battle of Armageddon, and the Second Coming of the Lord, is all in the Power of the Lord and not at all in man.

This erroneous Kingdom Now teaching proclaims that the world is getting better and better, with some even claiming that we are now in the Millennial Reign. The Bible doesn't teach any such thing.

In fact, the world is not getting better and better, but rather, worse and worse. Society as a whole cannot be changed and for Christianity to think that it can change society only proves the Biblical ignorance of such people. Society is corrupt. God has not called us to save society, but rather, to save men out of society.

In fact, society is so corrupt that Jesus Christ in the Second Coming, even as we have just quoted to you from the great Prophet Daniel, is going to destroy it all.

Soon to come upon this world is the very opposite of that which is claimed by those who preach *"Kingdom Now."* The church, instead of getting spiritually stronger, is getting spiritually weaker. In fact, if the truth be known, the modern church is not heading toward apostasy, it has already apostatized (I Tim. 4:1; Rev. 3:14-22).

Some of the last words that Paul wrote proclaim this particular time. He said:

THEY SHALL TURN AWAY THEIR EARS FROM THE TRUTH

"For the time will come when they will not endure sound Doctrine *('sound Doctrine' pertains to overriding principles: the Salvation of the sinner, and the Sanctification of the Saint; the Cross is the answer for both, and is the only answer for both)*; but after their own lusts shall they heap to themselves teachers, having itching ears *(refers to the people who have ears that 'itch' for the smooth and comfortable word, and are willing to reward handsomely the man who is sufficiently compromising to speak it; hearers of this type have rejected the Truth and prefer to hear the lie)*;

"And they shall turn away *their* ears from the Truth *(those who follow false teachers not only turn away their ears from the Truth, but see to it that the ears are always in a position such that they will never come in contact with the Truth)*, and shall be turned unto fables. *(If it's not the 'Message of the Cross,' then it is 'fables' [I Cor. 1:18])*" (II Tim. 4:3-4).

THE MESSAGE OF THE CROSS

Jesus Christ is the Source of all things that we receive from God, while the Cross is the Means by which these things are given to us. It remains for us that the Cross of Christ ever be the Object of our Faith, which then gives latitude for the Holy Spirit to work on our behalf.

The Holy Spirit works entirely within the framework of the Finished Work of Christ. In other words, it is the Cross of Christ which gives the Holy Spirit the Means to do all that He does for us (Rom. 8:1-2, 11).

When we speak of the Cross of Christ, we aren't speaking of a wooden beam, but rather, the price that He there paid and the Victory that He there won. The Scripture plainly tells us how that Victory was won and what that Victory was.

COMPLETE IN HIM

"And you are complete in Him *(the satisfaction of every spiritual want is found in Christ, made possible by the Cross)*, which is the Head of all principality and power *(His Headship extends not only over the Church, which voluntarily serves Him, but over all forces that are opposed to Him as well [Phil. 2:10-11])*:

"In Whom also you are circumcised with the Circumcision made without hands *(that which is brought about by the Cross [Rom. 6:3-5])*, in putting off the body of the sins of the flesh by the Circumcision of Christ *(refers* to the old carnal nature that is defeated by the Believer placing his Faith totally in the Cross, which gives the Holy Spirit latitude to work)*:

BURIED WITH HIM AND RAISED WITH HIM

"**Buried with Him in Baptism** *(does not refer to Water Baptism, but rather to the Believer baptized into the Death of Christ, which refers to the Crucifixion and Christ as our substitute [Rom. 6:3-4])*, **wherein also you are risen with *Him* through the Faith of the operation of God, Who has raised Him from the dead.** *(This does not refer to our future physical Resurrection, but to that spiritual Resurrection from a sinful state into Divine Life. We died with Him, we are buried with Him, and we rose with Him [Rom. 6:3-5], and herein lies the secret to all Spiritual Victory.)*

NAILING IT TO HIS CROSS

"**And you, being dead in your sins and the uncircumcision of your flesh** *(speaks of spiritual death [i.e., 'separation from God'], which sin does!)*, **has He quickened together with Him** *(refers to being made spiritually alive, which is done through being 'Born-Again')*, **having forgiven you all trespasses** *(the Cross made it possible for all manner of sins to be forgiven and taken away)*;

"**Blotting out the handwriting of Ordinances that was against us** *(pertains to the Law of Moses, which was God's Standard of Righteousness that man could not reach)*, **which was contrary to us** *(Law is against us, simply because we are unable to keep its precepts, no matter how hard we try)*, **and took it out of the way** *(refers to the penalty of the Law being removed)*, **nailing it to His Cross** *(the Law with its decrees was abolished in Christ's Death, as if Crucified with Him)*;

TRIUMPHANT

"*And* having spoiled principalities and powers *(Satan and all of his henchmen were defeated at the Cross by Christ Atoning for all sin; sin was the legal right Satan had to hold man in captivity; with all sin atoned, he has no more legal right to hold anyone in bondage)*, He *(Christ)* made a show of them openly *(what Jesus did at the Cross was in the face of the whole universe)*, triumphing over them in it. *(The triumph is complete and it was all done for us, meaning we can walk in power and perpetual Victory due to the Cross)*" (Col. 2:10-15).

Regrettably and sadly, the world has ever tried to fashion another God, meaning they are not satisfied with the God of the Bible. They want a God of their own choosing and making. As well, and sadder still, the church has ever tried to substitute another sacrifice in the place of the Sacrifice of Christ. Either road leads to destruction!

HEALING IN HIS WINGS

The great Prophet Malachi prophesied of the Second Coming some 400 years before the First Coming of Christ. He said:

"But unto you who fear My Name shall the Sun of Righteousness arise with healing in His Wings; and you shall go forth, and grow up as calves of the stall. *('But unto you who fear My Name,' refers to the small remnant of Mal. 3:16. It refers to all who, from the very beginning, have truly lived for God. 'Shall the Sun of Righteousness arise with healing in His Wings,' pertains to the Second Advent of Christ, when He will come back, bringing healing to every person on Earth, not only for physical sickness, but for spiritual sickness, as well!*

"*Here, Christ is compared to the 'Sun,' with its healing*

rays of light coming over the Earth [Isa. 30:26]. As well, the word 'wings' does not refer, at least in this case, as wings would normally be understood, but actually refers to something that is overspreading. The Hebrew word is 'kanaph,' which means 'an edge or extremity.' When Christ comes back in what is referred to as the 'Second Coming,' healing rays will be coming from Him in a way that can only be compared with the 'Sun.'

"The last phrase is a symbolism expressing great joy. When calves are released from the stall into a sunny field, they skip for joy.)

ARMAGEDDON

"And you shall tread down the wicked; for they shall be ashes under the soles of your feet in the day that I shall do this, says the LORD of Hosts. *(The proud now treat as dirt beneath their feet the confessors of Messiah's Name. In the future, that position will be reversed. 'In the day that I shall do this, says the LORD of Hosts,' pertains to the coming Kingdom Age, when Righteousness shall prevail, with Christ ruling supremely over the entirety of the Earth. Now, and sadly so, unrighteousness prevails. But, in the coming Glad Day, Righteousness will be the order of all mankind)"* **(Mal. 4:2-3).**

WHAT IS THE PURPOSE OF
THE SECOND COMING?

The Second Coming has many and varied purposes! Some of them are:
• **To rescue Israel from the Antichrist (Ps. 2).**
• **Actually, to kill the Antichrist, thereby, putting his soul and spirit, along with that of the false prophet, into Hell itself (Rev. 19:20).**
• **To completely smash this world system, which has been**

ruled by Satan himself, fallen Angels, and demon spirits (Dan. 2:44-45).

• To set up a Kingdom on Earth which will fill the entirety of the Earth with *"the Knowledge of the Lord, covering the Earth, as the waters cover the sea"* (Isa. 11:9).

• To set Himself up as the President of the entirety of the world with *"the government of the world upon His Shoulder"* (Isa. 9:6).

• To restore Israel to her rightful place as the priestly nation of the world (Ezek., Chpts., 40-48).

• To lock away Satan with all of his fallen Angels and demon spirits in the bottomless pit, which will rid the world of his activity at that time (Rev. 20:7-10).

• To show the world what Righteousness will accomplish, with peace and prosperity being the lot of every human being on the face of the Earth (Isa. 11:1-5).

• To abolish all sickness by virtue of the fruit that grows on the trees that grow beside the River that proceeds out from under the Temple in Jerusalem (Ezek., Chpt. 47).

• To abolish all war, which the world has never seen before, with the exception of the 33 year lifespan of our Lord in His First Advent (Lk. 2:14).

WHAT IS THE DIFFERENCE IN THE RAPTURE AND THE SECOND COMING?

The Rapture and the Second Coming aren't two parts of one Coming, as some teach, but rather, two distinct and different Comings altogether. Some of the differences are as follows:

• The two Comings will be separated by seven or more years (Dan. 9:27; II Thess. 2:6-12; I Thess. 5:9-11).

• At the Rapture, our Lord will come for His Saints (I Thess. 4:13-18). At the Second Coming, our Lord will come with His Saints (Rev. 19:14; Jude 14-15).

• At the Rapture, our Lord will not come all the way to the Earth (I Thess. 4:17), while at the Second Coming, our Lord will most definitely come all the way to the Earth, here to abide forever (Zech. 14:4).

• At the Rapture of the Church, all the sainted dead will be resurrected, and along with all of those who are alive, will be given Glorified Bodies (I Cor. 15:49-57). At the Second Coming, all the Saints, and that includes all who have ever lived, even from the time of Adam and Eve, will already have Glorified Bodies, having been given to us at the Resurrection (Rev. 19:14).

• At the Rapture, our Lord will come to take His Church out of the world (I Thess. 4:13-18). At the Second Coming, our Lord will come with His Church in order to take over the world (Rev., Chpt. 19).

• At the Rapture, our Lord will not come to stay. At the Second Coming, He will come for the purpose of staying (Isa., Chpts. 2, 9, 11).

WHERE WILL JESUS COME ON EARTH AT THE SECOND COMING?

His landing place, so to speak, will be the Mount of Olivet. The great Prophet Zechariah told us when He will come, which will be in the very midst of the Battle of Armageddon, and where He will come. He said, and I quote directly from THE EXPOSITOR'S STUDY BIBLE:

"Then shall the LORD go forth, and fight against those nations, as when He fought in the day of battle. *('Then' is the key word!*

1. 'Then': when Israel will begin to cry to God for Deliverance, knowing that He is their only hope.

2. 'Then': when half of Jerusalem has fallen and it looks like the other half is about to fall.

3. 'Then': when it looks like every Jew will be annihilated, with two-thirds already killed.

4. 'Then': when it looks like the Promises of God made

to the Patriarchs and Prophets of old will fall down.

5. 'Then': when it looks like the Antichrist will win this conflict, which will make Satan the lord of the Earth.

THE SECOND COMING

" *'Then shall the LORD go forth,' refers to the Second Coming, which will be the most cataclysmic event that the world has ever known. 'And fight against those nations,' pertains to the nations under the banner of the Antichrist, which have set out to destroy Israel, and actually with annihilation in mind.*

" *'As when He fought in the day of battle,' probably refers to the time when the Lord led the Children of Israel out of Egypt by way of the Red Sea [Ex. 14:14; 15:3]. This was Israel's first battle when Jehovah Messiah 'went forth' and fought for them. Israel then passed through a valley between mountains of water; in this, their last battle, they will escape through a valley between mountains of rock, which the next Verse proclaims.)*

THE MOUNT OF OLIVET

"And His Feet shall stand in that day upon the Mount of Olives, which is before Jerusalem on the east, and the Mount of Olives shall cleave in the midst thereof toward the east and toward the west, and there shall be a very great valley; and half of the mountain shall remove toward the north, and half of it toward the south. *(The first phrase refers to Christ literally standing on the Mount of Olives, which will be His landing point at the Second Coming, fulfilling the prediction of the two Angels at His Ascension [Acts 1:10-11]. 'And the Mount of Olives shall cleave in the midst thereof toward the east and toward the west,' actually speaks of a great topographical change, which Israel will use at that hour as a way of* *escape from the Antichrist. With every road blocked, the Lord will open a way through the very center of the mountain, as He opened a path through the Red Sea.*

" 'And there shall be a very great valley,' refers to the escape route of Israel. 'And half of the mountain shall remove toward the north, and half of it toward the south,' refers to the wall of rock on either side of escaping Israel, which makes it similar to the wall of water on either side when Israel escaped Egypt.)

"And you shall flee to the valley of the mountains; for the valley of the mountains shall reach unto Azal: yea, you shall flee, like as you fled from before the earthquake in the days of Uzziah king of Judah: and the LORD my God shall come, and all the Saints with you. *('And you shall flee to the valley of the mountains,' should read 'through the valley.' As stated, this will be Israel's escape route from the Antichrist. 'For the valley of the mountains shall reach unto Azal,' probably refers to Bethezel, mentioned in Mic. 1:11 as a village on the east of Olivet.*

" 'Yea, you shall flee,' is that the people might not be involved in the judgments which shall fall upon the enemy. The phrase, 'Like as you fled from before the earthquake in the days of Uzziah king of Judah,' also pertains to an earthquake which the Lord will use to produce this phenomenon.

" 'And the LORD my God shall come, and all the Saints with you,' pertains to the Lord coming at this particular time, which will have caused the cataclysmic events in the first place. The Passage, 'All the Saints with you,' refers to every Saint of God who has ever lived being with the Lord at the Second Coming [Rev. 19:14].)

"And it shall come to pass in that day, that the light shall not be clear, nor dark *('And it shall come to pass in that day,' refers to the very day that Christ appears on Earth, during the Battle of Armageddon. At that time, the day* *will be extended, thereby giving the Antichrist no respite)*:

"But it shall be one day which shall be known to the LORD, not day, nor night: but it shall come to pass, that at evening time it shall be light. *(The entirety of the Battle of Armageddon will last many days; however, the 'day' mentioned here will probably be extended to last approximately 24 hours)*" (Zech. 14:3-7).

THE TESTIMONY OF THE ANGELS

When Jesus ascended to Heaven after His Resurrection, at the time of His Ascension the record proclaims two Angels making the following statement:

"And while they looked steadfastly toward Heaven as He went up *(these statements are important because they affirm His actual Ascension testified to by eyewitnesses)*, behold, two men stood by them in white apparel *(these two 'men' were actually Angels)*;

"Which also said, You men of Galilee, why do you stand gazing up into Heaven? *(This does not mean that it was only men who were present, but rather that this was a common term used for both men and women.)* this same Jesus, which is taken up from you into Heaven *(refers to the same Human Body with the nail prints in His Hands and Feet, etc.)*, shall so come in like manner as you have seen Him go into Heaven *(refers to the same place, which is the Mount of Olivet)*" (Acts 1:10-11).

WHAT WILL BE THE FIRST THING JESUS WILL DO WHEN HE COMES BACK?

The first thing Jesus will do when He comes back is rescue Israel, which account we have just quoted from Zechariah 14:4-7. The second thing He will do is kill the Antichrist along with the false prophet.

DANIEL

Daniel said concerning the Antichrist, ". . . *he shall also stand up against the Prince of princes (the Lord Jesus Christ); but he shall be broken without hand,"* meaning that the Lord Himself will kill the Antichrist (Dan. 8:25).

EZEKIEL

The great Prophet also said concerning the Antichrist, *"You shall fall upon the open field: for I have spoken it, says the Lord GOD"* (Ezek. 39:5).

JOHN

John the Beloved gave perhaps the greatest description of the Second Coming of any of the great Prophets or Apostles. He said:

> "And I saw Heaven opened *(records the final Prophetic hour regarding the Second Coming, without a doubt the greatest moment in human history)*, and behold a white horse *(in effect, proclaims a war horse [Zech. 14:3])*; and He Who sat upon him *was* called Faithful and True *(Faithful to His Promises and True to His Judgments; He contrasts with the false Messiah of Rev. 6:2, who was neither faithful nor true)*, and in Righteousness He does Judge and make war *(refers to the manner of His Second Coming)*.

A DESCRIPTION

> "His Eyes *were* as a flame of fire *(represents Judgment)*, and on His Head *were* many crowns *(represents the fact that He will not be Lord of just one realm; He will be Lord of all realms)*; and He had a Name written,

that no man knew, but He Himself *(not meaning that it is unknown, but rather, it is definitely unknowable; it will remain unreachable to man, meaning that its depths can never be fully plumbed).*

"And He *was* clothed with a vesture dipped in Blood *(speaks of the Cross where He shed His Life's Blood, which gives Him the right to Judge the world)*: **and His Name is called The Word of God.** *(His revealed Name is the Word of God, for He revealed God in His Grace and Power to make Him known, so the Believer can say, 'I know Him.')*

"And the armies *which were* in Heaven followed Him upon white horses *(these 'armies' are the Saints of God, in fact, all the Saints who have ever lived, meaning we will be with Him at the Second Coming)*, **clothed in fine linen, white and clean.** *(Harks back to Rev. 19:8. It is the Righteousness of the Saints, all made possible by the Cross.)*

ARMAGEDDON

"And out of His Mouth goes a sharp sword *(represents Christ functioning totally and completely in the realm of the Word of God)*, **that with it He should smite the nations** *(refers to all the nations that will join the Antichrist in his efforts to destroy Israel; it is the Battle of Armageddon)*: **and He shall rule them with a rod of iron** *(refers to the fact that the Lord of Glory will not allow or tolerate in any shape, form, or fashion that which 'steals, kills, and destroys')*: **and He treads the winepress of the fierceness and wrath of Almighty God** *(refers to the Battle of Armageddon)*.

KING OF KINGS, AND LORD OF LORDS

"And He has on *His* Vesture and on His Thigh a Name written, KING OF KINGS, AND LORD OF LORDS *(proclaims the fact that there will be no doubt as to Who He actually is)*.

"And I saw an Angel standing in the sun *(proclaims the fact that Faith believes what is written, even if the mind cannot comprehend what is written)*; and he cried with a loud voice, saying to all the fowls who fly in the midst of Heaven *(denotes, as is obvious, supremacy over the Creation)*, Come and gather yourselves together unto the supper of the Great God *(this is symbolic, but it is spoken in this way to proclaim the magnitude of that coming time [Ezek. 39:2, 11-12])*;

JUDGMENT

"That you may eat the flesh of kings, and the flesh of captains, and the flesh of mighty men, and the flesh of horses, and of them who sit on them, and the flesh of all *men, both* free and bond, both small and great. *(This proclaims the fact that the Power of Almighty God doesn't blink at those on this Earth who consider themselves to be 'great.' The Judgment will be identical for all [Ezek. 39:18-20].)*

THE ANTICHRIST

"And I saw the beast *(John saw the Antichrist leading this mighty army; this is the 'man of sin' mentioned by Paul in II Thess., Chpt. 2)*, and the kings of the Earth, and their armies *(refers to all the Antichrist could get to join him; it includes the 'kings of the East' of Rev. 16:12)*, gathered together to make war against Him Who sat on the horse, and against His Army *(refers to Christ and the great Army of Heaven which is with Him; as stated, this is the Battle of Armageddon [Ezek., Chpts. 38-39])*.

THE LAKE OF FIRE

"And the beast was taken, and with him the false prophet who wrought miracles before him *(refers to both of them falling in the Battle of Armageddon)*, **with which he deceived them who had received the mark of the beast, and them who worshipped his image** *(pertains to Satan's chief weapon, which is deception)*. **These both were cast alive into a Lake of Fire burning with brimstone** *(thus is the destiny of the Antichrist and the false prophet, and all who follow them)*.

VICTORY

"And the remnant were slain with the sword of Him Who sat upon the horse, which *sword* **proceeded out of His Mouth** *(the Lord Jesus will speak the Word in the Battle of Armageddon, and whatever He speaks will take place)*: **and all the fowls were filled with their flesh.** *(This proclaims the end of this conflict. The Antichrist and his hoards will announce to the world what they are going to do regarding Israel, but the end result will be buzzards gorging on their flesh)*" **(Rev. 19:11-21).**

AN OLD TESTAMENT EXAMPLE

The invasion of Judah by Sennacherib, king of Assyria, is the example of which we speak.

Sennacherib invaded Judah and took all of that land with the exception of Jerusalem, which is exactly what the Antichrist will do. In fact, as it regards the Antichrist, he will actually subdue half of Jerusalem with the other half looking to fall at any moment (Zech. 14:2).

Sennacherib proposed the invasion of Jerusalem, but something happened that stopped everything.

Hezekiah, King of Judah, and a Godly king at that, sought the help of the Lord at this most trying time. As well, the great Prophet Isaiah stood shoulder to shoulder with the king, with the Lord telling the great Prophet:

"Behold, I will send a blast upon him (upon Sennacherib),

and he shall hear a rumor, and shall return to his own land; and I will cause him to fall by the sword in his own land" (II Ki. 19:7).

Concerning this event, one of the greatest Miracles recorded in the Old Testament took place. The Scripture says:

"And it came to pass that night, that the Angel of the LORD went out, and smote in the camp of the Assyrians an hundred fourscore and five thousand *(185,000)*: and when they arose early in the morning *(when the inhabitants of Jerusalem arose)*, behold, they *(the Assyrians)* were all dead corpses. *(Only one Angel did this! Such is the Power of God. How it was done, we aren't told!)*" **(II Ki. 19:35).**

In fact, this great Miracle is looked at by the Lord as one of the greatest in history with it being recorded three times, and in detail, in the Word of God (II Ki. 18:13-37; 19:37; II Chron., Chpt. 32; Isa. 36:1-22; 37:1-38).

PSALM 126

Even though the author of Psalm 126 is not known, still, it was written after the great Miracle performed by the Lord regarding the defeat of Sennacherib.

It also typifies the defeat of the Antichrist, of which the entirety of the scenario involving Sennacherib serves as a type.

There was no way that Israel could defeat the Assyrian Monarch. Their destruction was certain, but God intervened by sending an Angel who killed 185,000 of the soldiers of Sennacherib in one night. In fact, the Second Coming of Jesus Christ, typified by the Angel, will wreak havoc on the Antichrist exactly as the Angel did those long years ago. Concerning this event, the Psalmist said:

LIKE A DREAM

"When the LORD turned again the captivity of Zion,

we were like them who dream. *(This pictures the deliverance of Jerusalem from Sennacherib. It was so glorious that it all seemed like a dream [II Ki. 19:20-35].)*

"Then was our mouth filled with laughter, and our tongue with singing: then said they among the heathen, The LORD has done great things for them. *(The deliverance of Jerusalem was so outstanding that it was noticed by all the heathen round about, with them giving glory to God. The Lord sent one Angel and destroyed 185,000 Assyrians in one night [II Ki. 19:35].)*

THE LORD HAS DONE GREAT THINGS

"The LORD has done great things for us; whereof we are glad.

"Turn again our captivity, O LORD, as the streams in the south. *(To 'turn again our captivity' is a figure of speech for the restoration of prosperity.)*

"They who sow in tears shall reap in joy.

"He who goes forth and weeps, bearing precious seed, shall doubtless come again with rejoicing, bringing his sheaves with him. *(Paul said, 'This Seed is Christ' [Gal. 3:16]. The 'sheaves' are symbolic of the harvest which, at long last, is Righteousness)*" **(Ps. 126:1-6).**

The laughter and joy that filled the hearts of those in Jerusalem when they learned of the defeat of Sennacherib is a picture, if you will, a portrayal, of what will happen in Jerusalem as it regards the Second Coming of the Lord. In fact, and as we have stated, this great event, which took place about 2,700 years ago, was a portrayal, at least as far as such could be, of what is going to happen when Jesus Christ comes back. The joy and laughter will fill the hearts of the survivors in Israel. Their Messiah has come, the True Messiah, the Real Messiah, not the imposter they foolishly accepted some seven years earlier.

WHO WILL BE WITH JESUS WHEN HE COMES BACK?

The Apostle Paul had something to say about this:

"And to you who are troubled rest with us *(unfortunately, the trouble will continue until Jesus comes; we will then 'rest')*, when the Lord Jesus shall be revealed from Heaven with His mighty Angels *(refers to the Second Coming, which is different from the Rapture)*,

VENGEANCE

"In flaming fire taking vengeance on them who know not God *(gives us the manner of the Second Coming)*, and who obey not the Gospel of our Lord Jesus Christ *(who have rejected Christ and the Cross)*:
"Who shall be punished with everlasting destruction from the Presence of the Lord *(pertains to the Lake of Fire, which will be everlasting)*, and from the Glory of His Power *(power to Save, but rejected, and, therefore, the end is 'everlasting destruction')*;

GLORIFIED

"When He shall come to be Glorified in His Saints *(all Saints will praise Him, and will do so continually)*, and to be admired in all them who believe *(Christ will be the Center and Focal Point of all Things)* (because our testimony among you was believed) in that day. *(They believed the Testimony of Paul regarding Christ and the Cross and, therefore, will be with Christ forever)*" **(II Thess. 1:7-10).**

So, we are told in Verse Seven that the Lord's mighty Angels will accompany Him at the Second Coming. How many there will be with Him, we aren't told. But, please remember, only one Angel was enough to kill 185,000 Assyrians, so what will happen when hundreds of thousands, if not millions, of Angels accompany our Lord back to this Earth!

THE SAINTS OF GOD

As well, we are told that every Believer who has ever lived will accompany Christ back to this Earth at the Second Coming. John the Beloved wrote:

"And the armies *which were* in Heaven followed Him upon white horses *(these 'armies' are the Saints of God, in fact, all the Saints who have ever lived, meaning we will be with Him at the Second Coming)*, clothed in fine linen, white and clean. *(Harks back to Rev. 19:8 which says, 'and to her [the Church] was granted that she should be arrayed in fine linen, clean and white: for the fine linen is the Righteousness of Saints.' Angels are not spoken of in this fashion)*" (Rev. 19:14).

WHAT WILL THE SECOND COMING BE LIKE?

The Second Coming will be, without a doubt, the most cataclysmic event the world has ever known. The heavens are going to put on a display of fireworks, so to speak, in celebration of His Coming. In other words, the Creator is coming back to take charge of His Creation. Concerning this, the Scripture says:

"Immediately after the tribulation of those days *(speaks of the time immediately preceding the Second Coming)* shall the sun be darkened, and the moon shall not give her light *(the light of these orbs will be dim by comparison to the light of the Son of God)*, and the stars shall fall from Heaven *(a display of Heavenly fireworks at the Second Coming)*, and the powers of the Heavens shall be shaken *(will work with the Son of God against the Antichrist, at the Second Coming)***:**

"**And then shall appear the sign of the Son of Man in Heaven** *(pertains to the Second Coming, which will take place in the midst of these Earth and Heaven shaking events)***: and then shall all the tribes of the Earth mourn** *(concerns all the nations of the world which possibly will see this phenomenon by television)***, and they shall see the Son of Man** *(denotes Christ and His human, Glorified Body)* **coming in the clouds of Heaven with power and great glory** *(lends credence to the thought that much of the world will see Him by television as He makes His descent)*" **(Mat. 24:29-30).**

JOHN THE BELOVED

John wrote and said:

"**Behold, He comes with clouds** *(the Second Coming of Christ is the chief theme of this Book; the word 'clouds' represents great numbers of Saints who will accompany the Lord back to the Earth)***; and every eye shall see Him** *(refers to all who will be in the immediate vicinity of Jerusalem, and possibly even billions who may very well see Him by television)***, and they** *also* **which pierced Him** *(the Jews, and they will then know beyond the shadow of a doubt that Jesus is Messiah and Lord)***: and all kindreds of the Earth shall wail because of Him. Even so, Amen.** *(The 'wailing' will take place because of the Judgment Christ will bring upon the world for its sin and shame)*" **(Rev. 1:7).**

THE BATTLE AND THE SECOND COMING

When it says, *"every eye shall see Him,"* **it could be referring to those in the vicinity of Jerusalem; however, from the**

terminology given in all the Scriptures we have quoted, the inference is that the entirety of the world, per se, will see Him. If, in fact, that is the case, it will be because of television.

At the time of the Battle of Armageddon, the Antichrist, wanting the entirety of the world to see his great victory over Israel and their annihilation, will, no doubt, have every television network in the world recording all of these events. Multiple tens of thousands of cameras will be recording every victory of the man of sin, giving a blow-by-blow account, with it unfolding before the eyes of the world.

At a point in time, someone is going to look up and they are going to witness a sight that the world has never seen before. I can hear the announcers now saying it in their languages and their tongues, as the signal goes back to their various countries, as to how that the heavens are literally filled with something which they cannot quite identify.

No doubt, at the beginning, they will think this is another weapon brought to bear by the Antichrist to wrap up his great victory. However, the closer that it gets, they are going to recognize that there are horses in the heavens. It seems impossible, but there are millions and millions of them, all with riders, and all coming toward the Earth.

THE EXPLANATION!

No doubt, the announcers will try to explain what they see, but will finally give up and just tell the people, *"You can see for yourselves."* Thousands of cameras will be turned toward the heavens, with billions of people watching all over the world, a phenomenon, a sight, such as the world has never seen before.

As the announcers try to relate what is taking place, no doubt, one will eventually say, and then be joined by hundreds, if not thousands, of other announcers, *"It's a mighty army that's coming from Heaven, and the leading Person is so ignited with Glory, that His Light is brighter than the sun and the moon combined."* Then it will happen!

THE WEAPONRY OF OUR LORD

At this time, hundreds of thousands, if not millions, of meteorites are going to be used by the Lord to destroy the army of the Antichrist. It will be a barrage like nothing the world has ever seen. In fact, there will be no defense against it. The Lord will use the elements to defeat the man of sin, all being televised by virtually every nation in the world, as billions view this event. It is the Second Coming of our Lord and it is the greatest event in human history.

The whole world will watch what looked like certain victory for the antichrist turned into certain defeat, and in just a few moments of time. Israel's Messiah is coming back. When He comes back the Second Time, He will not come back to be spit upon, beaten, cursed and reviled, and hung on a Cross, but rather, He will come back crowned *"King of kings and Lord of lords."* Zechariah said, *"Then shall the LORD go forth, and fight against those nations, as when He fought in the day of battle"* (Zech. 14:3).

When He comes back accompanied by millions of Angels and every Saint of God who has ever lived, He will touch down on the Mount of Olivet, which will cause it to cleave down the middle, in effect, opening up (Zech. 14:4).

WHAT WILL ISRAEL DO AT
THE SECOND COMING?

That's a good question!

Israel will know at that time, and beyond the shadow of a doubt, that this is their Messiah. But, as to Who exactly He is, of that they aren't certain. Concerning this momentous time, the Scripture says they will say:

"And one shall say unto Him, What are these wounds in Your Hands? Then He shall answer, Those with which I was wounded in the house of My friends.

(In these Passages, the false prophets are placed beside the True Prophet, the Lord Jesus Christ. They, before the Coming of the Lord, too oftentimes were rewarded, while He, as each True Prophet, was greatly opposed, even crucified. The false prophets thrust themselves forward and claimed reverence and position; He Himself, the greatest of the Prophets, did not claim to be a professional Prophet — that was not His Mission in coming to Earth — but became a Bond-servant and a Shepherd; made and appointed such in the Divine Purpose of Redemption. For man having sold himself into slavery, it was necessary that Christ should take that position in order to redeem him.

THE WOUNDS

"*'And one shall say unto Him,' refers to the moment of recognition, as outlined in Zech. 12:10, where it says, 'And they shall look upon Me Whom they have pierced, and they shall mourn for Him.' This will be immediately after the Second Coming, with the Antichrist now defeated and Christ standing before Israel. They will then know, beyond the shadow of a doubt, that He is the Messiah; then will they ask, 'What are these wounds in Your Hands?'*

"*These wounds, which He will ever carry, will be an instant and constant reminder of Who He is and what was done to Him, which presents Him as the Sin-Bearer of the world. Even though He was the Redeemer of all mankind, still, this shows how He was treated by man, especially by His Own.*

"*'Then He shall answer,' will be an answer that will cause their terrible 'mourning' of Zech. 12:10-14. It will also be the cause of the 'Fountain opened to the House of David and to the inhabitants of Jerusalem for sin and for uncleanness' [Zech. 13:1].*

"*'Those with which I was wounded in the house of My friends,' proclaims His Crucifixion and those who did it to Him. The words, 'My friends,' are said in irony)*" **(Zech. 13:6).**

THE MESSIAH REVEALED TO ISRAEL

"And I will pour upon the House of David and upon the inhabitants of Jerusalem, the Spirit of grace and of supplications: and they shall look upon Me Whom they have pierced, and they shall mourn for Him, as one mourns for his only son, and shall be in bitterness for Him, as one that is in bitterness for his firstborn. *('And I will pour . . .' refers to the Lord pouring out fire upon Zion's adversaries, but the Holy Spirit upon her inhabitants [II Thess., Chpt. 1]. If one is to notice, the Messiah Himself is speaking in the entirety of this Chapter as far as the word 'pierced'; then the Holy Spirit points to the moral effect produced by the revelation. 'Upon the House of David,' proclaims the Promise originally given to David concerning his seed upon the Throne of Israel [II Sam. 7:12-16].*

THE SPIRIT OF GRACE

"The phrase, 'I will pour upon them the Spirit of Grace,' concerns the goodness of God and means they are no longer trusting in their Law, but instead, the 'Grace of God,' which is found only in the Lord Jesus Christ. 'And I will pour upon them the Spirit of Supplications,' speaks of Israel supplicating the Lord and the Lord supplicating the Father on their behalf. The word means 'to ask humbly and earnestly.'

MOURNING

" 'And they shall look upon Me Whom they have pierced,' identifies who and what they are and Who He is. 'And they shall mourn for Him, as one mourns for his

only son,' now proclaims the moral effect produced by this Revelation, as given by the Holy Spirit. They will then make their supplications to Him for Mercy and Forgiveness. 'And shall be in bitterness for Him,' means 'a sense of intense shame.' It speaks of True Repentance.

THE FIRSTBORN

"The last phrase, 'as one who is in bitterness for his firstborn,' refers to the loss of an only son, the firstborn. In effect, they killed their own son, and the firstborn at that, which meant that the family line could not continue; it was, in fact, destroyed, at least as far as the Covenant was concerned; however, this 'Son,' or 'Firstborn,' rose from the dead. Even though they would not accept it then, they will accept it now — and because He lives, they shall live also!)

ISRAEL'S REPENTANCE

"In that day shall there be a great mourning in Jerusalem, as the mourning of Hadad-rimmon in the valley of Megiddon. *(As Zech. 12:10 proclaims, there is personal 'mourning,' with national 'mourning' in Verse 11, and domestic 'mourning' in Verses 12 through 14. Every man will feel himself guilty of piercing Immanuel, which is the way they should feel.*

"The last phrase refers to King Josiah being killed in this place [II Chron. 35:22-25]. His reign was the one gleam of light in the gloom that covered the nation from Manasseh to the captivity. Consequently, there was great 'mourning' respecting his death.)

DOMESTIC MOURNING

"And the land shall mourn, every family apart; the

family of the House of David apart, and their wives apart; the family of the house of Nathan apart, and their wives apart;

"The family of the house of Levi apart, and their wives apart; the family of Shimei apart, and their wives apart *(the House of David and Nathan speaks of the princely line of Israel, while the family of Levi and Shimei speaks of the Priests. Consequently, these two Verses proclaim a personal and general Repentance on the part of both the civil and Spiritual leadership)*;

ALL THE FAMILIES

"All the families that remain, every family apart, and their wives apart. *('All the families that remain,' speaks now of the balance of Israel. Judah's repentance and conversion will not be motivated by fear of punishment, but by the overwhelming sense of guilt affecting the heart, when they recognize that their Deliverer is Jesus Whom they crucified, and that all along, despite their hatred and their conduct, He kept on loving them!)*" (Zech. 12:10-14).

THE FOUNTAIN OF CLEANSING FOR ISRAEL

"In that day there shall be a fountain opened to the House of David and to the inhabitants of Jerusalem for sin and for uncleanness. *('In that day,' occurs eighteen times from Zech. 9:16 through 14:21. This shows how precious 'that day' is to the Messiah's Heart. In that day, His Victory over the enemies of His People will be great, but greater will be His moral Victory over His People themselves.*

"*The Christian's true triumphs are God's triumphs over him, and God's triumphs over His People are their only victories. Such was Jacob of old, who represented*

Israel in that coming Glad Day. The conversion of the Apostle Paul illustrates the future conversion of Israel. He hated Jesus, but on the Damascus Road, he looked upon Him Whom he had pierced, mourned, and wept.

AN OPEN FOUNTAIN

"The phrase, 'In that day there shall be a fountain opened,' does not mean that it is first opened there, but that Israel will only begin to partake of it 'in that day,' i.e., the beginning of the Kingdom Age. This fountain was historically opened at Calvary, but will be consciously opened to repentant Jews in the future day of her Repentance. For the fact and function of that fountain only becomes conscious to the awakened sinner.

CHRIST'S ATONING WORK

"A true sense of sin and guilt in relationship to God awakens the sense of the need of cleansing, and so, the shed and cleansing Blood of the Lamb of God becomes precious to convicted conscience. As well, the ever-living efficacy of Christ's Atoning Work, with its power to cleanse the conscience and the life, is justly comparable to a fountain and not to a font. The sense of the Hebrew Text is that this Fountain shall be opened and shall remain open.

IF JERUSALEM, THEN ANYONE!

" 'To the House of David and to the inhabitants of Jerusalem for sin and for uncleanness,' portrays the possibility that, of all sinners, the Jerusalem sinners may be accounted the greatest. It was Jerusalem that stoned the Prophets and crucified the Messiah; therefore, great sinners may hope for pardon and cleansing in this Fountain opened for the House of David.

CHRIST JUDGES SIN

"The entrance of Christ judges sin, unmasks its true character, and arouses a moral consciousness which approves that judgment. That entrance dominates, adjusts, disciplines, instructs, and cleanses man's affections, relationships, and desires. All of this must be cleansed, not only in Israel of a future day, but also in any and all of who come to Christ. That Fountain is open to all!)" **(Zech. 13:1).**

WILL CHRIST COME TO STAY?

Yes, Christ will come to stay! Even as we shall study in the Chapter on the coming Kingdom Age, our Lord will be the President of the world. In fact, the world at that time will have a one-world government with Jesus Christ at its head and Israel as the leading priestly nation of the world.

"Consider Him, let Christ your pattern be,
"And know that He has apprehended thee;
"To share His very life, His Power Divine,
"And in the likeness of your Lord to shine."

"Consider Him; so shall you, day by day,
"Seek out the lowliest place, and therein stay,
"Content to pass away, a thing of naught,
"That glory to the Father's Name be brought."

"Shrink not, O Child of God, but fearless go,
"Down into death with Jesus: you shall know,
"The power of an endless life begin,
"With glorious liberty from self and sin."

"Consider Him, and thus your life shall be,
"Filled with self-sacrifice and purity,
"God will work out in you the pattern true,

"And Christ's example ever keep in view."

"Consider Him, your great High Priest above,
"Is interceding in untiring love,
"And He would have you thus within the veil,
"By Spirit — breathes petitions to prevail."

"Consider Him, as you run this race,
"Keep ever upward looking in His Face;
"And thus transformed, illumined you shall be,
"And Christ's own image shall be seen in thee."

CHAPTER SIX

What Is The Kingdom Age?

QUESTION:

WHAT IS THE KINGDOM AGE?

ANSWER:

As we have been studying, up unto the Second Coming of the Lord, the world has experienced the most horrific time that it has ever seen in all of its history. In fact, Jesus said, and concerning this coming time:

> "For then shall be great tribulation *(the last three and one half years),* such as was not since the beginning of the world to this time, no, nor ever shall be. *(The worst the world has ever known, and will be so bad that it will never be repeated)*" (**Mat. 24:21**).

That dark time, however, will be interrupted, and abruptly so, by the Second Coming of the Lord. This, the Second Coming, will usher in the greatest time of prosperity the world has ever known in all of its history. Then *"the Earth shall be full of the Knowledge of the LORD, as the waters cover the sea"* (Isa. 11:9). This will be so because the Lord Jesus Christ will be reigning Personally from Jerusalem, actually serving as the President, so to speak, of the entirety of the world.

WHAT IS THE KINGDOM AGE?

The *"Kingdom Age"* is sometimes referred to as the *"Millennial Reign."* Actually, the word *"Mille"* means one thousand. In fact, the great Prophet Isaiah had more to say about the coming Kingdom Age than any other Prophet, although, basically, all mentioned it in one way or the other. John the Beloved said the following about this coming event:

LIVE AND REIGN WITH CHRIST
A THOUSAND YEARS

"And I saw Thrones, and they sat upon them, and judgment was given unto them *(refers to the 24 Elders who represent the entire Plan of God, which pertains to the Redeemed of all ages; we aren't told who these men are)*: and I *saw* the souls of them who were beheaded for the witness of Jesus, and for the Word of God, and which had not worshipped the Beast, neither his image, neither had received *his* mark upon their foreheads, or in their hands *(categorizes the Tribulation Saints who gave their lives for the cause of Christ; the idea is that these will be included in the first Resurrection of Life, and will enjoy all its privileges)*; and they lived and reigned with Christ a thousand years. *(This is the Kingdom Age.)*

THE FIRST RESURRECTION

"But the rest of the dead lived not again until the thousand years were finished. *(This pertains to all the unsaved, in fact, all those who lived and died since the dawn of time. The souls and spirits of these people are now in Hell [Lk. 16:19-31].)* This *is* the First Resurrection *(proclaims the fact that these two Resurrections, the Resurrection of the Just and the Resurrection of the Unjust, will be separated by 1,000 years).*

"Blessed and Holy *is* he who has part in the First Resurrection *(this is the Resurrection of Life, which will include every Saint of God who has ever lived from Abel to the last Tribulation Saint; all will be given Glorified Bodies)*: on such the second death has no power *(the 'second death' is to be cast into the Lake of Fire, and to be there forever and forever [Rev. 2:8]; all who are washed in the Blood of the Lamb need not fear the second death),* but they shall be Priests of God and of Christ, and shall

reign with Him a thousand years. *(All Believers who have part in the First Resurrection will at the same time serve as mediators, so to speak, between the population of the world and God and Christ. The 'thousand years' portrays the Kingdom Age, when Christ will reign supreme over the entire Earth)"* **(Rev. 20:4-6).**

JESUS

Our Lord mentioned these two Resurrections, but gave very little information as to what they were. He said:

"Marvel not at this *(these statements, as given by Christ, left the religious leaders of Israel speechless)***: for the hour is coming, in the which all who are in the graves shall hear His Voice** *(speaks of the Resurrection of Life and the Resurrection of Damnation; again, these statements proclaim Christ as the Lord of both life and death)***,**
"And shall come forth *(portrays both Resurrections, as we shall see, and according to His 'Voice')***; they who have done good, unto the Resurrection of Life** *(pertains to the First Resurrection, or as commonly referred, 'The Rapture' [I Thess. 4:13-18])***; and they who have done evil, unto the Resurrection of Damnation** *(this last Resurrection will take place approximately a thousand years after the First Resurrection of Life [Dan. 12:2; Rev., Chpt. 20])"* **(Jn. 5:28-29).**

SEVEN FEASTS OF THE MOSAIC LAW

Those seven Feasts are:
- **The Passover;**
- **Unleavened Bread;**
- **Firstfruits;**
- **Pentecost;**
- **Trumpets;**

- Atonement; and,
- Tabernacles.

All of these Feasts portray Christ in either His atoning, intercessory, or mediatorial work.

THE PASSOVER

Christ is our Passover by virtue of Calvary. Paul said: *"For even Christ our Passover is Sacrificed for us"* (I Cor. 5:7).

UNLEAVENED BREAD

The Feast of Unleavened Bread, which was meant to be a part of Passover week, typified Christ in His Perfection. In other words, He never sinned by word, thought, or deed, all typified by the *"unleavened bread."*

Leaven is a form of rot which brings about fermentation. Paul said:

"Therefore let us keep the feast *(is meant to serve as a symbol of the Jewish Passover, when all leaven was purged from the household)*, not with old leaven *(old sins committed before conversion)*, neither with the leaven of malice and wickedness *(refers to the ways of the world from which the Child of God has been delivered)*; but with the unleavened *bread* of sincerity and truth. *(Can only be attained by one's Faith being anchored solely in the Sacrifice of Christ)*" (I Cor. 5:8).

Christ had to be perfect in order to serve as the Sacrifice that God would accept, which He did!

FIRSTFRUITS

The Feast of Firstfruits portrays Christ as the Resurrection and the Life. Again, Paul said:

"But now is Christ risen from the dead *(so says the Holy Spirit)*, **and** become the Firstfruits of them who slept.** *(The Resurrection of Christ guarantees the Resurrection of all Saints.)*

"For since by man *came* death *(refers to Adam and the Fall in the Garden of Eden, and speaks of spiritual death, separation from God)*, by Man *came* also the Resurrection of the dead.** *(This refers to the Lord Jesus Christ Who atoned for all sin, thereby, making it possible for man to be united once again with God, which guarantees the Resurrection.)*

CHRIST THE FIRSTFRUITS

"For as in Adam all die *(spiritual death, separation from God)*, even so in Christ shall all be made alive.** *(In the first man, all died. In the Second Man, all shall be made alive, at least, all who will believe [Jn. 3:16]).*

"But every man in his own order *(Christ first, and then all Believers thereafter)*: **Christ the Firstfruits** *(He was the First One to be raised from the dead, never to die again)*; afterward they who are Christ's at His coming.** *(This pertains to the Rapture of the Church, not the Second Coming [I Thess. 4:13-18])*" **(I Cor. 15:20-23).**

PENTECOST

Pentecost took place fifty days after Passover. Actually, *"Pentecost"* is a Hebrew word which means *"fifty"* or *"fiftieth."* This Feast portrays Jesus as the Baptizer with the Holy Spirit. John the Baptist said of Jesus:

"I indeed baptize you with water unto Repentance *(Water Baptism was an outward act of an inward work already carried out)*: but He *(Christ)* Who comes after me is mightier than I, Whose Shoes I am not worthy to bear: **He shall baptize you with the Holy Spirit, and** *with* **fire** *(to burn out the sinful dross [Acts 2:2-4])*:

"Whose fan *is* **in His Hand** *(the ancient method for winnowing grain)***, and He will thoroughly purge His Floor** *('purging it, that it may bring forth more fruit' [Jn. 15:2])***, and gather His Wheat into the garner** *(the end product as developed by the Spirit)***; but He will burn up the chaff with unquenchable fire.** *(The wheat is symbolic of the Work of the Spirit, while the chaff is symbolic of the work of the flesh)***" (Mat. 3:11-12).**

All four of the Feasts mentioned above have been fulfilled by Christ. The remaining three are yet to be fulfilled.

THE FEAST OF TRUMPETS

The Feast of Trumpets symbolized Israel being called to war or to celebration (Lev. 25:9; Num. 10:1-10). The Feast of Trumpets will be fulfilled at the Resurrection. Paul said:

"In a moment, in the twinkling of an eye *(proclaims how long it will take for this change to take place)***, at the last trump** *(does not denote by the use of the word 'last' that there will be successive trumpet blasts, but rather denotes that this is the close of things, referring to the Church Age)***: for the trumpet shall sound** *(it is the 'Trump of God' [I Thess. 4:16])***, and the dead shall be raised incorrupt-ible** *(the Sainted Dead, with no sin nature)***, and we shall be changed** *(put on the Glorified Body)***" (I Cor. 15:52).**

The Trumpet here blown will not only signal the occasion of the Resurrection of the Sainted Dead, which is an event so Earth-shaking as to defy all description, but, as well, it will signal that Israel is about to engage in war. This will take place when the Antichrist shows his true colors, thereby, attacking Israel, which will take place at the midpoint of the Great Tribulation.

The Feast of Trumpets, denoting joy and celebration, will be fulfilled at the Second Coming when Christ comes to rescue Israel and to annihilate the Antichrist, etc. As should be obvious, the latter proclaims tremendous joy.

THE FEAST OF ATONEMENT

Actually, the Great Day of Atonement was the only fast day of the year as it regarded the Law of Moses; however, a great Feast followed.

The Great Day of Atonement was when the High Priest went into the Holy of Holies, placing blood on the Mercy Seat, which served as Atonement for Israel. Actually, on this day He went in three times. The first time was to fill the Holy of Holies with Incense, and the second time was to take blood and apply it to the Mercy Seat for himself. Even though he was the High Priest, still, he was a sinful man. The third time he was to place blood on the Mercy Seat for the whole of Israel.

In essence, that has already been done by Christ which, in a sense, took place at the Cross of Calvary when He shed His Precious Blood; however, it will actually not be complete, one might say, until Israel accepts Christ as Saviour, Messiah, and Lord, which she will at the Second Coming.

At that time, the great Prophet Zechariah said:

"In that day there shall be a fountain opened to the House of David and to the inhabitants of Jerusalem for sin and for uncleanness" (Zech. 13:1). Then, the Feast of Atonement will be complete. Actually, as stated, in Christ the Feast of Atonement is complete and was done so at Calvary's Cross, but its effects are not complete until Israel accepts Him as Saviour, Messiah, and Lord.

FEAST OF TABERNACLES

The Feast of Tabernacles represents the coming Kingdom Age, which we are now studying. Israel celebrated this Feast yearly or, at least, was supposed to. Whether they understood the thousand-year Millennial Reign or not is open to question.

During the coming Kingdom Age, the entirety of the world, meaning every nation, will send delegations to Jerusalem *"to keep the Feast of Tabernacles."* It will be a time of rejoicing such as the world has never known before. The great Prophet Zechariah said the following about this coming time:

WORSHIP AT JERUSALEM

"And it shall come to pass, that every one who is left of all the nations which came against Jerusalem shall even go up from year to year to worship the King, the LORD of Hosts, and to keep the Feast of Tabernacles. *(This 'Feast of Tabernacles' was a delightful week of holiday in the month of October at the close of the year's toil, and was kept, at least it was supposed to be kept, all during the time of the Mosaic Law [Ex. 23:16; Lev. 23:33-43; Deut. 16:13]. This 'Feast' will be re-instituted in the Kingdom Age, which will be kept not only by Israel, but also, by all the other nations of the world.)*

THE FEAST OF TABERNACLES IN THE
KINGDOM AGE WILL BE MANDATORY

"And it shall be, that whoso will not come up of all the families of the Earth unto Jerusalem to worship the King, the LORD of Hosts, even upon them shall be no rain. *(This Scripture tells us that even though Jesus Christ is 'King' and 'LORD of Hosts,' still, there will be some in the Earth, despite all the tremendous blessings and prosperity, who will not accept Him as Saviour and Lord, who, therefore, will not properly serve Him. To be sure, they will not be allowed to foment rebellion, wickedness, or evil, but will be forced to subscribe to the letter of the Law, if not the spirit. In other words, they will not be allowed to entertain the evil thoughts of their hearts. Also, all of this proclaims the Truth that the coming Kingdom Age will not be ruled by force, but rather by love; and yet force will be used where it is absolutely necessary.*

LORD OF THE ELEMENTS

"The phrase, 'Even upon them shall be no rain,' speaks of these recalcitrant leaders of nations who will not desire to be subservient to the 'King,' i.e., the Lord Jesus Christ. The Lord will then take care of the situation by stopping the rain, which will hinder the harvests, which will be felt by the people. The people will then take active measures to see to it that their appointed leaders from henceforth obey the Law of the Lord.)

PUNISHMENT

"And if the family of Egypt go not up, and come not, who have no rain; there shall be the plague, wherewith the LORD will smite the heathen who come not up to keep the Feast of Tabernacles. *(This speaks of the nations of the world which did not depend on rain, as 'Egypt,' being dealt with in another fashion. As to exactly what this 'plague' will be, we aren't told!)*

"This shall be the punishment of Egypt, and the punishment of all nations that come not up to keep the Feast of Tabernacles. *(The certitude of its affliction is especially repeated in this Verse. In other words, this Law will not be abrogated, despite who the people are, as it is so often presently. As well, inasmuch as it is the Lord Who makes the decisions in these cases, one can be certain that the judgment, if needed, will be fair and equitable.)*

HOLINESS UNTO THE LORD

"In that day shall there be upon the bells of the

horses, HOLINESS UNTO THE LORD; and the pots in the LORD's house shall be like the bowls before the Altar. *(The idea of this Verse and the following is that, in this coming day in Israel, even the most common things used by men shall be signified as holy, whether used in work, profit, or ornament. All shall be consecrated to God's Service.*

" 'In that day shall there be upon the bells of the horses, HOLINESS UNTO THE LORD,' signifies the same inscription used upon the golden plate of the mitre [hat] of the High Priest [Ex. 28:36]. Then, only the High Priest, Who was a Type of Christ, carried this inscription, whereas now, even the lowliest things, as 'bells of the horses,' will be signified as such! Such is meant to portray the atmosphere which will guarantee the action of the preceding Verses. It is 'HOLINESS UNTO THE LORD'; and the Lord will not allow it to be changed by the evil hearts of wicked men.

"The phrase, 'Shall be like the bowls before the Altar,' concerns the Vessels which held the blood of the victims in Old Testament times for sprinkling upon the Altar, and were considered of superior sanctity. The Prophet announces that now all shall be holy, the lowest equal to the highest.)

THE SACRIFICE

"Yes, every pot in Jerusalem and in Judah shall be holiness unto the LORD of Hosts: and all they who sacrifice shall come and take of them, and seethe therein: and in that day there shall be no more the Canaanite in the House of the LORD of Hosts. *(These two Verses speak of the entirety of the Land of Israel being holy unto the Lord, and not just a designated part, as the Temple of old! As is obvious here, the 'Sacrificial System' will be re-instituted; but, as of old, it will not Save. It will be strictly for a memorial [6:14].*

" *'And in that day there shall be no more the Canaanite in the House of the LORD of Hosts,' means that there
will be no more a trafficker in the House of the LORD
[Jn. 2:14-16]. In other words, the Sacred Ministry will
cease to be adopted because of salaried profession or
other secular interests.*

*"The word 'Holy' [or 'Holiness'] simply means to be
set apart for sacred use. It is removed from the realm of the
common and moved to the sphere of the sacred)"* **(Zech.
14:16-21).**

VARIOUS HARVESTS

• **The first three Feasts were to be kept in April at the time
of the barley harvest.**

• **The Feast of Pentecost was to be kept in the latter part of
May or the early part of June, which was the time of the wheat
harvest.**

• **The last three Feasts were to be kept in October, which
was the time of the fruit harvest.**

WHAT WILL THE KINGDOM AGE BE LIKE?

**During that time, Satan, all fallen Angels, and demon spir-
its will be locked away in the bottomless pit. The Scripture
says concerning this:**

"And I saw an Angel come down from Heaven *(continues with the idea that Angels are very prominent in the
Plan and Work of God)***, having the key of the bottomless pit** *(speaks of the same place recorded in Rev. 9:1;
however, there the key is given to Satan, but this Angel
of Rev. 20:1 'has the key,' implying that he has had it all
along; more than likely, God allows this Angel to give the
key to Satan in Rev. 9:1)* **and a great chain in his hand**
*(should be taken literally)***.**

BOUND FOR A THOUSAND YEARS

"And he laid hold on the dragon, that old serpent, which is the Devil, and Satan *(as a 'dragon,' he shows his power; as a 'serpent,' he shows his cunning; as the 'Devil,' he is the accuser; and as 'Satan,' he is the adversary)*, and bound him a thousand years *(refers to being bound by the great chain carried by the Angel)*,

THE BOTTOMLESS PIT

"And cast him into the bottomless pit, and shut him up, and set a seal upon him *(speaks of the abyss being sealed to keep him there)*, that he should deceive the nations no more, till the thousand years should be fulfilled: and after that he must be loosed a little season. *(At the end of the thousand-year period, Satan will be loosed out of his prison. He will make another attempt to deceive the nations, in which he will not succeed. We aren't told how long this 'little season' will be)*" (Rev. 20:1-3).

Without Satan, fallen Angels, and demon spirits functioning on the Earth, one can well imagine how different the atmosphere will be. So, this, the binding of Satan, seems to be the first thing that will take place upon the return to this Earth of our Lord. Except, as stated, for one small uprising at the end of this thousand-year period, Satan's day is over.

ISRAEL

After Satan, the very first thing our Lord will do, it seems, is to restore Israel to her rightful place and position. Of course, this could not happen until Israel accepted Him as Saviour, Messiah, and Lord, which she will do, and which we have already addressed in the last Chapter.

GOD WILL JUDGE ISRAEL'S ENEMIES

Even though the following is quite voluminous, I felt it imperative that we include it in this section because it addresses itself directly to the restoration of Israel. In fact, this Thirty-sixth Chapter of Ezekiel tells us of the material restoration of Israel, which will take place in the coming Kingdom Age, and the Thirty-seventh Chapter of Ezekiel tells us the manner in which the Spiritual Restoration will be brought about.

As stated, even though this is quite voluminous, I felt it necessary that we include both Chapters in this section, which includes all the notes as well from THE EXPOSITOR'S STUDY BIBLE.

"Also, thou son of man, prophesy unto the mountains of Israel, and say, You mountains of Israel, hear the Word of the LORD *(this Prophecy is divided into two parts, with Ezek. 36:1-15 connecting with the previous Chapter, and the second part beginning with Ezek. 36:16 and closing at Ezek. 37:14. The subject of the first part is Israel's restoration)*:

"Thus says the Lord GOD; Because the enemy has said against you, Aha, even the ancient high places are ours in possession *(this 'enemy' was Edom)*:

"Therefore prophesy and say, Thus says the Lord GOD; Because they have made you desolate, and swallowed you up on every side, that you might be a possession unto the residue of the heathen, and you are taken up in the lips of talkers, and are an infamy of the people *(the sense of Ezek. 36:3 is that the heathen charged Jehovah with inability to protect His Land)*:

THE FUTURE RESTORATION OF ISRAEL

"Therefore, you mountains of Israel, hear the Word of the Lord GOD; Thus says the Lord GOD to the mountains, and to the hills, to the rivers, and to the valleys, to the desolate wastes, and to the cities that are forsaken, which became a prey and derision to the residue of the heathen who are round about *(God chastens His People, as this Verse proclaims, but destroys their enemies)*;

"Therefore thus says the Lord GOD; Surely in the fire of My Jealousy have I spoken against the residue of the heathen, and against all Idumea, which have appointed My Land into their possession with the joy of all their heart, with despiteful minds, to cast it out for a prey. *(Edom not only proposed to take 'My Land,' but to do so with a 'gleeful joy,' and with 'despiteful minds,' i.e., 'with contempt of soul,' meaning that Edom held Judah and Judah's God Jehovah in contempt.)*

PROPHESY

"Prophesy therefore concerning the land of Israel, and say unto the mountains, and to the hills, to the rivers, and to the valleys, Thus says the Lord GOD; Behold, I have spoken in My Jealousy and in My Fury, because you have borne the shame of the heathen *(the key to this Verse is the phrase, 'You have borne the shame of the heathen,' which means that the shame of God's People is temporary, while that of their enemies is perpetual. The Law of Retribution is demanded by the absolute Righteousness of God. The judicial visitations of God cannot possibly be one-sided. That which has been meted out to Israel for their sin will be meted out to Edom, as well as all other opposing nations)*:

THE WORD OF THE LORD

"Therefore thus says the Lord GOD; I have lifted up My Hand, Surely the heathen who are about you, they shall bear their shame. *(The certitude is found in the phrase, 'I have lifted up My Hand,' which refers to God taking an oath that what He has stated about the heathen and their punishment will come to pass.)*

"But ye, O mountains of Israel, you shall shoot forth your branches, and yield your fruit to My People of Israel; for they are at hand to come. *(The phrases, 'O mountains of Israel' and 'The everlasting hills' of Gen. 49:26, are terms expressive of the moral elevation of Israel over the physical elevation of Edom.)*

BLESSING

"For, behold, I am for you, and I will turn unto you, and you shall be tilled and sown *(as the Lord said that He was 'against Edom' [35:3], He, conversely, says of Israel, 'I am for you')*:

"And I will multiply men upon you, all the House of Israel, even all of it: and the cities shall be inhabited, and the wastes shall be built *(as the Lord outlined the destruction of Edom and other nations, He here outlines the coming blessing and prosperity of 'the House of Israel')*:

"And I will multiply upon you man and beast; and they shall increase and bring fruit: and I will settle you after your old estates, and will do better unto you than at your beginnings: and you shall know that I am the LORD. *(This pertains to the coming Kingdom Age.)*

"Yes, I will cause men to walk upon you, even My People Israel; and they shall possess you, and you shall be their inheritance, and you shall no more henceforth bereave them of men. *(Edom said they would possess the Land. They are indicative of the modern Palestinians. The Lord says, 'My People Israel shall possess you,' i.e., the Land.)*

"Thus says the Lord GOD; Because they say unto you, Your land devours up men, and has bereaved your nations *(concerning Israel, the heathen spread the evil* report that the Land of Israel had devoured its inhabitants and was, therefore, cursed!)*:

SAYS THE LORD GOD

"Therefore you shall devour men no more, neither bereave your nations any more, says the Lord GOD. *(The idea of the Verse is this: the great Spiritual Conflict between light and darkness has brought about the terrible contest for the Land of Israel, which began immediately upon its inception, and which has continued throughout its history.*

"Upon the return of Christ, the cause of this conflict will be removed; hence, it will 'devour men no more, neither bereave the nations.')

"Neither will I cause men to hear in you the shame of the heathen any more, neither shall you bear the reproach of the people any more, neither shall you cause your nations to fall any more, says the Lord GOD. *(This was not fulfilled, not even in the slightest, upon the return of the Exiles from their bondage, but will be fulfilled totally in the coming Kingdom Age.)*

ISRAEL'S PAST SINS AND JUDGMENTS

"Moreover the Word of the LORD came unto me, saying,

"Son of man, when the House of Israel dwelt in their own land, they defiled it by their own way and by their doings: their way was before Me as the uncleanness of a removed woman. *(The 'uncleanness' pictures the vileness of the sinner in God's Sight. The first statement of Ezek. 36:29 declares the ability of the Saviour to fully cleanse the sinner.*

" 'As the uncleanness of a removed woman,' refers to a

woman's monthly period, and was used as an example of Israel's uncleanness.)

SCATTERED AMONG THE HEATHEN

"Wherefore I poured My Fury upon them for the blood that they had shed upon the land, and for their idols wherewith they had polluted it *(this Verse proclaims that the idol worshipped produced the shedding of blood and the offering up of little children in human sacrifices. Because of this, the anger of the Lord knew no bounds)*:

"And I scattered them among the heathen, and they were dispersed through the countries: according to their way and according to their doings I judged them. *(This not only concerned Ezekiel's day, but also concerned itself with A.D. 70, when Titus destroyed Jerusalem. This was done because they had shed 'the Blood of Christ.')*

I HAD PITY

"And when they entered unto the heathen, whither they went, they profaned My Holy Name, when they said to them, These are the People of the LORD, and are gone forth out of His Land. *('These are the People of the LORD,' is the key phrase to this Verse. Their being defeated caused the heathen to conclude that Jehovah had either behaved capriciously toward His People and cast them off, or had proved unequal to the task of protecting them. In either case, the honor of Jehovah had been lessened in the mind and tarnished by the words of the heathen. This had been brought about by Israel's sin.)*

"But I had pity for My Holy Name, which the House of Israel had profaned among the heathen, whither they went. *(The idea is: the Lord will restore Israel, but not because of any good in them, but because of good in Himself.)*

THE REGATHERING AND
RESTORATION OF ISRAEL

"**Therefore say unto the House of Israel, Thus says the Lord GOD; I do not this for your sakes, O House of Israel, but for My Holy Name's sake, which you have profaned among the heathen, whither you went.** *(This Scripture further reinforces the statement regarding Ezek. 36:21, in that the Lord is not doing what He is doing for Israel's sake, but instead 'for His Holy Name's sake.')*

"**And I will sanctify My great Name, which was profaned among the heathen, which you have profaned in the midst of them; and the heathen shall know that I am the LORD, says the Lord GOD, when I shall be sanctified in you before their eyes.** *(God's Acts of Grace toward guilty men — solely because of His Name as Saviour and not because of any moral excellence in them — are shown in Ezek. 36:21-23 and 32. The sinner's only claim for Life and Righteousness is the admitting of his sinfulness and not his righteousness, of which he has none.)*

I WILL CLEANSE YOU

"**For I will take you from among the heathen, and gather you out of all countries, and will bring you into your own land.** *(This Passage was not fulfilled when the Children of Israel came back from Babylonian captivity, and has not even been fulfilled as of yet! It will be fulfilled immediately after the Second Coming of Christ.)*

"**Then will I sprinkle clean water upon you, and you shall be clean: from all your filthiness, and from all your idols, will I cleanse you.** *(The word 'then' marks the time for the fulfillment of these Prophecies. Israel, as a nation, will not be won to Christ until the Antichrist is defeated by the Second Coming of Christ. Israel 'then' will accept Christ as Saviour, Lord, and Messiah.)*

A NEW HEART

"A new heart also will I give you, and a new spirit will I put within you: and I will take away the stony heart out of your flesh, and I will give you an heart of flesh. *(This speaks of the New Birth, and totally refutes the claims of those who say that modern Israel will not be restored, and that they have no part or parcel in the Gospel program, presently or in the future.)*

"And I will put My Spirit within you, and cause you to walk in My Statutes, and you shall keep My Judgments, and do them. *('And I will put My Spirit within you,' refers both to regeneration, as carried out by the Holy Spirit at the time of one being Born-Again, and also to the Baptism with the Holy Spirit, which was first evidenced on the Day of Pentecost [Acts 2:1-4]. The entrance of the Holy Spirit is made possible solely by the Cross of Christ [Jn. 14:17], and the 'Statutes' and 'Judgments' fall into the same category. In other words, one can keep those only by and through the Power of the Holy Spirit, Who works exclusively within the framework of the Finished Work of Christ, which demands the constant Faith of the Believer [Rom. 6:3-5; 8:1-2, 11; Lk. 9:23-24].)*

I WILL BE YOUR GOD

"And you shall dwell in the land that I gave to your fathers; and you shall be My People, and I will be your God. *(The conflict regarding the Land of Israel will be solved only when Christ comes back. All hinges on Christ, as all always hinges on Christ.)*

"I will also save you from all your uncleannesses: and I will call for the corn, and will increase it, and lay no famine upon you. *(Regeneration, not reformation — a new heart, and not a changed heart — is essential to Salvation.)*

"And I will multiply the fruit of the tree, and the

increase of the field, that you shall receive no more reproach of famine among the heathen.

"Then shall you remember your own evil ways, and your doings that were not good, and shall loathe yourselves in your own sight for your iniquities and for your abominations. *(The effect of Grace is self-judgment, which will then make possible the Blessing of Ezek. 36:30.)*

THE WASTES SHALL BE BUILT

"Not for your sakes do I this, says the Lord GOD, be it known unto you: be ashamed and confounded for your own ways, O House of Israel. *(All that is done for the Child of God is done 'for Christ's sake' [Eph. 4:32; 1 Jn. 2:12].)*

"Thus says the Lord GOD; In the day that I shall have cleansed you from all your iniquities I will also cause you to dwell in the cities, and the wastes shall be built. *(Israel's conversion to Christ will precipitate their Blessing. Only when all iniquities have been 'cleansed' can the individual then 'dwell' in the inheritance, with the 'wastes' then being reclaimed, i.e., 'built.')*

NO MORE DESOLATION

"And the desolate land shall be tilled, whereas it lay desolate in the sight of all who passed by. *(For nearly 2,000 years, the Land of Israel lay 'desolate.' This was the Promised Land, and yet, there was little semblance of that which originally was. It is now beginning to be restored, but will not fully be made right until the Coming of the Lord.)*

"And they shall say, This land that was desolate is become like the Garden of Eden; and the waste and desolate and ruined cities are become fenced, and are inhabited. *(Tyre and Assyria claimed to be like the Garden of Eden. But this similitude belongs only to Israel [Ezek. 28:13; 31:8-9; Isa. 51:3].)*

THEY SHALL KNOW THAT I AM THE LORD

"Then the heathen who are left round about you shall know that I the LORD build the ruined places, and plant that that was desolate: I the LORD have spoken it, and I will do it. *(All that the Lord says He will do in this Verse is predicated on Israel's acceptance of Him as Lord and Saviour.)*

"Thus says the Lord GOD; I will yet for this be enquired of by the House of Israel, to do it for them; I will increase them with men like a flock. *('I will yet for this be enquired of by the House of Israel,' refers to the coming Great Tribulation of the future, which will bring them to utter desolation and threatened annihilation, which will precipitate their crying to Him for Deliverance. This will bring Israel to a full Repentance and dependence upon God [Isa., Chpt. 64; Zech. 12:10; 13:1; Mat. 23:37-39; Rom. 11:25-29].)*

"As the holy flock, as the flock of Jerusalem in her solemn Feasts; so shall the waste cities be filled with flocks of men: and they shall know that I am the LORD. *(The theme of these Chapters is the relationship between Jehovah and His People. Hence, there are no details given respecting the First Advent. The Chapters present a general picture of the Last Days, of the rebirth of Israel, and of her enjoyment of Earthly Glory and Blessing, which will take place in the coming Kingdom Age)*" **(Ezek. 36:1-38).**

THE SPIRITUAL RESTORATION OF ISRAEL

Before the material restoration addressed in Chapter 36 can take place, there has to be a Spiritual Restoration which, of course, is the most important. Chapter 37 of this great Book of Ezekiel tells us how this will happen.

THE VISION OF THE VALLEY OF DRY BONES

"The Hand of the LORD was upon me, and carried me out in the Spirit of the LORD, and set me down in the midst of the valley which was full of bones *(as the last Chapter graphically spoke of Israel's coming Restoration, Chapter 37 graphically portrays the spiritual manner of that Restoration)*,

"And caused me to pass by them round about: and, behold, there were very many in the open valley; and, lo, they were very dry. *(The repetition of 'behold' fastens the attention upon the two facts — that the bones were very many and very dry. 'Very dry,' speaks of a total absence of spirituality.)*

"And He said unto me, Son of man, can these bones live? And I answered, O Lord GOD, You know. *(Ezekiel's answer to the question of the Lord, 'O Lord GOD, You know,' signifies that within the realm of human endeavor the task was impossible!)*

PROPHESY UPON THESE BONES

"Again He said unto me, Prophesy upon these bones, and say unto them, O you dry bones, hear the Word of the LORD. *(The Prophet is told to 'Prophesy upon these bones,' meaning that the Lord will give a 'Word' which will guarantee their Restoration and Revival; however, such could only be done according to the 'Word of the LORD.')*

"Thus says the Lord GOD unto these bones; Behold, I will cause breath to enter into you, and you shall live *(the 'breath' spoken of is the same breath as when God 'breathed into his nostrils the breath of life,' respecting Adam, and he 'became a living soul' [Gen. 2:7]. The life that is spoken of in this Passage is national life and Spiritual*

Life. National life of the nation has already begun, having its beginning in 1948 and continuing. However, Spiritual Life will begin in the coming Great Tribulation, when 144,000 Jews will accept Christ as their Saviour. But the fullness of Spiritual Life will not come until the Second Coming [Zech. 13:1, 9]):

YOU SHALL KNOW THAT I AM THE LORD

"And I will lay sinews upon you, and will bring up flesh upon you, and cover you with skin, and put breath in you, and you shall live; and you shall know that I am the LORD. *('You shall live,' i.e., 'you shall come to life again, so shall you get to know that I am Jehovah.' God demonstrates His Existence and Power by raising the dead [Jn. 5:21; Rom. 1:3; 4:17; II Cor. 1:9].)*

"So I prophesied as I was commanded: and as I prophesied, there was a noise, and behold a shaking, and the bones came together, bone to his bone. *('There was a noise,' in the Hebrew actually says, 'a voice.')*

SAY TO THE WIND

"And when I beheld, lo, the sinews and the flesh came up upon them, and the skin covered them above: but there was no breath in them. *(As stated, national Israel began in 1948; however, the phrase, 'But there was no breath in them,' signifies the fact that national Israel presently has no Spiritual Life.)*

"Then said He unto me, Prophesy unto the wind, prophesy, son of man, and say to the wind, Thus says the Lord GOD; Come from the four winds, O breath, and breathe upon these slain, that they may live. *('Prophesy unto the wind,' actually says in the Hebrew, 'Prophesy unto the Spirit.' 'Come from the four winds,' actually says in the Hebrew, 'Come from the four breaths.*

"The number 'four' is symbolic of 'fourfold,' denoting an absolute, total, and complete Restoration.)

AN EXCEEDING GREAT ARMY

"So I prophesied as He commanded me, and the breath came into them, and they lived, and stood up upon their feet, an exceeding great army. *(As the preceding Verses spoke of Israel's national identity, now this Verse speaks of Israel's Spiritual Identity, signifying their Spiritual Revival, which will take place at the Second Coming.*

"The phrase, 'And stood upon their feet,' speaks of Spiritual Life enabling such. For a long time, even over 2,000 years, Israel has not 'stood upon their feet' spiritually. But in that coming Glad Day, they shall! Then they shall be an 'exceeding great army,' but an 'exceeding great army' for the Lord.)

THE WHOLE HOUSE OF ISRAEL

"Then He said unto me, Son of man, these bones are the whole House of Israel: behold, they say, Our bones are dried, and our hope is lost: we are cut off for our parts. *('The whole House of Israel,' speaks of the entirety of the thirteen Tribes. The latter part of this Verse, 'behold, they say,' refers to the latter half of the coming Great Tribulation. At that time, it will look like the entirety of their nation will be totally destroyed, with 'hope lost' and 'cut off for our parts.' This has reference to Zechariah's Prophecy, when he said, 'two parts therein shall be cut off and die' [Zech. 13:8].)*

I WILL BRING YOU INTO THE LAND OF ISRAEL

"Therefore prophesy and say unto them, Thus says the Lord GOD; Behold, O My People, I will open your

graves, and cause you to come up out of your graves, and bring you into the land of Israel. *(As Prophecy sometimes does, the previous Verse spoke of the last few months or even weeks before the Coming of the Lord and, therefore, the relief of Israel, whereas this Verse goes back even to World War II and forward.)*

"And you shall know that I am the LORD, when I have opened your graves, O My People, and brought you up out of your graves *('And brought you up out of your graves,' has reference in totality to the fact that Israel, and for all practical purposes, in the Battle of Armageddon is all but totally destroyed; actually, there is no Earthly way they can be salvaged. However, there is a Heavenly Way! And that Heavenly Way is Christ)*,

MY SPIRIT

"And shall put My Spirit in you, and you shall live, and I shall place you in your own land: then shall you know that I the LORD have spoken it, and performed it, says the LORD. *(This Passage signals the great Revival that will take place in Israel at the Coming of the Lord. Zechariah gave in greater detail the happening of this great moving of the Holy Spirit [Zech. 12:10-14; 13:1, 9].)*

ISRAEL AND JUDAH REJOINED

"The Word of the LORD came again unto me, saying *(now begins the second Prophesy predicting the unity of the nation, and its happy settlement under the Government of the Messiah)*,

"Moreover, thou son of man, take thee one stick, and write upon it, For Judah, and for the Children of Israel his companions: then take another stick, and write upon it, For Joseph, the stick of Ephraim and for all the House of Israel his companions *(the 'two sticks' represent the two Houses of Israel, the Northern Confederation of Israel, sometimes called Ephraim or Samaria, and the Southern Kingdom known as Judah. 'His companions,' refers to Benjamin and Levi, and also possibly Simeon, being joined with Judah. The other Tribes pertained to Ephraim)*:

JOIN THEM TOGETHER

"And join them one to another into one stick; and they shall become one in your hand. *(This Verse predicts that both Kingdoms will now become one Kingdom, signifying one people, which can only be brought about by the 'Hand of the Lord,' which means that they will never again be divided.)*

"And when the children of your people shall speak unto you, saying, Will you not show us what you mean by these? *(This Prophecy, which incorporates the balance of the Chapter, predicts the future union of the Tribes, their Restoration to the Land of Israel, and their settlement there under One Shepherd, and teaches that a Divinely wrought union is real and enduring, and brings its subjects into fellowship with God, and disposes them around a Divine center.)*

THE MESSIAH AND DAVID

"Say unto them, Thus says the Lord GOD; Behold, I will take the stick of Joseph, which is in the hand of Ephraim, and the Tribes of Israel his fellows, and will put them with him, even with the stick of Judah, and make them one stick, and they shall be one in My Hand. *(When God takes groups of His Servants and unites them, they actually become one in His Hand. This means that not only is the old division gone, but the cause of division has also been erased.)*

"**And the sticks whereon you write shall be in your hand before their eyes.** *(It is amazing that the Lord would take something that simple, such as 'sticks,' to express and portray something of such vital consequence [I Cor. 1:27].)*

I WILL BRING THEM INTO THEIR OWN LAND

"**And say unto them, Thus says the Lord GOD; Behold, I will take the Children of Israel from among the heathen, whither they be gone, and will gather them on every side, and bring them into their own land** *(the total fulfillment of this will take place in the coming Kingdom Age)***:**

"**And I will make them one nation in the land upon the mountains of Israel; and one King shall be King to them all: and they shall be no more two nations, neither shall they be divided into two kingdoms any more at all.** *('In the Land,' refers to the Land of Israel, as promised to Abraham [Gen. 12:7]. Its boundary on the west is the Mediterranean; on the south, the Suez Canal, which includes the Arabian Peninsula; on the east, the Euphrates River; on the north, Lebanon.)*

THEY WILL BE MY PEOPLE
AND I WILL BE THEIR GOD

"**Neither shall they defile themselves any more with their idols, nor with their detestable things, nor with any of their transgressions: but I will save them out of all their dwellingplaces, wherein they have sinned, and will cleanse them: so shall they be My People, and I will be their God.** *(This will take place almost immediately after the Second Coming of Christ.)*

DAVID THE KING

"**And David My Servant shall be king over them;**

and they all shall have One Shepherd: they shall also walk in My Judgments, and observe My Statutes, and do them. *(David was ever looked at as the example for all the kings of Israel, and will consequently serve in this capacity under Christ forever.)*

"And they shall dwell in the land that I have given unto Jacob My Servant, wherein your fathers have dwelt; and they shall dwell therein, even they, and their children, and their children's children for ever: and My Servant David shall be their prince for ever. *(This Passage goes back to the Messianic Promise of II Sam. 7:12-16. Some have concluded that the name 'David' refers to the Messiah; however, the Holy Spirit uses the phrase, 'My Servant David,' but never once is Christ called 'My Servant David.' So, it is obvious that King David is the one predicted here to be 'their prince forever.')*

A NEW AND EVERLASTING COVENANT

"Moreover I will make a Covenant of Peace with them; it shall be an Everlasting Covenant with them: and I will place them, and multiply them, and will set My Sanctuary in the midst of them for evermore. *(The setting of the 'Divine Sanctuary' in Jerusalem will cause the heathen to know that God has especially chosen Israel for His Peculiar Treasure. This Sanctuary is described in Ezek., Chpts. 40-48.)*

"My Tabernacle also shall be with them: yes, I will be their God, and they shall be My People. *(This 'Tabernacle' refers to an ozone type of covering, much greater than presently, which will be during the Millennium, when the light of the Sun will be increased sevenfold and the light of the moon will be as the present light of the Sun [Isa. 4:5].)*

"And the heathen shall know that I the LORD do sanctify Israel, when My Sanctuary shall be in the midst

of them for evermore. *(God's Presence with Israel is the sign that He is with them and that the world must, and in fact will, recognize this approval)"* **(Ezek. 37:1-28).**

The regathering of Israel and the Spiritual and material Restoration will be one of the greatest Miracles, if not the greatest, ever performed by our Lord. That's the reason that Satan will try to destroy Israel in the coming Great Tribulation. So much is said in the Bible about the restoration of these people that if the Evil One can prove those great Prophecies to be false, he will have won the day.

Some will ask the question, *"Cannot Satan read the Bible?"* Yes, he can, and it predicts his destruction; however, the truth is, he simply doesn't believe the Bible, even as most of the world does not believe it presently.

Concerning the things that will take place in the coming Kingdom Age, the following presents some of these wondrous Miracles that are going to be carried out on this Earth at that time.

THE LORD JESUS CHRIST

The great Prophet Isaiah said:

"The word that Isaiah the son of Amoz saw concerning Judah and Jerusalem. *(The word 'saw,' as used here by Isaiah, basically means the same thing as 'Vision.')*
"And it shall come to pass in the last days, that the mountain of the LORD's House shall be established in the top of the mountains, and shall be exalted above the hills; and all nations shall flow unto it *(Verses 2 through 4 in this Chapter correspond to Mic. 4:1-3. Micah's Prophecy was 17 years later than Isaiah's. Some wonder if the latter Prophet borrowed from the former, but this shows a want of intelligence. When God repeats a message, the repetition emphasizes its preciousness to Him and its importance to man.*

"In both of the Prophecies, Isaiah and Micah, the Lord reveals the character of the Kingdom He proposed to set up on the Earth; in the latter, it is repeated to the nations. All of this will take place in the coming Kingdom Age.)

NO MORE WAR

"And many people shall go and say, Come you, and let us go up to the mountain of the LORD, to the House of the God of Jacob; and He will teach us of His Ways, and we will walk in His Paths: for out of Zion shall go forth the Law, and the Word of the LORD from Jerusalem. *(The 'Law,' as referred to here, has no reference to the Law of Moses, but rather to instruction, direction, and teaching. Again, this is the coming Kingdom Age, when the Messiah, 'The Greater than Solomon,' will rule the world by Wisdom, Grace, and Love.)*
"And He shall judge among the nations, and shall rebuke many people: and they shall beat their swords into plowshares, and their spears into pruning hooks: nation shall not lift up sword against nation, neither shall they learn war anymore. *(The words, 'judge among,' should read 'arbitrate between', and 'rebuke' would have been better translated 'decide the disputes of.' Man's courts of arbitration are doomed to failure, but, to Messiah's Court, success is promised here)*" **(Isa. 2:1-4).**

THE RESTORATION OF ISRAEL
WILL BLESS THE WORLD

Psalm 67, of which we shall quote, contains a pertinent piece of information. It speaks of Israel fully restored, which will then occasion great blessing to the world. In other words, until Israel is in her rightful place as the Spiritual Leader of the world under Christ, the world will not be blessed. Psalm 67

tells us what will happen:

"**God be merciful unto us, and bless us; and cause His Face to shine upon us; Selah.** *(The 'shining of God's Face upon us' is one of the most beautiful Passages found in the Bible. It signifies the Blessings of God upon the person or the people in question.)*

THE WAY OF THE LORD

"**That Your Way may be known upon Earth, Your saving health among all nations.** *(The Prophetic Doctrine that the Salvation of the world depends upon the Restoration of Israel [Rom., Chpt. 11] is repeated in the last two Verses of this Psalm, as it is affirmed in these first two Verses. This repetition emphasizes its importance.)*

PRAISING THE LORD

"**Let the people praise You, O God; let all the people praise You** *(as prosperity covers the entirety of the Earth, and in every capacity, and we speak of the Kingdom Age, all the people will then definitely praise the Lord)*,

"**O let the nations be glad and sing for joy: for You shall judge the people righteously, and govern the nations upon Earth. Selah.** *(Many nations of the world presently are in deep poverty. All of that will change when Jesus rules and reigns Personally from Jerusalem.)*

"**Let the people praise You, O God; let all the people praise You.** *(This is a repetition of Ps. 67:3, given by the Holy Spirit in a double manner that all may know the significance that God places on His People praising Him.*

"*At this time, only a very small number of people throughout the Earth praise the Lord. In fact, only a small number in the Church praise the Lord. In the Millennial Kingdom, the entirety of the Earth ['all people'] shall 'praise You.')*

THE INCREASE

"Then shall the Earth yield her increase; and God, even our own God, shall bless us. *(A most remarkable revelation is given to us in this Passage. Much of the world presently is plagued by drought, famine, and starvation.*

"With Israel in her proper place, and the kingdoms of this world praising the Lord, then the 'Earth shall yield her increase,' and there shall be abundance for all!)

"God shall bless us; and all the ends of the Earth shall fear Him. *(To use an old Pentecostal phrase, 'It's Blessing Time!')*" (Ps. 67:1-7).

THE BLESSING OF THE LORD

"In that day shall the Branch of the LORD be beautiful and glorious, and the fruit of the Earth shall be excellent and comely for them who are escaped of Israel. *(This is the coming Millennial Reign. The phrase, 'are escaped of Israel,' refers to the remnant which shall escape the future Tribulation and the Battle of Armageddon. The 'Branch of the LORD' is Christ.)*

A HOLY PEOPLE

"And it shall come to pass, that he who is left in Zion, and he who remains in Jerusalem, shall be called holy, even everyone that is written among the living in Jerusalem *(Israel, after a long night of thousands of years, will finally come home, but at great price [Zech. 14:16-21])*:

THE SPIRIT OF BURNING

"When the Lord shall have washed away the filth of the daughters of Zion, and shall have purged the blood of Jerusalem from the midst thereof by the Spirit of

Judgment, and by the Spirit of Burning. *(This speaks of the conversion of the Remnant, immediately after the Battle of Armageddon and the Second Coming. Israel, at that time, will be Saved by accepting Jesus as Saviour.*

"The 'Spirit of Judgment' and the 'Spirit of Burning' have to do with the Office Work of the Holy Spirit. He will deal with Israel in Him bringing them to Christ in exactly the same manner that He has dealt with all men.)

GOD'S GLORY RESTORED

"And the LORD will create upon every dwelling place of Mount Zion, and upon her assemblies, a cloud and smoke by day, and the shining of a flaming fire by night: for upon all the glory shall be a defense. *(In that coming Glad Day, Jerusalem, and especially the Temple area, will be totally different from anything the world has ever known.*

"Hovering over Mount Zion will be a 'pillar of cloud by day' and 'fire by night,' which will be eternal symbols and manifestations of His Presence. As Ezekiel said, 'The LORD is there' [Ezek. 48:35].)

"And there shall be a tabernacle for a shadow in the daytime from the heat, and for a place of refuge, and for a covert from storm and from rain. *(All of this is Christ: the 'Tabernacle,' the 'Shadow,' the 'Place of Refuge,' and the 'Covert.'*

"All of this proves that Israel is going to be restored. In fact, the Church Age has almost come to its conclusion. It is being phased out, which will conclude with the Rapture, and Israel will then be restored [Rom., Chpt. 11])" **(Isa. 4:2-6).**

THE TYPE OF GOVERNMENT IN
THE COMING KINGDOM AGE

"And there shall come forth a Rod out of the stem

of Jesse, and a Branch shall grow out of his roots *(this Verse has to do with the Incarnation, with the balance of the Chapter referring to the glorious reign of Christ during the Millennium. The word 'Rod,' in this instance, refers to a 'tender branch,' which means a tender shoot sprouting out of the root of a dead, fallen tree, referring both to humanity in general and Israel in particular. Jesse was David's father, and through this family the Messiah would come; and so He did!)*:

THE SPIRIT OF THE LORD

"And the Spirit of the LORD shall rest upon Him *(upon Christ)*, **the Spirit of Wisdom and Understanding, the Spirit of Counsel and Might, the Spirit of Knowledge and of the Fear of the LORD** *(this proclaims the Perfection of the Holy Spirit in all His attributes listed here resting upon the Messiah)*;

"And shall make Him of quick understanding in the Fear of the LORD: and He shall not judge after the sight of His Eyes, neither reprove after the hearing of His Ears *(the words, 'quick understanding,' would probably have been better translated 'the breath of His nostrils shall be in the Fear of the LORD.' It suggests a disposition instinct with delight in God and fragrant with God [Gen. 8:21]. As a result, His Judgment of all things will be perfect)*:

RIGHTEOUSNESS

"But with Righteousness shall He judge the poor, and reprove with equity for the meek of the Earth: and He shall smite the Earth with the rod of His Mouth, and with the breath of His Lips shall He kill the wicked. *(The 'smiting of the Earth' might be better stated 'the oppressor of the land,' referring to the Antichrist. The word 'reprove'* *means 'to set right with equity' or 'to administer justice on behalf of the meek.')*

"And Righteousness shall be the girdle of His Loins, and Faithfulness the girdle of His Reins. *(This Verse presents Immanuel as Priest. The 'loins' speak of the physical, with the 'reins' speaking of the heart and, therefore, the Spiritual. For the first time, the human family in Christ will witness perfection. In fact, the Man Christ Jesus will be girdled with Perfection.)*

CONDITIONS DURING THE MILLENNIUM

"The wolf also shall dwell with the lamb, and the leopard shall lie down with the kid; and the calf and the young lion and the fatling together; and a little child shall lead them. *(The character and nature of the planet, including its occupants and even the animal creation, will revert to their posture as before the Fall.)*

"And the cow and the bear shall feed *(feed together)***; their young ones shall lie down together: and the lion shall eat straw like the ox.** *(This Passage plainly tells us that the carnivorous nature of the animal kingdom will be totally and eternally changed.)*

"And the sucking child shall play on the hole of the asp, and the weaned child shall put his hand on the cockatrice' den. *(Even though some of the curse will remain on the serpent in the Millennium, in that he continues to writhe in the dust, still, the deadly part will be removed [Gen. 3:14].)*

THE EXTENT OF MESSIAH'S REIGN

"They shall not hurt nor destroy in all My Holy Mountain: for the Earth shall be full of the Knowledge of the LORD, as the waters cover the sea. *(The 'Holy Mountain' refers to the dwelling place of Christ during the*

Kingdom Age, which will be Jerusalem. And from that vantage point shall go out the 'Knowledge of the LORD,' which will cover the entirety of the Earth.)

GENTILES

"And in that day there shall be a root of Jesse, which shall stand for an ensign of the people; to it shall the Gentiles seek: and His rest shall be glorious. *(The words, 'in that day,' as in most cases, refer to the Great Tribulation, the Battle of Armageddon, the Second Coming of the Lord, and the coming Kingdom Age.*

"The 'root of Jesse' refers to David and the Promise made by the Lord to David in II Sam., Chpt. 7. Hence, Christ is really the 'root of Jesse,' the Son of David)" **(Isa. 11:1-10).**

THE WORLD WILL BE CHANGED
IN THE COMING KINGDOM AGE

"The wilderness and the solitary place shall be glad for them; and the desert shall rejoice, and blossom as the rose. *(This pertains to the coming Kingdom Age. The previous Chapter, which was the first part of this Prophecy, proclaims the cause of all sorrow, pain, heartache, and destruction, which is sin and man's rebellion against God, which will be destroyed by the Lord Jesus Christ; this Chapter, the concluding part of the Prophecy, portrays what God can do in a heart and life that is yielded to Him. As the Spiritual Renewal takes place in hearts and lives, the material, economic, domestic, and physical renewal will take place over the entirety of the Earth.)*

THE EXCELLENCY OF OUR GOD

"It shall blossom abundantly, and rejoice even with

joy and singing: the glory of Lebanon shall be given unto it, the excellency of Carmel and Sharon, they shall see the Glory of the LORD, and the excellency of our God. *('The Glory of the LORD, and the excellency of our God' is the cause of the 'abundant blossoming' and the 'rejoicing even with joy and singing.')*

STRENGTH

"Strengthen you the weak hands, and confirm the feeble knees. *(With these exceeding great and precious Promises, the servants of Truth are commanded to strengthen trembling and apprehensive Believers. With the 'Glory of the LORD' now paramount, even the 'weak' gain 'strength,' and 'feeble knees' are no longer so.)*

"Say to them who are of a fearful heart, Be strong, fear not: behold, your God will come with vengeance, even God with a recompense; He will come and save you. *(This Passage expresses again the Doctrine of the Coming of the Lord Jesus Christ. As well, this Verse points to the period predicted in II Pet. 3:10 and Rev. 19:11-21. However, we greatly shortchange the Scriptures if we limit this Passage only to the Second Coming of Christ. Its words are pointed at every Child of God in every period.*

"The sentence, 'He will come and Save you,' actually says, 'He will come Himself to Save you.' There is One Alone Who can Save, and He must do it Himself; to do it, He must 'come to us.')

MIRACLES

"Then the eyes of the blind shall be opened, and the ears of the deaf shall be unstopped. *(Isa. 35:5-6 had a fulfillment in the Messiah's First Advent, but their moral and plenary fulfillment belong to His Second and future Advent. Christ did not work Miracles in His First Advent as mere wonders, but because it was predicted here that when He came, He would work Miracles of this nature; hence, His performing these particular Miracles proved Him to be the predicted Messiah. But His rejection postponed to the future the wonders and blessings of this entire Chapter.)*

STREAMS IN THE DESERT

"Then shall the lame man leap as an hart, and the tongue of the dumb sing: for in the wilderness shall waters break out, and streams in the desert. *(The entire complexion of that future Glad Day [the Millennium] will be changed. Sickness and disease will be at an end. 'Then' the 'lame man' will not only be able to walk, but will have such freedom of movement that he will be able to 'leap as an hart.' 'Then' the 'bound tongue' will not only be able to speak, but 'sing,' as well!*

"However, in the spiritual sense, this has even a greater meaning! Due to the Fall, men have been 'spiritually lame' as well as 'spiritually dumb.' 'Then' all such will 'dance in the Spirit' and 'sing His praises'!

"Due to the Fall, the world is a 'wilderness.' But at that time, the 'waters' and 'streams,' signifying the Holy Spirit, will make the 'desert blossom as the rose.')

SPRINGS OF WATER

"And the parched ground shall become a pool, and the thirsty land springs of water: in the habitation of dragons, where each lay, shall be grass with reeds and rushes. *('Jackals' make their home in the sandy desert. They will be banished and their haunts turned into verdant meadows. Many nations of the world presently cannot now feed themselves due to 'parched ground.' This Passage proclaims the fact that all the Earth will then* *become fertile. 'Springs of water' will burst through the desert floor, which will then be turned into a garden. Areas deserted and given over to desolation will then be 'fat pastures' grazed by cattle.)*

THE WAY OF HOLINESS

"And an highway shall be there, and a way, and it shall be called The Way of Holiness; the unclean shall not pass over it; but it shall be for those: the wayfaring men, though fools, shall not err therein. *(The Scripture definitely predicts a literal 'highway' that will be built from Egypt through Israel to Assyria [Isa. 11:6; 19:23-25]; however, these Passages do not refer to that particular 'highway,' but to 'The Way of Holiness.'*
"It is proclaimed by the Holy Spirit that the 'Way' is 'Holiness.' Holiness characterizes all that God is and does.)

THE REDEEMED

"No lion shall be there, nor any ravenous beast shall go up thereon, it shall not be found there; but the redeemed shall walk there *(such proclaims the Truth that Satan, as a 'roaring lion,' shall not have access to 'The Way of Holiness'; demon spirits, i.e., 'ravenous beasts' also 'shall not be found there'; therefore, the Victory that every true Child of God earnestly desires is found in 'The Way of Holiness.'*
"Its complete fulfillment portrays the Millennial Reign, when Satan and all his minions of darkness will be locked away; consequently, only the 'redeemed' shall occupy this 'highway'):

EVERLASTING JOY

"And the ransomed of the LORD shall return, and

come to Zion with songs and everlasting joy upon their
heads: they shall obtain joy and gladness, and sorrow
and sighing shall flee away. *(Isa. 35:8-10 can be summed
up by saying, 'The unclean shall not pass over it, for He
shall be with them walking in the way; so even the simple
shall not go astray therein.' It shall be the Way of the Lord
[Mal. 3:1] and, therefore, not only will His companion-
ship exclude evil and assure arrival, but it will protect
from peril.*

*"With such a Keeper on the way and such a harbor at
the close, it is not to be wondered at that the ransomed of the
Lord shall be characterized by songs, joy, and by gladness.*

*" 'Sorrow and sighing shall flee away,' that is, the bliss
of the redeemed shall not in the perfect state be liable to
be broken as was the innocent joy of Eden's Garden)"*
(Isa. 35:1-10).

Even though most every Old Testament Book mentions the
coming Kingdom Age in some way, still, it is Isaiah, whom we
have repeatedly quoted, who gives us the greatest information
concerning conditions in that coming Glad Day. In fact, he is
referred to as the Millennial Prophet. He was quoted by Jesus
more so than any other Old Testament Prophet.

WHAT TYPE OF PEOPLE WILL BE ON EARTH
DURING THE KINGDOM AGE?

In essence, there will be three types of people on Earth dur-
ing the Kingdom Age. They are:
• **The Glorified Saints of God.** This will include every
Believer from the time of Abel to the last person Saved in the
Great Tribulation. This is what Jesus referred to as the First
Resurrection of Life. He said:
*"For the hour is coming, in the which all who are in the
graves shall hear His Voice, and shall come forth; they who have
done good, unto the Resurrection of Life"* **(Jn. 5:28-29).**

He also said, *"Blessed and Holy is he who has part in the First Resurrection: on such the second death has no power, but they shall be Priests of God and of Christ, and shall reign with Him a thousand years"* (Rev. 20:6).

All of this means that every Saint of God will have part in the First Resurrection of Life and will, in turn, at the Resurrection, be given a Glorified Body. That's why Jesus said that those who have part in the First Resurrection are blessed. The following are some particulars about the Glorified Body:

1. The Glorified Body will be identical to that which Christ had after His Resurrection and which He will have forever (I Jn. 3:2).

2. The Glorified Body will be physical, meaning it is flesh and bone; however, there will be no blood (Lk. 24:39). Where now the life of the flesh is in the blood, then the life of the flesh will be in the Spirit, i.e., *"The Holy Spirit."*

3. The Glorified Body will be able to make itself visible or invisible (Jn. 20:19-20).

4. The Glorified Body will not be hindered by walls or doors (Jn. 20:26).

5. The Glorified Body, it seems, will be able to travel by the speed of thought. In other words, it will think where it wants to be and then, all of a sudden, it's there, and irrespective of the distance. Peter told us of the day, which will be at the conclusion of the Kingdom Age, when the heavens and the Earth will be renovated by fire, in other words, made anew. At that time, all the Saints of God, plus everyone else on Earth, will have to be taken to Heaven, the Abode of God. While the Saints living on Earth at that time will be taken there by the Power of God, all the Saints with Glorified Bodies will go there simply by the speed of thought (II Pet. 3:10-13). While this will be unique for the ordinary Saints, it will be commonplace for those with Glorified Bodies.

6. While those with Glorified Bodies will be able to eat and drink as always, still, there is no indication that such is needed for the sustenance of life. Whereas blood was once the life of

the flesh, now, as stated, it is the Holy Spirit Who is the life of the flesh (Lk. 24:41-43).

As stated, the Glorified Body will be received at the Resurrection (Rapture). The Scripture says:

"... And the dead *(Sainted dead)* shall be raised incorruptible, and we shall be changed.

"For this corruptible must put on incorruption *(a Glorified Body with no sin nature)*, and this mortal *(subject to death)* **must** put on immortality *(will never die)*" (I Cor. 15:52-53).

7. As well, and as just stated, the Glorified Body will never age or die.

8. John said:

"... And it does not yet appear what we shall be *(our present state as a 'son of God' is not at all like that we shall be in the coming Resurrection)*: but we know that, when He shall appear *(the Rapture)*, we shall be like Him *(speaks of being Glorified)*; for we shall see Him as He is" (I Jn. 3:2).

Jesus died and was resurrected at 33 years of age. One might say that is the perfect age. So, understanding that we shall be like Him, this means that every Believer who has had a part in the First Resurrection will be 33 years of age. This means that every baby and every child who died before reaching the age of accountability, and every baby and every child below the age of accountability in believing homes when the Rapture takes place, will be changed and, thereby, changed to full maturity, i.e., *"33 years of age."*

• There will be millions of people who will come out of the Great Tribulation and will give their hearts and lives to Christ during the Kingdom Age. While these will be given Eternal Life, there is no record that they will be given Glorified

Bodies. In other words, they will not have had a part in the First Resurrection of Life. That's why Jesus said, *"Blessed is he who has part in the First Resurrection"* (Rev. 20:6). These individuals, which will, no doubt, number into many millions, will most definitely be Saved, at least those who accept Christ, and will enjoy the privileges of Eternal Life, but will not have a Glorified Body. During the Kingdom Age, these Saints will continue to marry and have children, just as people do now. Glorified Saints will not marry and, therefore, will not have children. Concerning this, Jesus said:

"The children of this world marry, and are given in marriage: but they which shall be accounted worthy to obtain that world, and the Resurrection from the dead, neither marry, nor are given in marriage: neither can they die anymore: for they are equal unto the Angels; and are the Children of God, being the Children of the Resurrection" (Lk. 20:34-36).

• The third group of people who will be on Earth during the Kingdom Age will be those who will not give their hearts and lives to Christ. It is almost unthinkable that such will be, especially considering that Satan and all fallen Angels and demon spirits are locked up in the bottomless pit, still, many will not accept Christ. They will be forced to obey the Law, but not forced to live for God. If they continue in that state, in other words, continuing to refuse Christ, they will lose their souls, with the conclusion being the Lake of Fire, where all other unbelievers will be consigned, along with Satan, fallen Angels, and demon spirits.

The Scripture doesn't tell us how many there will be of these individuals, but it does say the following:

Satan will be loosed out of his prison (the bottomless pit) for a short period of time at the conclusion of the Kingdom Age. The Scripture says that he *"shall go out to deceive the nations which are in the four quarters of the Earth, Gog and Magog, to gather them together to battle: the number of whom is as the sand of the sea"* (Rev. 20:8). No doubt, this number will be into the millions.

The main reason the Lord allows Satan this latitude is, it seems, to rid the Earth of all who oppose Christ; George Williams says:

"*The Creation Sabbath witnessed the first seduction, and the Millennial Sabbath will witness the last*"; the "*Gog and Magog*" spoken of by John is a Hebrew term expressive of multitude and magnitude; here it embraces all nations, "*the four quarters of the Earth.*" (George Williams, *The Students Commentary on the Holy Scriptures*, Grand Rapids, Kregel Publications, 1949, pg. 1054.)

The Scripture gives us no details whatsoever concerning this conflict, except to say, "*and fire came down from God out of Heaven, and devoured them*" (Rev. 20:9). As stated, this will take place at the very conclusion of the Kingdom Age and before the New Heavens and the New Earth.

WHAT ROLE WILL ISRAEL PLAY IN THE COMING KINGDOM AGE?

Israel, at that time, will be the leading nation in the world. In fact, it will be the Priestly nation. David will be its king and will be forever, all under the Lord Jesus Christ Who will reign personally from Jerusalem.

While Israel presently is about the size of the State of New Jersey, then it will be at least one hundred times larger. Its eastern boundary will be the River Euphrates, which means that part of Iraq will then be a part of the State of Israel. Its northern boundary will be Syria, which will include that country. Its southern boundary will be the Suez Canal, which takes in the Sinai plus the Arabian Peninsula, with the Persian Gulf being its extreme southeastern border. Considering that the Arabian Peninsula is now almost all desert, but then will be turned into a verdant garden, this will make Israel the most productive country in the world. It will be at least one hundred times larger then than now.

Chapters 40 through 48 of Ezekiel tell us of the duties of Israel during that coming time. In fact, and as stated, Israel will be the Priestly nation of the world.

WHY IS ISRAEL SO IMPORTANT?

Israel is so important because of the Promises that God made to Abraham.

The world during the time of Abraham was so taken up with the powers of darkness that, anymore, it had no knowledge or semblance of God. In fact, all the nations of the world of that time worshipped idols, i.e., *"demon spirits."* So, for the Lord to bring the Redeemer into the world, the Lord Jesus Christ, He would have to raise up a people who would trust Him and have Faith in Him. Those people would be the Jews, with their beginning in the loins of Abraham and the womb of Sarah. From this source He would raise up a nation of people who would be different than any people on the face of the Earth, and because they would be called by the Name of God, i.e., *"Jehovah."*

This was all necessary for Redemption. For man to be redeemed, a man would have to carry out this great task. The trouble was that all were fallen and, thereby, unqualified. So, for man to be redeemed, God would have to become Man, which He did, and we speak of the Lord Jesus Christ. But, although He would be born like any other child, He would be conceived not by an Earthly man, but by the Holy Spirit. This simply means that the Holy Spirit, in essence, said, *"Let there be . . .,"* and it was (Mat. 1:18; Lk. 1:26-35). For this to be, a people would have to be raised up for this very purpose. As stated, that people would come from the loins of Abraham and the womb of Sarah.

ABRAHAM

How that Abraham came to know the Lord, we aren't told. Some believe that it could have been Shem, Noah's son, who witnessed to him, and this very well could have been; however, there is no Scriptural proof one way or the other.

We do know that the family of Abraham was idol worshippers. Actually, the Jewish Targums state that not only was his family a worshipper of idols, but, as well, they manufactured these idols. In fact, Ur of the Chaldees was one of the most advanced cities in the world of its day. Somehow, the Word of the Lord came to Abraham and with such force and power that he would set out to obey what was demanded of him.

The following is the Abrahamic Covenant which has everything to do with the station and position of Israel and her importance in the mind of God as it regards the future. As a side issue, we learn from all of this how that God keeps His Word, and no matter how hard it might be to bring it to pass.

THE ABRAHAMIC COVENANT

"Now the LORD had said unto Abram *(referring to the Revelation which had been given to the Patriarch a short time before; this Chapter is very important, for it records the first steps of this great Believer in the path of Faith)*, Get thee out of your country *(separation)*, and from your kindred *(separation)*, and from your father's house *(separation)*, unto a land that I will show you *(refers to the fact that Abraham had no choice in the matter; he was to receive his orders from the Lord, and go where those orders led him)*:

A GREAT NATION

"And I will make of you a great Nation *(the Nation which God made of Abraham has changed the world, and exists even unto this hour; in fact, this Nation 'Israel' still has a great part to play, which will take place in the coming Kingdom Age)*, and I will bless you, and make your name great *(according to Scripture, 'to bless' means 'to increase'; the builders of the Tower of Babel sought to 'make us a name,' whereas God took this man, who forsook all, and 'made his name great')*; **and you shall be a blessing:** *(Concerns itself with the greatest blessing of all. It is the glory of Abraham's Faith. God would give this man the meaning of Salvation, which is 'Justification by Faith,' which would come about through the Lord Jesus Christ, and what Christ would do on the Cross. Concerning this, Jesus said of Abraham, 'Your father Abraham rejoiced to see My Day: and he saw it, and was glad' [Jn. 8:56].)*

IN YOU SHALL ALL FAMILIES
OF THE EARTH BE BLESSED

"And I will bless them who bless you *(to bless Israel, or any Believer, for that matter, guarantees the Blessings of God)*, **and curse him who curses you** *(to curse Israel, or any Believer, guarantees that one will be cursed by God)*: **and in you shall all families of the Earth be blessed.** *(It speaks of Israel, which sprang from the loins of Abraham and the womb of Sarah, giving the world the Word of God and, more particularly, bringing the Messiah into the world. Through Christ, every family in the world who desires blessing from God can have that Blessing, i.e., 'Justification by Faith')*" **(Gen. 12:1-3).**

THE SEED

The Covenant also stated:

"As for Me, behold, My Covenant is with you, and you shall be a father of many nations.

"Neither shall your name anymore be called Abram *(which means 'exalted father')*, **but your name shall be Abraham** *('father of the multitudes')*; **for a father of many nations have I made you.**

"And I will make you exceeding fruitful, and I will make nations of you, and kings shall come out of you *(He was saying to the Patriarch, and as stated, that He was able, whatever the need).*

"And I will establish My Covenant between Me and you and your seed after you in their generations for an Everlasting Covenant *(that means this Covenant is valid even to this moment and, in fact, ever will be; the Palestinians should learn that),* to be a God unto you, and to your seed after you *(this Covenant is linked to 'Justification by Faith,' which means that it is now a part of the New Covenant, which is also referred to as 'The Everlasting Covenant' [Heb. 13:20]).*

THE LAND OF CANAAN

"And I will give unto you, and to your seed after you, the land wherein you are a stranger, all the land of Canaan, for an everlasting possession; and I will be their God. *(The Jews, having forfeited their possession through rebellion against God, and especially their rejection of Jesus Christ, have caused a rupture; however, the Covenant still stands, and will come to full bloom in the coming Kingdom Age, which is not long off)"* (Gen. 17:4-8).

ISAAC

Abraham wanted Ishmael to be the principal one, in other words, that everything would go to Ishmael upon the death of Abraham, but the Lord said otherwise. The Scripture says:

"And God said unto Abraham, Let it not be grievous in your sight because of the lad, and because of your bondwoman; in all that Sarah has said unto you, hearken unto her voice; for in Isaac shall your seed be

called. *(It is labor lost to seek to make a crooked thing straight. Hence, all efforts after the improvement of nature are utterly futile, so far as God is concerned. The 'flesh' must go, which typifies the personal ability, strength, and efforts of the Believer, of which Ishmael was a result. The efforts of Abraham and Sarah to bring an heir into the world resulted in Ishmael, which was a work of the flesh, which God could not accept.*

"The Faith of the Believer must be entirely in Christ and what Christ has done at the Cross. Then, and then alone, can the Holy Spirit have latitude to work in our lives, bringing forth perpetual Victory [Rom. 6:14]. It must ever be understood, 'in Isaac [in Christ] shall your seed be called.')

ISLAM

"And also of the son of the bondwoman will I make a nation, because he is your seed. *(Out of this 'work of the flesh' ultimately came the religion of Islam, which claims that Ishmael is the promised seed, and not Isaac)"* **(Gen. 21:12-13).**

THE PROMISE

The reason that Israel is so important is because God made a promise to Abraham. Through many dangers, toils, and snares, Abraham kept his part of the Covenant, and to be sure, the Lord has kept, and will keep, His part of the Covenant. That's the reason Israel is so important!

WILL THERE BE SICKNESS AND DEATH ON EARTH DURING THE KINGDOM AGE?

Yes, there will be death during the Kingdom Age, but it will be in a very limited way. I think one can say from the Scriptures that there will be no sickness whatsoever on the Earth during the Kingdom Age. Concerning sickness, the Scripture tells us of a literal River that will have its origin under the newly built Temple in Jerusalem. It will flow out *"from under the right side of the House, at the south side of the Altar"* (Ezek. 47:1).

As the River goes forward, it will increase in depth and width, and at a given point, will divide, with part going to the Dead Sea, which will heal those waters, and the other part going to the Mediterranean.

The Scripture continues by saying, *"Behold, at the bank of the River were very many trees on the one side and on the other"* (Ezek. 47:7).

Considering that this literal River will flow into both the Mediterranean and the Dead Sea, which is a distance of approximately 50 miles from one to the other, and considering that trees will grow on both sides of this River, this means that there will be approximately 100 miles of trees.

To be sure, this River will have healing properties far beyond that which is normal. The Scripture says:

"And it shall come to pass, that everything that lives, which moves, whithersoever the Rivers shall come, shall live: and there shall be a very great multitude of fish, because these waters shall come thither: for they shall be healed *(this means the Dead Sea will be healed, meaning that now it will be filled with a great multitude of fish)*; and everything shall live whither the River comes" (Ezek. 47:9).

THE MEDICINE

And then the Scripture says:

"And by the River upon the bank thereof, on this side and on that side, shall grow all trees for meat, whose leaf shall not fade, neither shall the fruit thereof be consumed: it shall bring forth new fruit according to his months, because their waters they issued out of the Sanctuary: and the fruit thereof shall be for meat, and the leaf thereof for medicine. *(Now Ezekiel is shown the purpose of these miracle Trees which grow on either side of this River. These 'Trees' shall perpetually bring forth new fruit because they are nourished by waters issuing from the Sanctuary. The fruit will heal as well as nourish. Such is the character of a Life and Ministry based upon Calvary, and energized by the Holy Spirit.*

"In fact, the population of the world [which will include all, with the exception of the Glorified Saints] will continue to live perpetually by the means of the 'fruit' and the 'leaf' of these Trees. In other words, the aging process will be halted, with all sickness eliminated, and because of this 'medicine.' Glorified Saints will not need such)" (Ezek. 47:12).

THAT BEING THE CASE, HOW WILL THERE BE DEATH?

There will not be death due to the aging process or sickness, but only by execution. In other words, if individuals, during the time of the Kingdom Age, will not serve God and try to take peace from the Earth by rebelling against the Lord, they, no doubt, will be warned; however, if they fail to heed the warning, they will be executed.

ACCURSED

The great Prophet Isaiah also addressed himself to this situation. He said:

"There shall be no more thence an infant of days, nor an old man who has not filled his days: for the child shall die an hundred years old; but the sinner being

an hundred years old shall be accursed. *(During the coming Millennium, the Redeemed, with Glorified Bodies, and even those who have given their hearts to Christ at that time, as stated, will experience no death whatsoever. Even among the unredeemed, longevity of life, possibly even for hundreds of years, will be restored.*

"'But the sinner being an hundred years old shall be accursed,' means that any person living at that time who hasn't given his heart and life to Christ by the time he is 100 years old will be 'accursed,' meaning that, in all likelihood, he will not be Saved.)

ENJOY THE FRUIT OF THEIR LABOR

"And they shall build houses, and inhabit them; and they shall plant vineyards, and eat the fruit of them. *(This proves that ordinary natural life and living conditions on the Earth will continue in the Millennium. The idea of this Passage is that work and labor will bring forth fruit and not be cut off by death, sickness, or sin, as at the present. Men, then, can build, construct, labor, and enjoy the fruit of their labor.)*

"They shall not build, and another inhabit; they shall not plant, and another eat: for as the days of a tree are the days of My People, and My Elect shall long enjoy the work of their hands. *('My Elect,' speaks of Israel, but also, of all who have accepted Christ as their Saviour. 'Shall long enjoy the work of their hands,' actually speaks of eternity. The 'enjoyment' will never cease.*

"'For as the days of a tree are the days of My People,' refers to the longevity of certain types of trees, which are actually thousands of years old.

EXECUTED

"As is alluded to in this Passage, death will continue

through the 1,000-year Reign of Christ on Earth, but only for those who refuse to accept Christ and who commit sins worthy of death. If such is the case, as stated, they will be executed for the 'Law will go forth from Zion and the Word of the LORD from Jerusalem' [Isa. 2:3].)

TROUBLE WILL CEASE

"They shall not labor in vain, nor bring forth for trouble; for they are the seed of the blessed of the LORD, and their offspring with them. *(The phrase, 'their off-spring with them,' tells us that children will be born during the Kingdom Age, and actually will be born forever, even in the 'new Earth.' This will not pertain to the Glorified Saints, but rather to the Redeemed who are not Glorified, meaning they didn't have part in the First Resurrection, but will keep alive[1] forever by means of the Tree of Life [Rev. 22:1-3]. These will bring forth offspring.)*

INSTANT ANSWER TO PRAYER

"And it shall come to pass, that before they call, I will answer; and while they are yet speaking, I will hear. *(This Scripture proclaims the Truth that Christ will be the One Who will solve all problems, answer all questions, meet all needs, and right all wrongs. The answer will not be delayed, hindered, or denied!)*

THE NATURE OF THE ANIMAL KINGDOM WILL BE CHANGED

"The wolf and the lamb shall feed together, and the lion shall eat straw like the bullock: and dust shall be the serpent's meat. They shall not hurt nor destroy in all My Holy Mountain, says the LORD. *(Rom. 8:19-22 is based upon the last Verse of this Chapter. The animal* *creation will enjoy the beneficence of the Messiah's Government; but the serpent, i.e., Satan, shall be made to 'eat the dust.' This is a fine and striking idiom expressing his perpetual impotency and degradation [the language is figurative]. However, the snake, even though not having the curse lifted completely, will be rendered harmless, and instead of preying upon beasts, birds, or reptiles, shall be content with the food assigned it in the primeval decree.*

"*'They shall not hurt nor destroy in all My Holy Mountain, says the LORD,' is repeated from Isa. 11:9 word for word. In either case, we should not regard the subject of the sentence as limited to the animals only. The meaning is that there shall be no violence of any kind, done either by man or beast, in the happy period described)*" **(Isa. 65:20-25).**

WHY WILL THE SACRIFICIAL SYSTEM BE REINSTITUTED?

Yes, the Sacrificial System of little lambs and other types of clean animals will be reinstituted and practiced (Ezek. 40:39-43; 43:18).

Why?

Although reinstituted, as under the Old Covenant, the sacrifices do not now take away sin any more than they did then (Heb. 10:4). The sacrifices are merely symbolic and are meant to portray the Great Sacrifice made by Christ at Calvary. This is to never be forgotten. The daily offering of the sacrifices will be a constant ritual during the Kingdom Age so that the entire world will never forget.

That which Saved man, the shed Blood of Jesus Christ at Calvary, did not come cheaply or easily; therefore, it is thought of so highly in the Mind of God, and rightly so, that the never-ending repetition of sacrifices will constantly be offered as an ongoing reminder.

THE SIN OFFERING AND THE BURNT OFFERING

The great Book of Leviticus tells us that the Burnt Offering preceded the Sin Offering; in the coming Kingdom Age, it is reversed. Then, Faith praised in looking forward to the Sin Offering of Calvary; in the future day, Faith will praise looking back to Calvary. Thus, the great Sin Offering of the Lamb of God stands in the midst of the ages and is preceded and followed by praise.

Actually, there will be no Day of Atonement in Millennial Worship for the sacrifices then will recall the One All-Sufficing Atonement perfected at Golgotha.

The *"salt"* placed on the offerings typifies the fact that all of this is according to the Word of God.

WITHOUT BLEMISH

In the Kingdom Age, as under the Law and before, animals brought for sacrifice must not be animals that have died of natural causes or been killed by beasts, but instead, the healthiest of the healthy. Calvary, of which all of this was a Type, will be shown to be the Divine Center of God's Purposes of Grace and Wrath.

THE FEASTS OF PASSOVER
AND TABERNACLES

Ezekiel 45:21-25 portrays these two Feasts which will be kept every year in the coming Kingdom Age.

The two Feasts of Passover and Tabernacles will be marked by sevenfold offerings in contrast to the twofold ones of Leviticus. This is because these offerings will testify to the perfection of the cleansing for sin fulfilled at Calvary.

The character of worship in that future day and the sense of the sufficiency of Christ's Sacrifice of Himself as the Sin Offering and the Burnt Offering will be perfect. Thus, these two Feasts will celebrate the perfection and sufficiency of the

Atoning Work of Christ. Together with the Feasts of the Sabbath and the New Moon, they testify to the fulfillment of God's Promises to Israel in bringing them into rest and making them to be a light to the Gentiles (Isa., Chpts. 60, 66).

WILL EVERYONE BE FORCED TO LIVE FOR GOD IN THE KINGDOM AGE?

No!

In fact, those who do not accept Christ as Saviour and Lord, and there will be some who fall into that category, will not be forced to live for God, but they will be forced to serve the Lord. In other words, they will not be allowed to break the Laws of Righteousness which will envelop the entirety of the Earth in that day.

While most, no doubt, will come to Christ and be everlastingly Saved, the indication is that some will not.

The Scripture says that that *"number of whom is as the sand of the sea"* (Rev. 20:8). Compared to the entirety of the world at that time, perhaps the percentage will be small; however, that *"number"* could very well include many millions.

All of this portrays the incurable evil of the human heart. Think about it!

During the coming Kingdom Age, Satan, along with his fallen Angels and demon spirits, will be locked away in the bottomless pit. That means there will be no more temptation, at least as far as the Evil One is concerned. As well, the entirety of the world will know peace, prosperity and freedom as never before. In other words, the Lord will show the entirety of Planet Earth during that time what it could have been like all along but for sin. And, yet, in the midst of this worldwide prosperity, this worldwide freedom, this worldwide peace, still, some will not accept Christ as Savior and Lord.

As to the why of such a direction, one would have to ask as to why Abel served the Lord while his brother Cain didn't! One would have to ask as to why Jacob loved the Lord while his twin brother, Esau, didn't!

Man is a free moral agent. As such, he is free to serve the Lord or to reject the Lord. While the Lord will speak to men, deal with them, and move upon their hearts, still, He will not force men to live for Him. That must be of one's own free, moral choice. The Scripture still says, *"For whosoever shall call upon the Name of the Lord shall be Saved"* (Rom. 10:13).

"Whosoever" covers every individual. So, the Salvation Plan is before man. He has the capacity to either accept or reject. Only the Lord knows the reasons people reject the greatest life eternity has ever known. It is all in Christ.

"Nothing between my soul and the Saviour,
"Naught of this world's delusive dream;
"I have renounced all sinful pleasure,
"Jesus is mine; there's nothing between."

"Nothing between my soul and the Saviour,
"So that His Blessed Face may be seen;
"Nothing preventing the least of His Favor,
"Keep the way clear! Let nothing between."

"Nothing between, like worldly pleasure,
"Habits of life though harmless they seem,
"Must not my heart from Him ever sever,
"He is my all; there's nothing between."

"Nothing between, like pride or station,
"Self or friends shall not intervene,
"Though it may cost me much tribulation,
"I am resolved; there's nothing between."

"Nothing between, even many hard trials,
"Though the whole world against me convene;
"Watching with prayer and much self-denial,
"I'll triumph at last, with nothing between."

CHAPTER SEVEN

What Is The Perfect Age To Come?

QUESTION:

WHAT IS THE PERFECT AGE TO COME?

ANSWER:

• The account of this time, which will be without end, i.e., *"eternal,"* is found in the last two Chapters of the Book of Revelation.

• It will be the time when God will move His Headquarters, so to speak, from Heaven to Earth.

• Satan, all fallen Angels, and all demon spirits, plus every person who has rejected Christ, will be banished to the Lake of Fire forever and forever. In other words, in this Perfect Age, there will be no sin or sinners.

• The description given in the last two Chapters of Revelation concerning this coming time is filled with such phenomenal statements regarding what this time will be like as to defy all description.

• The way the Holy Spirit describes this coming time, which we will address more directly momentarily, lets us know that all of this is possible because of what Jesus did at the Cross of Calvary. We must never forget that!

THE BRIDGE

From the conclusion of the Kingdom Age to the beginning of the Perfect Age, several things will take place, which are of great consequence. They are:

• At the very end of the Kingdom Age Satan and, no doubt, his fallen Angels and demon spirits as well, will be loosed from the bottomless pit where they have been incarcerated for the past 1,000 years. Concerning this, the Scripture says:

"And when the thousand years are expired *(should have been translated, 'finished')*, **Satan shall be loosed**

out of his prison *(is not meant to infer a mere arbitrary act on the part of God; He has a very valid reason for doing this)*,

"And shall go out to deceive the nations which are in the four quarters of the Earth, Gog and Magog *(the main reason the Lord allows Satan this latitude is, it seems, to rid the Earth of all who oppose Christ; George Williams says: 'The Creation Sabbath witnessed the first seduction, and the Millennial Sabbath will witness the last'; the 'Gog and Magog' spoken of by John is a Hebrew term expressive of multitude and magnitude; here it embraces all nations, 'the four quarters of the Earth'),* **to gather them together to battle: the number of whom** *is* **as the sand of the sea** *(proclaims the fact that virtually all of the population at that particular time, which did not accept Christ during the Kingdom Age, will throw in their lot with Satan)*.

FIRE FROM HEAVEN

"And they went up on the breadth of the Earth, and compassed the camp of the Saints about, and the beloved city *(pictures Satan coming against Jerusalem with his army, which will be the last attack against that city)*: **and fire came down from God out of Heaven, and devoured them.** *(Stipulates that the Lord will make short work of this insurrection. In fact, very little information is given regarding this event, as is obvious.)*

THE LAKE OF FIRE

"And the Devil who deceived them was cast into the Lake of Fire and Brimstone *(marks the end of Satan regarding his influence in the world, and, in fact, in any part of the Creation of God)*, **where the Beast and the False Prophet** *are* *(proclaims the fact that these two were placed in 'the Lake of Fire and Brimstone' some one thousand*

years earlier [Rev. 19:20]), **and shall be tormented day
and night forever and ever.** *(This signifies the Eternity of
this place. It is a matter of interest to note that Satan's first
act is recorded in Gen., Chpt. 3 [the third Chapter from
the beginning], whereas his last act on a worldwide scale
is mentioned in Rev., Chpt. 20 [the third Chapter from the
end)"* **(Rev. 20:7-10).**

We are given very little information regarding this insurrection, except that it will be very short-lived.

THE GREAT WHITE THRONE JUDGMENT

At this point the Great White Throne Judgment will
convene.
• Jesus Christ will be the Judge. The Scripture says, *"For
the Father judges no man, but has committed all Judgment unto
the Son"* (Jn. 5:22).
• Whether this Judgment will be carried out in Heaven
or Earth, the Scripture doesn't say; however, it will probably
be Earth.
• No Saved person will be at this Judgment. Only the
unsaved will be there, which will include every unredeemed
person who has ever lived.
• The reason for this Judgment is to show all the unredeemed that the Judgment pronounced is fair and equal.
They will be judged from the Books where God keeps a record
of every sin committed, unless the sin is washed clean by the
Blood of Jesus Christ. There will be no reprieves at this Judgment. The Scripture says regarding this time:

THE LORD JESUS CHRIST

"And I saw a Great White Throne *(proclaims the
final Judgment of the unredeemed, which will take place
at the end of the Kingdom Age)*, **and Him Who sat on it**

(proclaims none other than God; however, we must under-stand that it is the Person of the Godhead, the Lord Jesus Christ [Mat. 25:31]; He is the Saviour today; He will be the Judge tomorrow), **from Whose Face the Earth and the Heaven fled away; and there was found no place for them.** *(This means a New Heaven and New Earth are in the offing.)*

ALL UNREDEEMED WILL STAND BEFORE GOD

"And I saw the dead, small and great, stand before God *(pertains to the second Resurrection, the Resurrec-tion of Damnation [I Cor., Chpt. 15; I Thess. 4:13-18; Jn. 5:29])*; **and the Books were opened: and another Book was opened, which is** *the Book* **of Life: and the dead were Judged out of those things which were writ-ten in the Books, according to their works** *(proclaims the manner of Judgment)*.

THE JUDGMENT

"And the sea gave up the dead which were in it; and death and Hell delivered up the dead which were in them *(points to the fact that every unredeemed person who has ever lived will face the Great White Throne Judg-ment; none will be exempted)*: **and they were Judged every man according to their works** *(records the fact that this Judgment is not arbitrary, but is based on abso-lute Justice)*.

THE LAKE OF FIRE

"And death and Hell were cast into the Lake of Fire *(combined, includes the wicked of all ages)*. **This is the second death** *(eternal separation from God and the Lake of Fire)*.

"And whosoever was not found written in the Book
of Life *(refers to the record of all the Redeemed)* was
cast into the Lake of Fire. *(This includes every single
individual who isn't Redeemed, beginning with Adam
and Eve. That is, if they didn't come back to God)*" (Rev.
20:11-15).

THE RENOVATION OF THE HEAVENS AND THE EARTH

We are told by the Holy Spirit through Simon Peter that at
the conclusion of the Kingdom Age the Lord is going to renovate the heavens and the Earth with fire, in other words, to
cleanse it.

More than likely, at that time the Lord will transfer all
on Planet Earth to Heaven while the Earth is being cleansed.
The word *"heavens"* probably refers to the starry space and
not Heaven itself, but if, in fact, Heaven, the abode of God, is
included, then all will have to be transported back to Earth during that particular time. Concerning this, the Scripture says:

FIRE

"But the Day of the Lord will come as a thief in the
night *(the conclusion of the Millennium; what will happen at that time will be unexpected, and for a variety of
reasons)*; in the which the Heavens shall pass away with
a great noise, and the elements shall melt with fervent
heat, the Earth also and the works that are therein shall
be burned up. *(This does not speak of annihilation, but
rather, passing from one condition to another.)*

THE DAY OF GOD

"*Seeing* then *that* all these things shall be dissolved
(the present is temporal), what manner *of persons* ought

ye to be in *all* **Holy conversation** *(lifestyle)* **and Godliness** *(pertains to the correct view of things)*,

"**Looking for and hasting unto the Coming of the Day of God** *(concerns the Coming Eternal, Perfect Earth, which will last in that condition forever and forever)*, **wherein the Heavens being on fire shall be dissolved, and the elements shall melt with fervent heat?** *('The Day of God' will be ushered in by the cataclysmic events of this Verse. There must be no sin left in the Universe.)*

"**Nevertheless we** *(Believers)*, **according to His Promise** *(the Lord has Promised that a new day is coming [Isa. 65:17])*, **look for new Heavens** *(this is the Promise!)* **and a new Earth, wherein dwells Righteousness.** *(This proclaims the condition of the Coming 'New Heavens and New Earth' [Rev., Chpts. 21-22])*" **(II Pet. 3:10-13).**

THE NEW HEAVENS AND THE NEW EARTH

"**And I saw a New Heaven and a New Earth** *('New' in the Greek is 'kainos,' and means 'freshness with respect to age'; when it is finished, it will be new, as is obvious, but the idea is it will remain new and fresh forever and forever because there is no more sin)*: **for the first Heaven and the first Earth were passed away** *(refers to the original Creation, which was marred by sin; 'passed away' in the Greek is 'parerchomai,' and means 'to pass from one condition to another'; it never means annihilation)*; **and there was no more sea** *(refers to the giant oceans, such as the Pacific and the Atlantic; however, there will continue to be lakes, bodies of water, rivers, streams, etc.).*

NEW JERUSALEM

"**And I John saw the Holy City, New Jerusalem** *(presents a New City for this New Earth)*, **coming down from God out of Heaven** *(in effect, God will change His*

Headquarters from Heaven to Earth), **prepared as a Bride adorned for her husband** *(proclaims the Eternal Home of the Redeemed as a dwelling place)*.

GOD WILL DWELL WITH MAN

"And I heard a great Voice out of Heaven saying *(according to the best manuscripts, the Voice now heard was heard 'out of the Throne')*, **Behold, the Tabernacle of God *is* with men, and He will dwell with them, and they shall be His people, and God Himself shall be with them, *and be* their God.** *(Finally proclaims that which God intended from the beginning.)*

NO MORE SORROW

"And God shall wipe away all tears from their eyes *(actually says in the Greek, 'every teardrop,' and refers to tears of sorrow)*; **and there shall be no more death, neither sorrow, nor crying, neither shall there be any more pain** *(addresses sin and all its results)*: **for the former things are passed away** *(refers to the entire effect of the Fall)*.

TRUE AND FAITHFUL

"And He Who sat upon the Throne said *(presents, for the second time in this Book, God Himself as the Speaker)*, **Behold, I make all things new** *(refers to the fact of changing from one condition to another)*. **And He said unto me, Write: for these words are true and faithful.** *(All said is 'true,' and God will be 'faithful' to bring it all to pass as well.)*

ALPHA AND OMEGA

"And He said unto me, It is done. I am Alpha and Omega, the beginning and the end. *(The mighty declaration*

'Finished' heard at the morning of Creation, at Calvary, and now repeated here for the last time, closes all Prophecy. What He began, He now finishes.) **I will give unto him who is athirst of the fountain of the Water of Life freely.** *(This statement doesn't pertain to the coming Perfect Age, for all then will have the Water of Life, but rather, to the present. This 'fountain of the Water of Life' is tied directly to the Cross of Calvary in that it is free to all who will believe [Jn. 3:16].)*

THE OVERCOMER

"He who overcomes shall inherit all things *(the only way one can overcome is to place one's Faith exclusively in the Cross of Christ, which gives the Holy Spirit latitude to work in one's life, bringing about the Fruit of the Spirit)***; and I will be his God, and he shall be My son.** *(The overcomer is adopted into the Family of God and God treats him as a son, exactly as He does His Son, the Lord Jesus Christ.)*

THE LAKE OF FIRE

"But the fearful, and unbelieving, and the abominable, and murderers, and whoremongers, and sorcerers, and idolaters, and all liars *(all of this corresponds with the 'works of the flesh,' as outlined in Gal. 5:19-21)***, shall have their part in the lake which burns with fire and brimstone: which is the second death** *(proclaims the eternal destiny of Christ-rejecters).*

NEW JERUSALEM

"And there came unto me one of the seven Angels which had the seven Vials full of the seven last plagues, and talked with me, saying, Come hither, I will show

you the Bride, the Lamb's Wife. *(By use of the word 'Lamb,' we are taken back to the Cross, which has made all of this possible.)*

"And he carried me away in the Spirit to a great and high mountain *(the 'Spirit' referred to here is the Holy Spirit)*, and showed me that great city, the Holy Jerusalem, descending out of Heaven from God *(John saw it 'descending,' meaning that it is coming down to Earth; this will be after the Lord has made the 'New Heavens and New Earth,' in fact, when God changes His Headquarters from Heaven to Earth)*,

"Having the Glory of God *(this is what makes the city what it is)*: and her light *was* like unto a stone most precious, even like a jasper stone, clear as crystal *(presents the radiance of God's Glory)*;

THE HOLY CITY

"And had a wall great and high *(this wall is 216 feet high, counting 18 inches to the cubit; it is decorative only)*, *and* had twelve gates *(signifies three gates on the North, three on the South, three on the East, and three on the West; the gates on each side will be about 375 miles apart from each other)*, and at the gates twelve Angels *(proclaims the Glory of the City, and as well the Glory of God's Government)*, and names written thereon, which are *the names* of the Twelve Tribes of the Children of Israel *(proclaims the fact that 'the Lamb's Wife' is made up of every single Believer, whether on this side or the other side of the Cross; every gate will have the name of one of the Twelve Tribes; as well, this tells us how precious Israel is to the Heart of God)*:

THE GATES

"On the east three gates *(will probably have the*

names *Joseph, Benjamin, and Dan)*; **on the north three gates** *(will probably have the names Reuben, Judah, and Levi)*; **on the south three gates** *(will probably have the names Simeon, Issachar, and Zebulun)*; **and on the west three gates** *(will probably have the names Gad, Asher, and Naphtali).*

"And the wall of the city had twelve foundations *(the way of Salvation was shown to the Jews, hence, the gates and the names of the Twelve Tribes inscribed on those gates; however, the Foundation of Salvation was not really given until after the Cross, because it could not be given until after the Cross)*, and in them the names of the twelve Apostles of the Lamb.** *(On each foundation is the name of one of the Twelve Apostles. The Foundation of the Salvation Message is based 100% on Christ and the Cross, hence, the word 'Lamb' being used.)*

"And he who talked with me *(this is not the Angel who talked with John in Rev. 21:9; the one now speaking identifies himself as a Prophet [Rev. 22:9])* had a golden reed to measure the city, and the gates thereof, and the wall thereof.** *(The measuring is done for a reason. It reveals the perfection, fulfillment, and completion of all God's Purposes for His Redeemed People.)*

MEASUREMENTS

"And the city lies foursquare, and the length is as large as the breadth: and he measured the city with the reed, twelve thousand furlongs** *(translates into about 1,500 miles per side).* **The length and the breadth and the height of it are equal.** *(This presents astounding dimensions. It is about half the size of the United States, regarding length and breadth. If that is not enough to take one's breath away, it will also be 1,500 miles tall. The mind cannot comprehend this, but Faith believes.)*

THE WALL AND THE FOUNDATIONS

"And he measured the wall thereof, an hundred *and* forty *and* four cubits *(translates into about 216 feet, that is if we are using 18 inches to the cubit; as stated, the wall is strictly for ornamentation)*, *according to* the measure of a man, that is, of the Angel. *(The designation of 'Angel' is sometimes given to men, God, and the Creatures we refer to as Angels. This man, as Rev. 22:9 proclaims, is a Prophet.)*

PURE GOLD

"And the building of the wall of it was *of* jasper *(presents a precious stone of several colors)*: and the city *was* pure gold, like unto clear glass *(takes us beyond the imagination, beyond comprehension! but yet, this is literal)*.

PRECIOUS STONES

"And the foundations of the wall of the city *were* garnished with all manner of precious stones *(describes beauty upon beauty)*. The first foundation was jasper; the second, sapphire; the third, a chalcedony; the fourth, an emerald;
"The fifth, sardonyx; the sixth, sardius; the seventh, chrysolite; the eighth, beryl; the ninth, a topaz; the tenth, a chrysoprasus; the eleventh, a jacinth; the twelfth, an amethyst. *(The flooding of color in that incomparable City is beyond imagination. All of these stones named here are exquisite in color.)*

A PEARL

"And the twelve gates *were* twelve pearls *(probably means each gate, which is about 216 feet tall, is made of untold thousands of pearls)*; every several gate was

of one pearl *(seems to indicate that this particular gate, which is probably every third or fourth one, is made out of one gigantic pearl)*: **and the street of the city** *was* **pure gold, as it were transparent glass** *(refers to the fact that not only are all the buildings of 'pure gold,' [Rev. 21:18], but even the streets are made of pure gold)*.

THE LAMB

"And I saw no Temple therein *(refers to a Temple such as in Old Testament times; actually there is a literal Temple in the New Jerusalem, but it will not serve the same purpose as the Temple on Earth [Rev. 3:12; 7:15; 11:19; 14:15, 17; 15:1-8; 16:1, 17])*: **for the Lord God Almighty and the Lamb are the Temple of it.** *(Before the Cross, a Temple on Earth was necessary because God could not dwell with man at that time, at least directly. Since the Cross, the Holy Spirit can dwell within man because the terrible sin debt has been paid [Jn. 14:17; I Cor. 3:16].)*

THE LAMB IS THE LIGHT

"And the city had no need of the sun, neither of the moon, to shine in it *(proclaims the fact that the Creator is not in need of His Creation; God has need of nothing, but all have need of God)*: **for the Glory of God did lighten it, and the Lamb** *is* **the Light thereof.** *(The word 'Lamb' signifies that all of this is made possible for Believers as a result of what Christ did at the Cross.)*

THE NATIONS OF THAT WORLD

"And the nations of them which are Saved shall walk in the light of it *(should have been translated, 'and the nations shall walk by means of its light'; the words* *'of them which are Saved' are not actually in the best manuscripts; in fact, there will be no one in the world in that day who isn't Saved)*: **and the kings of the Earth do bring their glory and honour into it.** *(This refers to leaders of nations, whatever they might be called at that particular time. All will give Glory to God, and all will Honor the Lord, and do so forever.)*

NO NIGHT THERE

"And the gates of it shall not be shut at all by day *(in fact, they will never be shut)*: **for there shall be no night there.** *(This speaks of the City only, for outside the City there will be day and night eternally [Gen. 1:14-18; 8:22; Ps. 89:2-3; Jer. 31:35-36].)*

THE LAMB'S BOOK OF LIFE

"And they shall bring the glory and honour of the nations into it *(proclaims a Righteous commerce, and in every capacity).*

"And there shall in no wise enter into it any thing that defiles, neither *whatsoever* **works abomination, or** *makes* **a lie** *(this means that all sin is forever banished, and will never return)*: **but they which are written in the Lamb's Book of Life** *(refers to the Book of the Redeemed; the word 'Lamb' refers to the fact that all are Saved by placing their Faith and Trust in Christ and what He did for us at the Cross)***" (Rev. 21:1-27).**

Chapter 21 presents to us great and grand particulars of the New Jerusalem. Chapter 22 is far more personal.

THE WATER OF LIFE

"And he showed me a pure river of Water of Life,

clear as crystal *(symbolic of the Holy Spirit [Jn. 7:37-39])*, **proceeding out of the Throne of God and of the Lamb.** *(This 'Water of Life' is made possible by what Jesus did at the Cross, hence, the word 'Lamb.')*

THE TREE OF LIFE

"In the midst of the street of it *(proclaims the fact that this 'pure River of Water of Life, clear as crystal,' flows in the middle of this street of pure gold)*, **and on either side of the river,** *was* **there the Tree of Life** *(the fruit of this Tree of Life must be eaten every month, and we're speaking of the part of the population who doesn't have Glorified Bodies)*, **which bear twelve** *manner of* **fruits,** *and* **yielded her fruit every month** *(we have the number 'twelve' again, which signifies the Government of God as it relates to the manner of Eternal Life; there are twelve different types of fruit, but we aren't told what they are)*: **and the leaves of the tree** *were* **for the healing of the nations.** *(This pertains to the stopping of any type of sickness before it even begins. As stated, the population on Earth, which will never die and will not have Glorified Bodies, will need these things. These are they who were Saved during the Kingdom Age, and thereafter.)*

NO MORE CURSE

"And there shall be no more curse *(a curse was placed on the Earth at the Fall; it is being said here that there will be no more curse because there will be no more sin)*: **but the Throne of God and of the Lamb shall be in it** *(the authority of rulership will be as great with God the Son as it is with God the Father; in fact, by the use of the word 'Lamb,' we are made to realize that all of this is made possible because of what Jesus did at the Cross)*; **and His**

Servants shall serve Him *(the idea is that every Believer in the Perfect Age will so love the Lord and the Lamb that they will gladly 'serve Him')*:

HIS NAME

"And they shall see His Face *(shows intimate relationship)*; **and His Name** *shall be* **in their foreheads** *(refers to ownership; we were bought 'with a price,' and that price was the Blood of the Lamb)*.

NO NIGHT

"And there shall be no night there *(this speaks of the New Jerusalem only, for night and day will be in the balance of the Earth forever)*; **and they need no candle, neither light of the sun; for the Lord God gives them light** *(presents the Source of this Light)*: **and they shall reign forever and ever.** *(It has never been known for servants to 'reign' like kings; however, these servants shall!)*

FAITHFUL AND TRUE

"And he said unto me, These sayings *are* **faithful and true** *(proclaimed in this fashion simply because many of the statements made are so absolutely astounding they defy description)*: **and the Lord God of the Holy Prophets sent his Angel to show unto His Servants** *(the Greek word 'Aggelos' is translated 'Angel' here, but should have been translated 'Messenger'; we know this man is not an Angel, nor is he Christ)* **the things which must shortly be done** *(is not speaking of John's day, but rather, the setting of the Vision is a time frame which has not come about even yet; it will take place immediately after the Rapture of the Church; from that point forward, which is what is meant here, we have 'the* *things which must shortly be done,' referring to the Great Tribulation).*

THE PROPHECY OF THIS BOOK

"**Behold, I come quickly** *(has more to do with the manner of His Coming than anything else; when He does come, which will be at the height of the Battle of Armageddon, it will be sudden, even immediate)*: **blessed** *is* **he who keeps the sayings of the Prophecy of this Book.** *(This is the only Book in the world that gives a preview of the future. Consequently, every Believer ought to study the Book of Revelation as much as they do any other Book in the entire Bible.)*

THE SAYINGS OF THIS BOOK

"**And I John saw these things, and heard** *them (presents an impeccable witness).* **And when I had heard and seen, I fell down to worship before the feet of the Angel which showed me these things.** *(John, it seems, will make the same mistake twice.)*

"**Then says he unto me, See** *you do it* **not** *(presents the same words used by the previous man when John did the same thing [Rev. 19:10])*: **for I am your fellowservant, and of your Brethren the Prophets, and of them which keep the sayings of this Book.** *(He evidently is one of the Great Prophets of the Old Testament, who eagerly awaits the fulfillment of these Prophecies as well)*: **worship God** *(includes both God the Father and God the Son.)*

THE TIME IS AT HAND

"**And he said unto me, Seal not the sayings of the Prophecy of this Book** *(refers to the fact that the things given in this Book are meant to be known and understood;*

they are not hidden truths): **for the time is at hand** *(speaks of the immediate fulfillment of the events, which were to happen in consecutive order from John's day to eternity; it began with the Church Age, which is now almost over; the Great Tribulation will follow, concluding with the Second Coming, which will usher in the Kingdom Age, followed by the Perfect Age).*

THE UNRIGHTEOUS AND THE RIGHTEOUS

"He who is unjust, let him be unjust still: and he which is filthy, let him be filthy still *(proclaims the fact that men are building up their destiny by the actions and habits of their lives)*: **and he who is Righteous, let him be Righteous still: and he who is Holy, let him be Holy still.** *(Records that which the Spirit of God can bring about in a person's life, irrespective that they have once been 'unjust and morally filthy.' This is all done through the Cross, and only through the Cross.)*

THE REWARD

"And, behold, I come quickly *(is not meant to portray the 'time' of His Coming, but rather, the suddenness of His Coming; the idea is that whatever we are at His Coming, whenever that Coming takes place, is what we will be forever)***; and My reward is with Me** *(the word 'reward' can either be positive or negative)***, to give every man according as his work shall be.** *(Our Faith, however placed, will produce a certain type of works. Only Faith in the Cross is accepted.)*
"I am Alpha and Omega *(presents the first letter in the Greek Alphabet [Alpha], and the last letter in the Greek Alphabet [Omega]; it is another way of saying, 'the first and the last,' which includes all in-between)***, the beginning and the end, the first and the last.** *(This*

doesn't mean Christ as God had a beginning, for He didn't. It is speaking of whatever is in question. Christ is the beginning of all things, and the end of all things.)

"Blessed *are* they *(presents the seventh and last Beatitude in the Book of Revelation)* **who do His Commandments** *(should have been translated, 'who washed their robes in the Blood of the Lamb'; the Greek Text used for the King James Version of the Bible was the Textus Receptus; it is the Text that Erasmus, the famous Renaissance scholar, published in A.D. 1516; it was the first New Testament Greek Text ever published; since 1516, the world of scholarship and Archaeology has discovered thousands of earlier Greek Texts; by comparing these thousands of Manuscripts, the scholars can easily ascertain the original Text the Apostle wrote)*, **that they may have the right to the Tree of Life** *(proclaims the fact that this 'right' can be attained in only one way, 'by washing our robes in the Blood of the Lamb')*, **and may enter in through the gates into the city** *(proclaims the Eternal abode of the Redeemed; we shall enter that city by means of His Grace, which is the Cross of Christ).*

WITHOUT

"For without *are* dogs *(homosexuals)*, **and sorcerers** *(witchcraft)*, **and whoremongers** *(pertains to all type of immorality)*, **and murderers** *(pertains not only to killing in cold blood, but as well, murdering one's reputation through gossip)*, **and idolaters** *(pertains to placing anything above God, or on a par with God; religion is the greatest idolatry of all)*, **and whosoever loves and makes a lie** *(refers to anything that's untrue).*

THE BRIGHT AND MORNING STAR

"I Jesus *(this short phrase is found only here in*

Scripture, emphasizing its importance; Christ is closing out the Book of Revelation here, but most of all, He is testifying to the Truth of what has been given) **have sent My Angel to testify unto you these things in the Churches.** *(The word 'Angel' here means 'Messenger,' and actually refers to the Pastors of the respective Churches in question, and actually for all time.)* **I am the Root and the Offspring of David** *(is meant to project the Incarnation of Christ)***, and the Bright and Morning Star.** *(The 'Morning Star' speaks of a new beginning that any person can have, irrespective of their present situation, if they will only look to Christ.)*

THE GREAT INVITATION

"And the Spirit and the Bride say, Come. *(This presents the cry of the Holy Spirit to a hurting, lost, and dying world. What the Holy Spirit says should also be said by all Believers.)* **And let him who hears say, Come.** *(It means if one can 'hear,' then one can 'come.')* **And let him who is athirst come** *(speaks of Spiritual Thirst, the cry for God in the soul of man)***. And whosoever will, let him take the Water of Life freely** *(opens the door to every single individual in the world; Jesus died for all and, therefore, all can be Saved, if they will only come)***.**

THE PROPHECY OF THIS BOOK

"For I testify unto every man who hears the words of the Prophecy of this Book *(proclaims the inerrancy of the Book of Revelation; in other words, John testifies that it is the Word of God)***, If any man shall add unto these things, God shall add unto him the plagues that are written in this Book** *(proclaims the fact that changing the meaning of the Prophecies in this Book can bring upon* *one the Judgment of God)***:**

THE BOOK OF LIFE

"And if any man shall take away from the words of the Book of this Prophecy *(the idea is that the 'words of the Prophecy' should not be changed in any manner, whether by addition or deletion)*, God shall take away his part out of the Book of Life, and out of the Holy City, and *from* the things which are written in this Book. *(This is a warning given to Believers, and should be understood accordingly!)*

I COME QUICKLY

"He which testifies these things *(proclaims the fact that the Office of the Messiah as Saviour is repeated again and again throughout the Prophecy; He is the Lamb Who was slain, and His Blood washes from sin, and Alone makes fit for entrance into the Eternal City)* says, Surely I come quickly *(leaves the Promise to come as the last Message from the Lord Jesus to the Believers' hearts; and on this sweet note, the Prophecy ends)*. Amen. Even so, come, Lord Jesus *(proclaims the answer of the True Church to the Promise of Christ regarding the Second Coming)*.

GRACE

"The Grace of our Lord Jesus Christ *(presents John using the very words of Paul in his closing benediction; Christ is the Source, but the Cross is the means)* be with you all. Amen. *(This proclaims the fact that it is the same Message for all, and is available to all. The word 'Amen' closes out the Book of Revelation, and, in fact, the entire Canon of Scripture, which took about 1,600 years to bring forth in its entirety. It gives acclaim to the*

Finished Work of Christ. It is done. And, thereby, all of Heaven, along with all the Redeemed, must say: 'Amen')" (**Rev. 22:1-21**).

THE LAMB OF GOD

Some seven times in the last two Chapters of Revelation, the Holy Spirit through John uses the word, the name, or the designation *"Lamb"* (**Rev. 21:9, 14, 22, 23, 27; 22:1, 3**).

Why?

There is no more Satan and sin, and no more demon powers and darkness, so why would the Holy Spirit use the designation *"Lamb,"* as it refers to the Son of God?

I'm sure there are many reasons; however, the main reason is that the inhabitants of that City, the duration of which will be forever and forever, are to ever remember and understand that all of this described to us in the last two Chapters of Revelation, which presents the Perfect Age, is made possible because of what Jesus Christ did at the Cross.

One might say that the Bible opens with the Cross (**Gen. 3:15**), and closes with the Cross, i.e., *"the Lamb."*

"For God so loved the world, that He gave His Only Begotten Son, that whosoever believes in Him should not perish, but have Everlasting Life" (**Jn. 3:16**).

"Living for Jesus a life that is true,
"Striving to please Him in all that I do;
"Yielding allegiance, glad-hearted and free,
"This is the pathway of Blessing for me."

"Living for Jesus Who died in my place,
"Bearing on Calvary my sin and disgrace;
"Such love constrains me to answer His call,
"Follow His leading and give Him my all."

"Living for Jesus wherever I am,

"Doing each duty in His Holy Name;
"Willing to suffer affliction and loss,
"Deeming each trial a part of my cross."

"Living for Jesus through Earth's little while,
"My dearest treasure, the light of His smile;
"Seeking the lost ones He died to redeem,
"Bringing the weary to find rest in Him."

"O Jesus, Lord and Saviour;
"I give myself to Thee,
"For You, in Your Atonement,
"Did give Yourself for me;
"I own no other Master,
"My heart shall be Your Throne;
"My life I give, henceforth to live,
"O Christ, for You alone."

Jimmy Swaggart
Books

Brother Swaggart, Here Is My Question . . .
Here are samples of some of the questions:
- Who is Satan, and where do demon spirits come from?
- What is Blaspheming the Holy Spirit?
- What is the difference between The Great White Throne Judgment and The Judgment Seat of Christ?
- What should be the Christian's position in respect to alcohol?
- Are homosexuals born that way?

09-097

Brother Swaggart, How Can I Understand The Bible?
The following are some of the subjects addressed:
- The Doctrine Of The Bible
- The Doctrine Of Grace
- The Doctrine Of *"Justification By Faith"*
- The Doctrine Of Our Lord Jesus Christ
- The Doctrine Of Satan
- The Doctrine Of Sin
- The Doctrine Of The Baptism With The Holy Spirit

09-100

Brother Swaggart, Here Is My Question About The Cross
The following are some of the subjects addressed:
- How Do I Apply The Cross To My Life Daily?
- How Does Satan Respond To The Message Of The Cross?
- Why Is The Cross Of Christ So Important As It Regards The Holy Spirit?
- How Do You Know That Romans 6:3-4 Speaks Of The Crucifixion, Instead Of Water Baptism?
- Why Is It That The Cross Doesn't Work For Me?
- How Does Christ Intercede For The Saints?

09-103